The Lives and Liberation of
Princess Mandarava

The Lives and Liberation of Princess Mandarava

The Indian Consort of Padmasambhava

Translated by
LAMA CHONAM AND SANGYE KHANDRO

Introduction by
JANET GYATSO

Wisdom Publications • Boston

Wisdom Publications
199 Elm Street
Somerville, Massachusetts 02144 USA

Library of Congress Cataloging-in-Publication Data

Bsam-gtan-gliṅ-pa Phrin-las-'gro-'dul-las-rab-bde-ba-rtsal.
 [Za-hor rgyal po'i sras mo Lha-lcam Man-dha-ra-wa'i rnam par thar pa. English]
 The lives and liberation of Princess Mandarava : the Indian consort of Padmasambhava
 / translated by Lama Chonam & Sangye Khandro.
     p.   cm.
 Includes bibliographical references and index.
 ISBN 0-86171-144-0 (alk. paper)
  1. Mandarava. Princess. 2. Padma Sambhava, ca. 717-ca. 762.
 3. Mandarava. Princess—Pre-existence. 4. Women Buddhists—India-
 -Biography—Early works to 1800. I. Chonam, Lama. II. Khandro,
 Sangye. III. Title.
 BQ972.A57B7513 1998
 294.3'4213—DC21   98-17766

ISBN 0-86171-144-0

10 09 08 07
6 5

Cover image: Mandarava, late 16th century, western Tibet.
Photo by John Bigelow Taylor, N.Y.C.

Wisdom Publications' books are printed on acid-free paper and
meet the guidelines for the permanence and durability of the
Committee on Production Guidelines for Book Longevity of the
Council on Library Resources.

Printed in the United States of America.

Table of Contents

Translator's Preface   ix

Introduction by Janet Gyatso   1

1. *Daughter of the King of Zahor, Princess Mandarava*   17

2. *The Daughter of King Indradeva*   22

3. *Marrying Prince Suryagarbha*   30

4. *In the Kingdom of Kanaka*   39

5. *In the Kingdom of Damaru*   45

6. *Enlightening the Kingdom of Damaru*   53

7. *In the Realm of the Gods*   58

8. *In the Naga Realm of Black Chandala*   61

9. *Daughter of the Demigod King*   65

10. *Shri Sagara*   67

11. *The Twenty-Five Manifestations*   70

12. *Blessings from the Dakinis*   72

13. *Seeing the Country of Her Birth*   76

14. *Choosing Her Mother and Father*   79

15. *Entering Her Mother's Womb*   82

16. *Paying Homage to Her Father and Mother*   86

17. *Aversion to Samsara*   92

18. *Perfecting the Outer Sciences*   97

19. *Liberating the Heretic Kyabsal Nagpo*   102

20. *Leading Three Hundred Noble Women to the Path of Dharma*   105

21. *The Death of Prince Pawode*   109

22. *Setting Five Hundred Women on the Path to Liberation*   113

23. *The Sacred Flesh of a Bodhisattva*   119

24. *A Vision of Vajrasattva*   122

25. *Taking Vows and Training in the Dharma*   128

26. *Meeting Master Padmasambhava*   131

27. *Subduing the King with Miracles*   135

28. *Freed from Imprisonment*   142

29. *Abandoning Samsara*   146

30. *Accomplishing Longevity in Maratika Cave*   152

31. *Subjugating Heretics in the Kingdom of Kotala*   155

32. *Conquering Elementals at the Charnel Ground*   162

33. *Bringing the Cannibals of Chamara to the Dharma*   166

34. *Eight Miracles in Eight Countries*   169

35. *Turning the Wheel of Dharma in Oddiyana*   179

36. *Turning the Wheel of Dharma in Shambhala*   182

37. *Becoming the Wisdom Dakini*   188

38. *Supplication to Mandarava's Emanations*   194

Epilogue   203
Table of Equivalents   207
Notes   219
About the Contributors   227

Publisher's Acknowledgment

Wisdom Publications gratefully acknowledges the generous support of the Hershey Family Foundation in sponsoring the publication of this book.

Translator's Dedication

Dedicated to the Dudjom Sangyum, Rigdzin Wangmo, a great primordial wisdom dakini living in this world today.

Translator's Preface

As spiritual practitioners we receive encouragement and inspiration by reading the lifestories of great and sublime teachers, and the inspiration we receive from their exemplary lives allows us to progress more swiftly along the path to liberation. Because the appearance of everything we can know and experience depends on causes and circumstances, ordinary individuals embarking on the path must do so through a gradual process. Princess Mandarava, however, already liberated from the cycle of suffering and perfectly omniscient, was not an ordinary individual. She intentionally emanated into realms of ordinary existence in order to inspire beings and lead them through this gradual process, teaching them how to practice through her example. The pages of this book present, for the first time, an English translation of the precious treasure text of Padmasambhava called *The Lives and Liberation of Princess Mandarava*. The accounts of Mandarava's remarkable lives illuminate the experiences of a great wisdom dakini who inspired everyone she met, turning their minds irrevocably toward liberation.

Princess Mandarava of Zahor is often depicted at the side of Guru Padmasambhava opposite his other principal consort, Kharchen Yeshe Tsogyal. Princess Mandarava was instrumental in the guru's accomplishment of immortality, and, as a result, she is usually depicted holding a long-life vase and arrow. Because of his relationship with Mandarava, Padmasambhava was able to extend the duration of his enlightened activities in this world and thus travel to the snow land of Tibet, where, according to Je Mipham Rinpoche, he remained some fifty-four years.

In the thirty-eight chapters of this revelation, the reader comes to know a *nirmanakaya* (enlightened manifestation) *dakini* (goddess) who chose numerous times to enter the world as an aristocrat. The purpose of this depiction is not to show us that only those of high status or wealth are fortunate enough to have such opportunities, but to reveal that Mandarava was able and willing to renounce that which is most difficult to renounce, namely attachment to the so-called pleasures of worldly life. In each of her lifetimes, she unflaggingly forsakes fame and pleasures to work for the benefit of others through example and skillful means. Her abandonment of the temporary pleasures that steal away precious time and opportunities for spiritual development mirrors the struggles facing modern day Dharma practitioners. Although Mandarava was a famous female practitioner, she ultimately defies gender distinctions, and her enlightened activities are timeless. The Dharma that Mandarava—and all sublime teachers like her—teach is the path that transcends all relative distinctions made by ordinary individuals based on the ordinary habits of the dualistic mind.

Great importance is placed on the purity and authenticity of lineage in the Vajrayana tradition. The great female practitioners within these lineages deserve our recognition. This can be accomplished by translating more of the lifestories of great female practitioners and important classical texts and commentaries written by women into the English language. The project of translating this particular text was originally inspired by the devotion of several disciples of Jetsunma Ahkon Lhamo. Jetsunma is the spiritual director of Kunzang Palyul Choling in Poolesville, Maryland and is an American woman recognized as an emanation of a famous dakini from Tibet by H.H. Penor Rinpoche, the present head of the Nyingma School of Tibetan Buddhism. Anxious to make the lifestory of Mandarava available to English language readers, Thubten Rinchen Palzang found the Tibetan text at the Library of Congress. Special thanks go to Susan Meinheit who lovingly cares for the vast Tibetan collection at the Library and helped locate the original text. My translation of this text would not have been possible without generous sponsorship provided by Thubten Jampal Wangchuk, Noel Jones, Sarah Stevens, W.W. and Eleanor Rowe, as well as dozens of others from the KPC Sangha. Since this text is written in the Ume (*dbu med*) Tibetan script and possesses many abbreviated words as well as spelling errors, the translation would not have been possible without the kind assistance of Lama

Choying Namgyal, better known as Chonam, who tirelessly worked with me, going through the text line by line. Lama Chonam's knowledge of the Dharma, Buddhist history, and the Tibetan language was indispensable in completing this difficult task. The rough draft was initially reviewed by W.W. and Eleanor Rowe, who spent countless hours meticulously editing the initial translation. Thubten Konchog Norbu coordinated the translation project and oversaw many of the small details. Because several years transpired since our initial efforts, Lama Chonam and I again reviewed the entire text for accuracy. Despite our best efforts, there may still be errors in the translation. For any such errors we offer our apologies and welcome any corrections or improvements that scholars may detect. I would like to acknowledge and express my gratitude to Arthur Azdair, who has been indispensable in these final stages of the preparation of the manuscript by overseeing, editing, and skillfully inputting all of our revisions and corrections. Finally I feel I must mention that the views and comparisons presented in the introduction that follows do not completely reflect my views and reasons for translating this precious revelation treasure. The basis for the difference of opinion centers around the interpretation of the feminine principle and how it pertains to the path of Vajrayana Buddhism.

The notion that Vajrayana Buddhism is male-oriented is misleading. Still, many women attempting to pursue the path may naturally become discouraged when they encounter the strong Tibetan cultural influence. The more Dharma takes root in the West, however, the easier it becomes to relate directly to the Dharma, which is perfectly pure and free from biased distinctions, rather than focusing on the habits of ordinary individuals from foreign cultures. It is my prayer that this book may be of some benefit in encouraging the many excellent female practitioners in the world to cultivate their noble qualities and, through the force of their practice, go on to become fully qualified teachers themselves. May this work bring immeasurable benefit to all living beings, who are all equal and able to realize their precious buddha nature.

Sangye Khandro
Tashi Choling
Ashland, Oregon 1998

Introduction

*T*he *Lives and Liberation of Princess Mandarava* is an extraordinary story
from the heart of Tibetan religious culture about the Buddhist liberation of a woman.[1] Recounted from the magisterial perspective of a female
buddha—Pandaravasini—and her emanations in the world, the story tells of
life after life of compassionate manifestations in samsaric trouble spots, where
the heroine uses her splendor, magical powers, and often her feminine
charms to tame demons and teach the Buddhist messages of impermanence,
compassion, and enlightened insight to all. This superwoman's story has a
fairytale quality that is counterbalanced by the real-life problems of women
in Indian and Tibetan society that the work repeatedly addresses: the
assumption that all women must marry, their control by the men in their
lives, and the lack of respect for them in society at large. In the final long
episode of the heroine's life as the consort of Padmasambhava, these themes
are writ large in her struggles with her parents and her censure by those
around her on account of her controversial relationship with the tantric master. She is finally victorious in these struggles, but only after an arduous path
of self-cultivation and self-expression.

The version of the story translated in this book dates from the turn of
the twentieth century, but the figure of Mandarava has long occupied a
chapter in the larger narrative of Buddhism's introduction of in Tibet, in
which Padmasambhava plays such a leading role. But like its counterpart, the
lifestory of the famous Tibetan female saint Yeshe Tsogyal (who also became

a consort of Padmasambhava), the tale of Mandarava and her previous lives goes far beyond its significance for Tibetan national history and identity.[2] It is replete with messages of encouragement for women of many Buddhist traditions. In order to appreciate the meaning that its exceptional, proto-femininist themes might have had for its traditional audience—that is, its readers, male and female alike, as well as the auditors of its oral renditions— some general background in the lifestory tradition in Tibet and in Buddhist literature might be helpful to convey a sense of the history and religious practices of the cultural milieu from which the work originates.

All lifestories in Buddhist literature model themselves on the lifestories of the Buddha, which began to be written by the first century B.C.E. Most importantly, the plot of Shakyamuni's lifestory, his steps to buddhahood and his enlightened activity thereafter, set the standard for all exemplary Buddhist lives. Mandarava's own story shares this basic orientation. The work translated here recounts how she first achieved enlightenment in the distant past as the buddha Pandaravasini (chapter 2). The process seems to be repeated in her last lifetime as Mandarava when she achieves the status of an immortal awareness holder (*vidyadhara, rig 'dzin*) after rigorous training at Maratika (chapter 30) and then wins the ultimate rainbow body at death (chapter 37). The explanation for the repetition may be that Mandarava's second enlightenment was meant as a display or model for others on the path. In any event, it is the lifestory of Mandarava that is recounted in most detail in this book and that serves most prominently as an exemplary life for the student. Many of its moments repeat similar moments in the lifestories of the Buddha: her deliberate choice of parents; the auspicious dreams of parents and other significant indications at her conception; her precocious words and signs of advanced realization at birth; the sights of old, sick, and dead people that dis-illusion her and inspire a renunciatory attitude; her escape from the palace and periods of ascetic practice; her later efforts to teach and train. The parallel of her story with that of the Buddha is especially obvious in the overview summary that the text itself provides at the close of chapter 1. When the reader recognizes these elements as typical themes in the lifestory of a Buddhist saint, it becomes an important sign that the life being told is going in the same direction and that the protagonist too is a Buddhist saint. Such conventions structure the large proportion of hagiographical and biographical literature in Tibet—a genre that, significantly, is labelled "full liberation [story]" (*rnam thar*). Hundreds of such works were produced in Buddhist Tibet; it is important, first of all, to place the work translated in this book within that tradition.

The impact that the story of liberation has on its readers and hearers has been given paramount importance since the inception of lifestory literature in Buddhism. The point was made early on in this tradition that the entire purpose of the Buddha's life was to demonstrate to others the paradigmatic steps on the path to enlightenment. The Buddha's own life in fact was characterized as repeating a basic pattern already in place in the lives of buddhas of past eras. In turn, it was projected that others who reached his level of buddhahood would subsequently go through much the same process. This expectation is then confirmed when elements in his lifestory are repeated in the lifestories of so many saints in Buddhist literature, as we see in the present work.

In Tibetan literature, the lifestory of an enlightened master is also said to have a positive impact by causing marvel and wonder in the reader. This is the expected response to narratives of fantastic powers, intergalactic travel, and scintillating meditative experience. Such features were well known in Indian story literature and became prominent in the Mahayana sutras and the Puranic renditions of the exploits of the Hindu deities and their avatars. Much of the cosmic, miraculous quality of Mandarava's story can be understood as influenced by this large and heterogenous tradition, as are many other Tibetan narrative cycles. Stories of the founders of lineages are particularly likely to contain such marvelous dimensions; they are certainly central to the cycle of stories surrounding Avalokiteshvara and his manifestations in Tibet, as well as to the lifestory tradition of Padmasambhava, with which the Mandarava story is directly connected.³ The idea is that the spectacular vision of a magnificent cosmic heritage will inspire faith in the religious practices the story represents.

But confidence (*yid ches*, or *nges shes*), a special notion often invoked in Tibetan discussions of the benefits of reading lifestory narratives, is equally induced by another corner of the biographical tradition in Tibet—namely, that which tends more toward the everyday. Connected, to be sure, to the miraculous tale tradition in Tibet just discussed, some biographical and especially autobiographical writing in Tibet achieves an exceptional level of candor and historical specificity that becomes the source of a different sort of confidence for the reader: it assures one that that one's difficulties are not unique to oneself, and it gives some indication of ways to overcome such obstacles on the religious path. Some of the realistically portrayed family and social problems that the various heroines in Mandarava's stories endure present such role models. Even the most realistic biographical writing in Tibet may strike Western minds as fantastic, not infrequently referring, for example, to the protagonist's past lives, as well as recounting special dreams and epiphanies. Reading this literature always impresses upon the modern student how differently the line between psychic and material realities is construed in Tibetan Buddhist culture than it is in the contemporary West.

A lifestory such as that of Mandarava is seen to possess efficacious powers of its own. The text serves ritual functions; reading or chanting it as a liturgy is an act of devotion to Mandarava, and is even used to invoke her visualized presence. Rehearsing the story enables one to visualize its characters and their world, and this act of imagination in turn evokes important experiences and opportunities for cultivation on the part of the reader/listener. Some sense of the expected effects of such transformations may be gained from pp. 201–2, where it is maintained that, as a result of reading the story of Mandarava, one's wishes will be fulfilled, one will be protected on journeys, evil spirits will be subdued, animals and agriculture will flourish, and even that disease and war will end.

What has been said so far describes the traditional views on virtually all hagiographical or biographical work in Tibetan religion. But what is distinctive about the particular work at hand, the account of the past and present lives of Mandarava? One of its most important features is that it is a story about a female. This can be said of only very few of the hundreds of lifestories in Tibetan literature. Indeed, the principal reason that Mandarava is important to Tibetans at all has to do precisely with her gender. She is never even said to have been in Tibet; her claim to fame, rather, is that she was a consort of Padmasambhava. And since Padmasambhava is probably the most important Buddhist teacher in Tibetan history, we need to note, first of all, that it is the lore surrounding Padmasambhava that provides the basic framework for the story of Mandarava.

Invited to Tibet to tame its wild demons by the eighth-century King

Trisong Detsen, Padamsambhava was a tantric master from an area of north-west India commonly called Oddiyana. Although several previous Tibetan kings had established some connections with Indian, Chinese, and other traditions of Buddhism, the powerful ruler Trisong Detsen is said to have been bent upon establishing it as the state religion. However, the scholarly Indian abbot Shantarakshita whom the king invited to Tibet was unable to impress and convert the anti-Buddhist factions (especially those in the spirit world) that opposed this conversion. The story goes that the learned abbot then recommended Padmasambhava as a master with the right charisma and power to handle the volatile Tibetan situation. Padmasambhava's hagiography is replete with graphic descriptions of his suppression and taming of Tibet's fierce spirits as he crosses the border from Nepal, not to mention his subsequent wrangles with the conservative Tibetan aristocracy. He finally succeeds in initiating the king and some of his retinue in several key tantric traditions and leading them through a series of esoteric meditations at the mountain cave retreats in central Tibet. Some of these meditations involve sexual yoga, and Padmasambhava takes as his principal consort and disciple in these yogas the Tibetan lady Yeshe Tsogyal, who had been one of King Trisong Detsen's own queens. It is also Yeshe Tsogyal who helps Padmasambhava hide many treasure texts (*gter ma*) in Tibet, earmarked for future generations, before the master at last leaves Tibet.

Mandarava plays little part in these events, but her story is sometimes told in the earlier chapters of Padmasambhava's lifestory, when she was his consort in India, prior to his sojourn in Tibet.[4] Since she has no apparent relation to Tibetans, one might wonder why her story is told at all, and particularly how she came to be the protagonist of the elaborate version of her present and past lives that is translated in this book; many other characters appear in the story of Padmasambhava whose full lifestories never appear. A significant part of the answer to this question revolves around the fact that Mandarava is female. Even if we were to regard her story only as an embellishment of the Padmasambhava narrative cycle, the fact that what provides this embellishment is female is most striking.

Many contemporary scholars are coming to believe that much of the impact that Padmasambhava is portrayed as having in Tibet relates to his transmission of the controversial techniques of tantric yoga to Tibetans; and a large part of what Padmasambhava represents to Tibetans has to do with his virtuosity in the practices of consort yoga. In particular, his liaison with the Tibetan queen Yeshe Tsogyal importantly sets the stage for the subversion of the traditional forms of patriarchy, kinship structures, and power relations that ensued as tantric religion gained sway in Tibetan culture. And although for Tibetans Padmasambhava's relationship with Yeshe Tsogyal is one of the primary markers of this cultural transformation, the fact that he also is depicted as having taught and practiced consort yoga with many other women only reinforces his image as the master of this esoteric tradition. As a very common Tibetan prayer says, Padmasambhava ever has "many dakinis circling around him." *Dakini* is a polysemous category of female figures, sometimes referring to goddesses, sometimes to human women, in tantric Buddhism. Mandarava, devoutly called the "head of one hundred thousand dakinis" in the opening to the current work, is the other main consort of Padmasambhava, the Indian counterpart of Yeshe Tsogyal. This is a key element of Mandarava's claim to fame in Tibet.

However, the Tibetan reader's interest in the story of Mandarava and her status as a dakini is not particularly motivated by a desire to glorify the legacy of Padmasambhava; her female gender has a great significance of its own. That is, Mandarava is a female heroine in her own right, and it would be accurate to say that her connection with the famous Padmasambhava serves to enhance her image, rather than vice versa. The function of Mandarava as a female heroine is most appropriately understood in light of the large numerical gap between the precious few female Buddhist heroines in Tibetan literature and lore and the much more numerous male heroes. Like the separate lifestory of Yeshe Tsogyal, the story of Mandarava translated in this book helps fill that gap by providing detailed narratives of what the life of a female Buddhist practitioner might entail and what a powerful female saint is like.

The female model presented by the story of Mandarava differs in significant respects from that of Yeshe Tsogyal. The latter, by virtue of being Tibetan and, relatively speaking, a much more historically locatable figure than Mandarava, is a more accessible role model with whom Tibetan female readers might identify than is the foreign and—certainly in this version of her story—far more deified figure of Mandarava. In some respects we might compare Mandarava's story more profitably to that of the female bodhisattva Tara. That narrative places at its the center the possibility of female enlightenment, as a counter to the view prevalent for several centuries in many sectors of the Buddhist world that buddhahood was limited to males.[5] Clearly in protest of that view, Tara constructs her initial vow to achieve buddhahood specifically to include the rider that in all of her future lives on the way to this goal she will always be female and attain the final fruit in a female body.[6] Mandarava's story of past and present lives instantiates this same goal: in all of the incarnations recounted here she is always a female, often struggling with typical female problems on the path, achieving enlightenment as a female buddha, and then manifesting herself as a female goddess/buddha to accomplish her many compassionate projects to help other sentient beings. In many ways, then, we can say that the Mandarava story, like that of Tara, has universal messages for all Buddhist women and is less tied to a specifically Tibetan cultural matrix than is the story of Yeshe Tsogyal, even though the latter also has universal messages for women as well. But in other respects the Mandarava and Yeshe Tsogyal stories have more in common, both going a great deal further than the story of Tara in drawing out the particular problems of female life on the one hand and in suggesting ways to capitalize on distinctive female virtues for Buddhist purposes on the other. The Mandarava and Yeshe Tsogyal stories also share a deep root in tantric practice and mythology, with very particular lessons to teach their readers about the nature of the dakini figure and her relation to her teachers, her consorts, and her disciples.

In considering all of these questions about the models and messages of a work like the lifestory of Mandarava, we must continue to wonder to what degree those messages were meant to inspire a female audience in particular, and whether the story's images were fashioned specifically as models for female identification, and to what extent, on the other hand, these served to edify all readers, regardless of gender. Such a question cannot be answered precisely for a variety of reasons, not the least of which is the current lack of sufficient historical and sociological information. But we can at least be sure that, given the many feministic themes in the work, the creators of the story of Mandarava clearly had gender-related issues in mind.

The work translated in this book is classed as a treasure text, a genre that has been fostered by a long tradition of treasure discoverers (*gter ston*). Such visionaries claim to recover works that were previously concealed by

Padmasambhava and several of his close disciples back in the late eighth or early ninth century. This particular text's status as a treasure is made explicit at the beginning and end of the work (see pp. 19–21, 203), where it is stated that Mandarava's story was originally conveyed by Padmasambhava to Yeshe Tsogyal, King Trisong Detsen, and his court. Yeshe Tsogyal in turn records and hides the work, as she is said to have done for most of Tibetan treasure literature.[7] On the occasion of the burial of a treasure, a prophecy is typically uttered regarding its future revelation. In the present case, several versions of the treasure are mentioned, each of which is predicted to be discovered by a particular discoverer. The discoverer of this particular version (the "intermediate version:" see p. 204) is a yogin named Samten Lingpa, who probably was born in 1871 (the "iron sheep year"). Unfortunately there is not much information available about his life, but it is known that soon after his revelation of the story of Mandarava, he appeared in the village of the family of the maternal grandmother of Khanpo Palden Sherab and Khanpo Tsewang, two scholars from Riwoche in eastern Tibet now living in the United States. His treasure text was later edited by Dorshul Tsewang Tendzin (mentioned on p. 205), at the time the main lama of Gochen Monastery, which is also the home monastery of the Khanpos. The relationship between that lama and the treasure discoverer is described briefly at the end of this work.

As already indicated, however, stories about Mandarava had long been in circulation before the revelation of this particular version. They are often recounted in the course of relating the life of Padmasambhava. One of the earliest summaries of her lifestory is given in the 12th century treasure discoverer Nyangral Nyima Ozer's hagiography of Padmasambhava. Other material can be found in the treasures of Orgyan Lingpa and Sangye Lingpa (both fourteenth century) and Padma Lingpa (fifteenth century); several other versions are referred to in the final pages of the current work.[8] Scholars have not recognized any independent evidence from Indian sources of a woman named Mandarava, not to mention any of the previous lives that are detailed in the current version of her story. Nonetheless the text contains allusions to a fascinating array of places and persons—some historical, some mythological—in the Indian subcontinent, and for the careful historian this work would surely provide many hints about the sacred geography and political actors of India's tantric Buddhist period.

Although the known versions of the lifestory of Mandarava from the

Tibetan treasure tradition follow the same overall outline, details vary. Few contain the accounts of her previous lives that are provided by Samten Lingpa's version. This narrative, spanning eons (see the summary of the episodes on pp. 195–201), is framed as the enlightened emanations of the female buddha Pandaravasini (*Tib.* Gökarmo), "She in White Garments," the consort of the famous buddha of the Western Paradise, Amitabha. In an important sense Pandaravasini is the true identity of Mandarava, although on occasion this strict identity is blurred when, for example, in chapter 22 Mandarava encounters an epiphany of her enlightened side as Pandaravasini, seemingly a separate figure.

The first eleven chapters of the work describe various previous lives of Mandarava, including the one in which she originally attained enlightenment as a buddha, followed by subsequent emanations in a variety of realms to teach a variety of types of beings. Many other lives than could be detailed are alluded to in the eleventh chapter, including a life as the goddess Singmo Gangadevi during the time of Shakyamuni.

The remainder of the text describes the life in which she is Mandarava, the consort of Padmasambhava. It would have taken place not long before the text's imputed recording by Yeshe Tsogyal. The account commences in chapter 12 by returning to the grand purpose of Mandarava's existence, which, significantly, is connected both to Buddha Shakyamuni and to the establishment of Buddhism in Tibet. It is ultimately related to the emanation activity of Pandaravasini's consort, Amitabha. The conditions of her particular life as Mandarava are traced to a prophecy by Kashyapa (a disciple of Shakyamuni), who predicts his own future life as Padmasambhava, and for whom Pandaravasini is aroused and consecrated so as to emanate herself as Mandarava. She is in this way cast as the true mother of herself, since her grand union with Amitayus produces a seed that descends upon the royal couple in the land of Zahor who are to become her human parents.

Zahor is an area in northeast India, also famous in Tibetan lore as the birthplace of Shantarakshita, and associated with some of the early origins of tantric Buddhism. The beautiful princess Mandarava, who is born to a royal couple in that land, is portrayed here as wise and virtuous. She eschews her many suitors, however, and wishes only to practice Buddhism, for which she finally wins her parents' consent. While in retreat she is visited by the tantric master Padmasambhava and becomes his devoted disciple. Although she and

Padmasambhava are persecuted by the conservative countryfolk and Mandarava's parents alike for their seemingly scandalous behaviour, the couple finally vindicate themselves by displaying their magical powers. The final chapters of Mandarava's lifestory recount her sojourns around the Indian religious landscape. She continually cultivates her yogic virtuosity and Buddhist realizations further under the tutelage of Padmasambhava. She also continues to hone her skills in taming beings, just as she had done in her past lives, in places such as Padmasambhava's birthplace, Oddiyana, and the hidden country of Shambhala. On the eve of Padmasambhava's trip to Tibet, she finally passes away after conveying final teachings to her disciples.

A closer look at a few of the details of this story as they are rendered by Samten Lingpa can provide insight into the work's messages about the path of female practitioners of Buddhism, its conceptions of female glory and power, its feminine and in some cases feminist sentiments, and its portrayal of the particular problems that females face in the world of Buddhism.

Perhaps most striking of all the positive images of the female that the work provides is the exceptionally positive characterization in chapter 2 of the womb and the experiences of the fetus therein. In marked contrast to a very standard strain throughout Buddhist literature that pictures the womb as dirty and the source of stain and pain for both mother and child,[9] the current text has the fetus speaking from her mother's womb, attesting to her experiences of bliss, conceiving of her mother's body as a pure realm and the placenta as a source of bliss, warmth, and softness. Attention might be called to the literal meaning of "Pandaravasini" itself, which names the very same "covering of white silk" that here euphemizes the placenta. The meaning of Pandaravasini's name thus suggests a powerful affirmation of the birthing process.

Certainly there is no discomfort with, and indeed a straightforward valorization of, feminine beauty throughout the story of Mandarava. Although she frequently has to take on a wrathful or frightening demeanor in her activities to subdue evil and to teach, her default countenance is one of classical feminine beauty. There seems to be a deliberate point in the repeated references to this virtue, as in chapter 3, where the princess Natyendri is said to have "gentle beauty, smiling face, and melodious speech," to be "lovely to behold," "exquisitely beautiful," and so on. Similar attributes are ascribed to other outstanding female characters throughout the work. A woman who turns out to be the prior incarnation of the famous female Nepalese teacher Shakyadevi is bedecked in jeweled ornaments, the first teacher of Mandarava is characterized several times as a beautiful woman, her precocious fellow female student is a dakini in the form of a youthful maiden, and Pandaravasini herself appears as an intoxicatingly beautiful goddess when she decides to reveal herself as an epiphany to her own emanation, Mandarava.

The very fact that Mandarava has many accomplished and serious female companions, teachers, and mentors itself makes an important set of womanist points. These come out most clearly in the protagonist's own accomplishments. Surely one of the most basic purposes of the work is to show how women can achieve anything—just as well, if not better than—men usually do in Buddhist hagiography. The female incarnations of Pandaravasini are teachers, debaters, and conquerors, overpowering enemies and binding demons by oath—not only by virtue of her wisdom and skill but also through her charisma and even brute strength. This is not to say, however, that all female figures in the text are characterized positively. The work personifies evil in both male and female form; the latter appear in the form of blood-thirsty *mamos* (an ancient Indic class of terrifying "mother" spirits), cannibal queens, evil dakinis, and other monstrous females. Still, positively portrayed female characters far outnumber their evil counterparts in the work, which outstrips virtually any other example of Buddhist literature in its emphasis upon wise and powerful female figures.

The positively imaged male figures in the story are few. The most prominent one of course is Padmasmabhava himself, and in fact it is in the context of Mandarava's relationship with him that a few hints of womanish weakness on her part can be discerned. For example, when she begs him to take her with him to Maratika, he feels he must warn her that she will need to be strong and courageous enough to retain her "pure vision" even when traveling in frightening environments (chapter 29). Feminine vulnerability in fact sometimes becomes a special burden, and she must even overcome foes who challenge her power by raping her (chapter 32). Still, Padmasambhava continues to assign her realms which it is her special duty to "tame," and several of the final chapters of the work seem to be precisely about her cultivation of the powers and skill to tame such realms effectively. But her precocious abilities, surpassing those of the more conventional heroes in the tale, are already more than evident in her early years. One striking example is found in chapter 22, when her wise comments not only convince her father to realize the futility of a war in which he is engaged, but even inspire him to write a letter that ends up causing all of the feuding parties to disarm.

The text's pro-female orientation prefigures what in modern times would be called feminist. On several occasions, wittily playing on the widely-acknowledged preference for sons over daughters in Indian society, the text portrays the birth of a child attended by all the auspicious signs that lead everyone to assume that a son has been born. But no, it turns out that the child is a girl (chapters 4, 16). In another life, the parents even perform rituals so that they will have a son, but they too end up with a daughter— albeit one who clearly is just as blessed and saintly as any boy would be (chapter 10). The text nonetheless overtly recognizes the special limits upon females in samsara (see p. 106–7). Most remarkably, this work rejoins the lifestory of Yeshe Tsogyal in courageously engaging the too-often repressed topic of rape. In the case of Yeshe Tsogyal, the heroine transforms her rape by seven brigands into an opportunity to teach them about the tantric trans-formation of bliss.[10] Mandarava instead takes a more defiant stance by deliberately provoking the ridicule and aggression of a group of butchers, displaying herself as a beautiful but husbandless vagrant. When they taunt and then try to rape her, this becomes the excuse for her to manifest herself as a wrathful dakini in order to extract their vow to stop taking the lives of oth-ers and to enter the Buddhist path (chapter 34). In addition to showing the heroine as capable of overcoming her male tormentors, this episode subverts the stereotype of the vulnerability of any woman who lacks a husband.

In any event, a strong critique of the conventional institution of mar-riage pervades the entire text, particularly the section on Mandarava. This theme is, of course, directly indebted to the monastic orientation of Buddhism overall, evident with respect to women as early as the *Therīgāthā*.[11] Like many of the women featured in that Pali account of the first Buddhist nuns, as well as many other female Buddhist heroines, Mandarava's rejection of marriage in favor of her desire to practice Buddhism is resisted by her par-ents. Thus her propensity for the Dharma simultaneously becomes the occasion for her separation from her parents. It also becomes the occasion for Mandarava to lecture her maidservants on the uselessness not only of hus-bands, but also of class status and wealth—again very much in line with the overarching anti-materialist stance of the ascetic strand in Buddhism (chapter 20). Mandarava eventually wins her father's approval to be a nun (her mother supports her daughter's wishes more readily), but only after escaping from her parents' home and finding a master to ordain her on her own. Her father still attempts to control Mandarava and to enforce conventional morality by virtually imprisoning her in a retreat house, surrounded by nun attendants but strictly guarded against any male intrusions. The castle is nonetheless penetrated by Padmasambhava, and for the rest of her life she follows the tantric path, rather than one of strictly celibate monasticism. Messages that subordinate the importance of family continue throughout the narrative, as when Padmasambhava lectures on the superiority of the Dharma over blood relatives (chapter 28). This irreverence for conventional norms and sexuality becomes almost humorous when, criticized again in another context for not having a husband, Mandarava's mocking response is to create a multitude of manifestations of herself, all of whom proceed to join in sexual union with all of the men in her presence.

Despite the work's critique of worldly family ties, the religious milieu represented here resolutely affirms the value of tantric consort yoga. The transformation from the celibate to the esoteric path in Mandarava's story is in fact typical of the tantric approach in Buddhism, which insisted that students at the advanced level should cultivate meditative awareness not only in isolated states of purity, but rather in every conceivable activity in the world. Hence tantric practices such as consort yoga are not only permissible for qualified practitioners, but are even said to be necessary on the path to enlightenment. This is one of the primary reasons for the tantric path's notable inclusion of female figures, in stark contrast to the exclusions of male-dominated institutions in most forms of monastic Buddhism. It is important to note, however, that the esoteric practices of consort yoga cannot be equated with conventional sex; and as already noted, the temporary partnerships entailed by the practice are also not to be conflated with the more worldly institution of marriage.

Nevertheless, the ethos of consort yoga sometimes does seem to translate into a greater valorization of couplehood. Several illustrations of this view are found in the stories of Mandarava's past lives, where royal couples are conceived of as acting in enlightened concert to benefit their subjects. In one past life, Mandarava exploits the acceptability of couplehood to achieve her own Buddhist aims, using her feminine charms to convert the prince who has fallen in love with her and promising to marry him only if he would change the evil ways of his kingdom. But the most sustained defense of the value of enlightened couplehood is found in Mandarava's own story, indeed in the explicit context of consort yoga. Although the text clearly acknowledges the disapproval that most conventional Buddhists would have had for her daring relationship with Padmasambhava, the cowherd who reports the couple's activities and the king who attempts to punish them are humiliated and shown to have been in the wrong. Mandarava is especially furious with her father for not recognizing the holy character of her tantric mate, to whose male body and beauty she defiantly sings an elaborate song of praise.

Mandarava goes on to receive detailed instructions in all of the relevant techniques of tantric yoga in Maratika cave in Nepal. The realizations she achieves in accordance with Padmasambhava's instructions are at the heart of the demonstrations of skill, charisma, and power that she displays in the final chapters of the work. In the end, her story presents its readers with a complex image of a woman engaged in a difficult process of self-cultivation. That the story is mythologized and deifies its characters reflects the religious vision of which it is a part. What would have been most striking to its traditional readers is the strength of its resolutely feminine heroine, who carved out a distinctive way to travel on the classical tantric path. Although we lack precise knowledge about the community of practitioners in the circle of Samten Lingpa, the discoverer of this work, we can assume that both the men and the women who were in that tantric circle took special inspiration from the exceptional hagiography revealed by their master.

Janet Gyatso
Department of Religion
Amherst College

The Lives
and Liberation of
Princess Mandarava

Daughter of the King of Zahor, Sister of the Divine,

According to the Oral Instructions of Guru Padmasambhava

called

A Precious Garland

or

The Origins of the Queen of the Dakinis, Upholder of Secret Mantra

The Chronicle of Dungmen, Goddess of Life

The Lives and Liberation of the Dakini Paltrengma:
Queen of One Hundred Thousand Dakinis

Namo Shri Mahadevi Dakini!

I.
Daughter of the King of Zahor,
Princess Mandarava

Primordial mother of original purity,
all-pervasive innate wisdom of the sphere of space,
emanating from the supreme paradises of the five buddha families,
principal among all dakinis,
mother of the bodhisattvas of the three times[1] without exception,
divine pure awareness holder[2] of the dance of miraculous display,
on the supreme path of longevity,
you are the goddess of all vajra buddha families![3]
I bow down to you, Mandarava!

Glorious yogini mother of the buddhas, from within the oceans of exalted pure realms, the play of your emanations appears in one hundred million embodied forms. Limitless beyond measure is the marvel of the indication of your presence throughout many aeons. According to the capability of sentient beings, you display the dance of the miraculous activity of mundane appearances. With stainless natural wisdom, you reveal the profoundly extensive essence of the path of maturity and liberation. You are well known as the mother of all the conquerors, who maintains virtue in the four states of existence. All the heirs of the buddhas without exception have bowed to your lotus feet and attained true realization. As the very basis for the appearance of all wisdom dakinis, like space itself, you are the queen consort of the space of truth. All the dakinis who have appeared in this world throughout the three times are only the clouds of your own radiance. Akshobhya-vira, your vajra major and minor marks reveal the expanse of the nature of emptiness. Like a great downpour of rain, you appear—for the benefit of beings—from the supreme realm of the nirmanakaya as the natural manifestation of the five families and the inconceivable magical net of perfectly arranged manifestations. As a dakini your enlightened powers are manifest in an infinitude of miraculous activity. Known as Mandarava, your fame encompasses the three realms of existence.[4] Unwavering from the essential nature, may you remain in the center of the lotus in my heart, indivisible and firm, until the heart of enlightenment is realized. Respectfully, I bow to you to encounter my own true nature.

By the blazing light of the sun of great compassion, the heavy stains of ignorance and the obscurity of distorted vision are cleared in an instant, and the ground and path of Dharma are actually realized. By completing the practice of the path, the result of absolute truth is perfected. May enlightenment occur naturally in the state of the originally pure primordial mother.

E ma ho! In the sphere of Akanishta, the Paradise of Dense Array, objective appearances is the palace of the blissful wisdom of emptiness, indivisible from the fields of the five buddha families and their five consorts. With unobstructed, perfect accomplishment in all directions and times, the buddhas and bodhisattvas are the natural manifestation of the enlightened embodiments of dharmakaya, sambhogakaya, and nirmanakaya.[5]

The display of these realms of places and sacred grounds is beyond ordinary conception. Upon one atomic particle dwell infinite emanations of the teacher and assembly, revealing the Dharma according to the individual needs of the regions in this world system. The display of sacred places is inconceivably astonishing. Realms of space, earth, and subterranean activity, with their own associated sacred power spots and grounds, are manifest as Tsantoha and others. These correspond to enlightened body, speech, mind, noble qualities, and enlightened activities, each one of which also comprises the other four.

Among these countless sacred grounds and lands, there is a realm known as Tibet, in which red-faced cannibals live. In the central province of Tibet, at the red cliff of Samye Peloling is the temple known as the Unchanging Spontaneously Present Palace of the Three Traditions, which is nondual with the Copper-colored Mountain Realm of Lotus Light. In the inner chamber of the temple, known as

Turquoise Crystal, the guru himself was seated along with the king and his disciples and subjects.

In the presence of Shakyadevi of Nepal, Nyangzatso, Tashi Kyidren, Kalasiddhi, Chogroza, myself, Yeshe Tsogyal of Kharchen, and several thousand fortunate disciples, Guru Rinpoche revealed the mandala of the Eight Herukas, which is the condensed essence of the buddhas, and bestowed the ripening and liberating essential transmissions and instructions. At this time, the nine karmic holders of the authoritative command, as well as five female disciples, offered many signs of devotion and homage. In particular we offered the most valuable precious jewels, including a sapphire the size of an eight year old's fist. The king and his subjects offered troves of wealth that had belonged to the naga king Nanda. Accompanying this mandala offering, a supplication was made:

"E ma ho! How wondrous! From Akanishta, the paradise of Amitabha, to the Potala realm of Arya Avalokiteshvara, to the land of Oddiyana, having abandoned birth in a womb, you were miraculously born from a lotus in Lake Dhanakosha, and, as the nirmanakaya son of the king, you are renowned as the Lake-born Vajra. As the sovereign of the miraculous enlightened activities of all the buddhas, you are surrounded by one hundred thousand dakinis from the land of Oddiyana. As a treasure of ripening and liberating transmissions of the secret mantra vajra vehicle, you are the sole protector of your worthy followers.

"O Lord Guru Padmasambhava, head of all pure awareness holders, great spiritual master, please direct your enlightened awareness toward us. Your enlightened activities have spanned twenty continents, including India and Tibet. The miracles you have performed to tame the minds of beings are astonishing beyond imagination. In the country of Zahor you encountered the goddess of long life known as Mandarava, one whose abilities to benefit sentient beings were more sublime than any other—a glorious woman whose fame pervades the three realms of existence. O Guru, I implore you, out of your great kindness and for the benefit of those who have gathered here and for those of future generations, please share with us the story of her life and liberation!"

Guru Padma smiled with great pleasure and, with his vajra speech like the melodious voice of the god Brahma, said, "Kye ho! Listen closely, nine possessors of karma and all you of excellent spiritual faculties.

Fortunate disciples who have made such a fine request, listen now with respect and attentiveness, and keep these words in mind!

"E ma ho! How astonishing! The originally pure buddha realm is the sacred arena of spontaneously present, self-originating, primordial wisdom. In Akanishta Paradise dwell the dharmakaya Samantabhadra, the embodiment of supreme method, and Samantabhadri, the mother of the sphere of truth. As the birthplace of all the buddhas of the three times and their heirs, their nature is the wisdom of emptiness, appearing as an unceasing manifestation of the five buddha families.

"Moreover, in the supreme buddha realm of Sukhavati, where the display of noble enlightened qualities surpasses ordinary comprehension, resides the buddha Amitabha, the king of all conquerors. Known in sambhogakaya form as the long-life buddha Amitayus, he is the father of the one thousand nirmanakaya buddhas of this aeon. His wisdom counterpart is the Goddess Pandaravasini, who reveals inconceivable displays of enlightened body, speech, mind, noble qualities, and miraculous activities in order to tame beings throughout all realms of the world.

"Although the ways in which these manifestations appear vary according to the individual needs of beings, they will continue even after this aeon ends. The way that a primordial wisdom dakini emanates in this world of ours is such that countless manifestations have and will come throughout the three times. One of them, the lotus family dakini Natyendri, is a longevity dakini and pure awareness consort who took the form of a female known in the human world as Mandarava.

"Unsurpassed in fame, she came into this world as a princess, yet was also famous as a realized being in the realm of the gods, where she propagated the teachings of secret mantra. In the realm of dakinis she disseminated an account of the lifestory of the Wisdom Garuda. In the land of Oddiyana, where ten thousand chapters of her lifestory were propagated, she became famous as Dungmen Tsedzin, Conchshell Mistress of Life. Nine hundred chapters spread forth in the country of Zahor. In India, she was well known as Shrimala, Rosary of Splendor, and there one hundred chapters of her lifestory were spread forth. In the country of the eight tribes, she was known as Buddhi Tsomo, and five hundred and ten chapters of her lifestory were propagated. In the cold-blooded realm of the Nagas she was known as Maitri Shridevi,

Glorious Goddess of Love, and one thousand chapters of her lifestory were disseminated there. Similarly, one hundred chapters of her lifestory were propagated in other continents, such as Maru Singhala, Tsoti Bigche, Lanka, Oddiyana, Bheta Soge, Shambhala, Kashmirakarabha, and the eight great charnel grounds. Until now, her names and lifestories of the past have not been revealed here in Tibet according to the wondrous level of absolute understanding. For posterity, I shall reveal the story of her lives and liberation in brief.

"Whoever sees, hears, recalls or encounters this biography will be placed on the path to perfect enlightenment. This account will include: her lifestory in seven paradises, the manner in which she intentionally manifested herself for the benefit of beings, how she entered the womb of her mother with the power of the fivefold state of clairvoyance, how she became disillusioned with samsara, how she practiced the six perfections and trained on the stages of the path, how she developed qualities through her practice of secret mantra, her accomplishment of the state of an immortal pure awareness holder, her attainment of enlightenment, her passage into nirvana, and the manner in which she intentionally reincarnated herself for the benefit of others. In all, there will be thirteen divisions."

Samaya

This completes the first chapter of
*The Lives and Liberation
of the Princess of Zahor, Mandarava,*
called *A Precious Garland.*

2.

The Daughter of King Indradeva

In the previous time of ten thousand and forty-two aeons, during the
aeon known as Bhaskara Sahasrakara, Illumination of One Thousand
Lights, in the country known as Kotamati, in the palace of Salapatra,
lived King Gyeche Tsugpupel. He was of a priestly caste, a worshipper
of the god Vishnu. His consort, Rinchen Nangche Dronme Ö, gave
birth to their son Bhaskarashri, the Glorious Illuminator. Beginning
with the reign of Bhaskarashri, each king for one thousand successive
generations of patriarchial descent possessed the major and minor marks
of perfection.

The last king in this line, Indradeva, took as his consort a wealthy
merchant's daughter, Taye Dzesema, Infinite Beauty. One time while
they were staying in the palace the king became aware that, close by, in
a turquoise lake one hundred miles deep and seven thousand miles in
circumference, was the palace of the naga king Malashi.

Surrounding this lake was a lovely forest with a clear pool extremely
pleasing to behold. The pool contained many piles of precious wish-
fulfilling gems. It was surrounded by many small lakes, beautifully
ornamented with an abundance of blooming lotus flowers. Wonderful
varieties of songbirds and cranes gathered there, and nectar bubbled
forth from many springs. In the middle of all this stood a square crystal
mountain called Nametotra. Clouds of five-colored light amassed at its
peak, and it resembled the mountains in the spontaneously accomplished pure realms.

Wishing to visit this sacred place, the king addressed his beautiful queen: "Listen, beautiful Dikari, mistress of pure secret noble qualities. Lady Taye Dzesema, please listen well! Northeast of this palace, among various countries, there is a valley with a great lake one hundred miles deep and seven thousand miles in circumference. This is the home of the naga king Malashi. The lake is surrounded by small ponds and pools, fields of flowers, and bubbling streams of nectar. A square crystal mountain called Nametotra is located there. Its peak, adorned with five-colored rainbow light, ascends to the realm of Brahma. There are hundreds of marvelous sights to delight the eyes! Let us go to this sacred place with a retinue of ministers and armies. Beat a great drum to gather this assembly and make all the necessary preparations for our journey, O friend of my heart!"

Accordingly, the honorable queen beat the assembly drum. The ministers and their hosts assembled instantly on the second floor of the palace. The wise minister Tratrashri respectfully asked the honorable queen why she had summoned the assembly. Speaking eloquently, he said, "E ma! How astonishing! Consort of the king, youthful daughter of the great merchant, your face is intoxicatingly beautiful. Sister of gods and men, simply gazing at you cannot possibly quench our desire. The great drum of the gods was miraculously created by Brahma. It resounds with the great melodies of peace, enrichment, dominion, and wrath.[6] At the beating of this great drum we who are endowed with the prodigious vitality of the gods have gathered here spontaneously. Please tell us why we were summoned. I respectfully request the guardian of your throat to release the conch of your voice!"

The queen replied: "Kye! Hark! Intelligent Minister Tratrashri and your assembly of officers, please listen! With his melodious voice, the ruler of this land of Kotamati, King Indradeva, has commanded us to visit a country to the northeast where the naga king Malashi dwells in his palace in the great lake of Namaru. This country is resplendent, like the realm of the gods! Its crystal mountain, Nametotra, is pervaded with the unobstructed radiance of five-colored lights. There are sparkling rivers of ambrosia and gardens of blooming lotuses. If you senior and junior ministers with your eightfold retinues wish to visit this incredible place that defies the imagination, resound the great drum to summon you here immediately! We must all adhere to the command of our king!"

After the queen finished speaking, she, the ministers, and their assemblies respectfully offered prostrations. They gathered their finest belongings, including silken scarves, brocade, and precious jewels, and presented them as a mandala offering to the king. Then they requested: "Namo! Homage. O Great King, sovereign of the gods, sole protector of the human race, the very merit of self and others, please pay heed! Having heard the sound of the great drum, we have gathered without delay! We have all understood the meaning of your command, which our precious queen has conveyed. Please tell us how best to prepare for this most desirable journey."

Hearing their request, the king replied: "From the time of Gyeche Tsugpupel until now, for a thousand royal generations, all the great kings in this lineage of Brahmin kings have made offerings to the nagas. In fact, there are many accounts of their journeys to make offerings to the great naga kings. Now, as we prepare for our journey and assemble our offerings, take care to gather the most excellent symbols: the supreme horse, the great elephant, the wish-fulfilling jewel known as Palasha, varieties of jewels, medicines, and musical instruments, dancers, singers, drum beaters, treasure vases, crops that need no harvest, grain, silk, parasols, canopies, victory banners, and various other decorations. Bring everything possible, omitting nothing! Wear your most luxurious clothing and adorn your hair with ornaments."

After the king had spoken, all the necessary preparations were made. As the eighth constellation appeared in the sphere of space, the earth seemed hallowed with exceptional beauty. The gardens were bursting with flowers in full bloom, and the elephants were bedecked with wish-fulfilling jewels and various embellishments. The king took his mount, followed by the queen, his ministers, and their subjects—all mounted on horses, banners hoisted, accompanied by musical instruments and conch shell horns. Filled with joy, satisfaction, and abundant good will, the great leader and his assembly arrived in the sacred place. As the women sang melodious songs, the men rushed forward, dancing and performing playfully and vigorously. Although they had come from many different regions and countries, they were one in a state of absolute joy. The king presented bountiful offerings of all the enjoyable substances, which they had gathered. Then the nagas displayed their pleasure by revealing their presence to the humans, and both humans and nagas savored the occasion together.

That evening, while the king and queen were preparing for sleep, the king, queen, and ministers all heard the strains of divine music. In the middle of the night, however, they learned that barbaric nagas were planning to harm them. The king picked up his wish-fulfilling jewel, known as Palasha, placed it on the crown of his head, and made this prayer: "E ma! Wish-fulfilling jewel that spontaneously accomplishes all needs and desires, you are the result of the prayers made by King Tsugpupel. If you are indeed the jewel known as Palasha, then eradicate the unruly, barbaric nagas who are plotting harm. Bestow the sacred spiritual attainments this instant!" Due to the force of this supplication and by the radiance of the wish-fulfilling jewel, many sparks of fire issued forth, penetrating the unruly nagas. Instantly they were reduced to ashes that dissolved into nonduality.

In the early hour of dawn, both the king and queen had dreams. The king dreamt of seven auspicious signs. A rosary of wish-fulfilling jewels dissolved into him, and a white stupa then arose from his crown. Orbs of rainbow light rays descended from space and dissolved into his heart. White lotus flowers bloomed from his teeth, and in his heart five-colored light rays blazed from a golden vajra. A youth appeared out of the lake, offering a silken scarf. Flowers bloomed from the palms of his hands and blossomed in the ten directions.

When the king awoke, he told the queen about his dream. She replied that she herself had dreamt that in the center of her chest was a swirling, tent-like orb of crystal light and that the king gave her a crystal vase. Red light rays streamed from her crown as she carried a five-pronged vajra on her shoulder. She held a katvanga,[7] from which many tridents began manifesting themselves. Then she heard a voice say that this would occur for many aeons. After hearing of her dream, the king replied that they both had received auspicious indications that must be deciphered by a holy clairvoyant.

After this, the host of ministers circumambulated the lake, and seven naga maidens immediately appeared before the king, each bearing a different wish-fulfilling jewel. The names of the jewels they held were Indranila,[8] Koshala, Kushtasukha, Parol Golwajom, Narayana Baladhara, Bage Kadog, and Mulagyen. The naga maidens offered all seven varieties of jewels to the king. Then they proclaimed: "Kye! O powerful king of the humans, King Indradeva! These seven amazing wish-fulfilling jewels are sent to you from our brother as his offering. Enjoy them and make regular and timely offerings to us!"

The king replied: "Kye! O seven fair maidens of the naga realm, what is your family name, your caste, and the name of your country? Which companions are you looking for and how are the people of your district? Please answer my questions and tell me honestly: what offerings would bring you the most pleasure?"

When he had spoken, the maidens replied: "Kye kye! Great king, you are a pleasure to look upon! Your strength and dexterity is equaled only by great Brahma himself, and you are as handsome as the sons of the gods. Your youth and endowments are like those of the god of wealth, Vaishravana. The splendor of your presence is beyond compare. We belong to the race of nagas, and our wealth and endowments are great. We are of royal caste, and our subjects are the eight classes of nagas. Our father's name is King Shiroratna, Crown Jewel. Our mother's name is Goddess Marichi, Mistress of Light. We seven are all daughters of the king, and our companions are sons of Brahma. Our subjects include a million female naginis. The offerings that please us are medicines, grains, precious jewels, and treasure vases."

Hearing this, the king offered them five varieties of medicine, grains, multitudes of jewels, crops that need no harvest, and treasure vases. The seven maidens then returned to their own abodes. The wish-fulfilling jewels that they had offered to the king were now carefully wrapped in silk brocade. Then the jewels were placed in a carriage and transported to the kingdom accompanied by banners and the sound of trumpets and musical instruments. The great king also returned with his queen, ministers, and retinue.

Upon their arrival, they held a giant celebration for the wondrous, auspicious gifts. The news of their fortune spread throughout the kingdom. As a sign of honor and praise, the wish-fulfilling jewels were respectfully placed above the royal victory banners. The king made regular offerings to the jewels, and the queen performed daily prostrations and circumambulations.

One night, as the king and queen were making love, a dazzling orange light, blindingly bright, appeared to them and then dissolved. The queen saw it dissolve into the forehead of the king, while the king saw it enter the throat of the queen. Three months later the queen began to feel uncomfortable and knew she was with child.

Once, when the king inquired about her health, they both heard pleasing words coming from her womb: "E ma! Father King of great kindness! Listen to what your child has to say. Blissful, blissful, I feel so blissful! This vessel, my mother's body, is a blissful paradise, a palace of the conquerors. This red and white bodhichitta nectar of male and female is the bliss of method and wisdom, the sun and the moon. This placental covering of white silk is the bliss of great warmth and the sensation of softness. This six-pointed source of dharma womb is the blissful birthplace of all the conquerors. The motion of the vital air within my mother's body is the blissful motion of twenty-six thousand vital energies. The central channel and the five principal networks of channels[9] are the bliss of the paradises of the five families and the three enlightened embodiments. The stages of development of the branches are the bliss of transcending the five paths and ten stages. The activity of my mother's bodily motions is the bliss of the dakinis' song and dance. I am the great consort Pandaravasini, blissfully appearing for the benefit of sentient beings. My essence originates from the father Akshobya, and emptiness is liberated from the lotus.

"This is the blissful caste of the king's daughter, the bliss of the paternal lineage of the self-originating vajra, the bliss of the activity that accomplishes the benefit of others, the bliss of the organs as the five wisdoms, the bliss of the self-clarity of realizing the liberation as one's own intrinsic awareness, and the bliss of offering happiness to the nagas. All this is now offered back to you, my father of great kindness."

Both the king and the queen were overcome with joy at these words. After ten months had passed, as the queen gave birth to her child, the space above her became filled with gods and goddesses, who bathed the child and sang auspicious songs as showers of flowers poured forth from the heavens. The nagas made offerings to the accompaniment

of musical instruments, songs, and dances. The king and ministers celebrated. While giving birth, the queen experienced bliss, and her
daughter was born in the rishi posture,[10] wearing silken garments.

The newborn child said: "Ah la la ho! In the palace of the sphere of
unchanging bliss, I am the ornamental goddess of the display of clear
light. I have accomplished the ten stages and five paths[11] in the womb
of my mother. I came from the great, expansive space of empty bliss. O
father and mother of great kindness, I respectfully bow to you and pray
to reciprocate your kindness!"

Having spoken thus, she prostrated reverently to her father and
mother. The king and queen in their delight named her Tushtikara-
devi, Goddess Bestower of Pleasure. They also named her
Pandaravasini, Lady of White Cloth, because she was born swathed in
silk, and Kirtibhadra, Famous Lady of Excellence, because the fame of
her birth was widespread. Then they invited the holy sage, hoping he
would indicate the most auspicious name, which he did. The king
beseeched him to indicate whether or not his daughter would be the
queen of a chakravartin.[12]

The sage replied: "This girl is a pure primordial wisdom dakini, a
mistress of great exaltation. She will liberate all realms of ordinary existence. As Pandaravasini, she is the mother of all the buddhas and their
heirs. The status of queen of a chakravartin is far beneath her. She is an
untainted embodiment of a supremely enlightened being. Since she is
such an object of devotional offering, do not regard her as one who
holds a place in samsara!"

Hearing these words, the king and all his subjects rejoiced. From
that time onward, the princess grew ever more beautiful. In one day's
time she developed to the same degree that took others a whole year.
In her eleventh year, she sat at the feet of the buddha Ratnashri and
entered the path of the Dharma. Buddha Ratnashri declared her to be
the vajra family consort, the female pure awareness holder who, for
eighty-nine thousand years, was fully enlightened and indivisible with
the Buddha of Unlimited Life, Amitayus. In accordance with this por-
tentous indication, she entered the path of Dharma. Renouncing
samsara in the place called Nametotra, she developed clairvoyance and
miraculous abilities beyond imagination. She turned the wheel of the
Dharma boundlessly for sixteen thousand fortunate disciples.

Meanwhile, in the Realm of Great Bliss, the fully ordained monk Dharmakara actualized enlightenment. Then Amitabha, the Buddha of Boundless Light, and his vast entourage, as well as immeasurable paradises arranged as the five sambhogakaya realms, acknowledged goddess Pandaravasini's enlightenment. They acknowledged her as the one who, for countless aeons of time while life expectancy was measureless, had remained indivisible with the protector Buddha Amitabha, enthroned as his enlightened wisdom consort. She had vowed to manifest herself in ways inconceivable to the mind in order to empty the depths of samsara.

Samaya

This completes the second chapter of
The Lives and Liberation
of the Princess of Zahor, Mandarava,
called *A Precious Garland,*

Telling the story of her birth as
the daughter of King Indradeva and
her attainment of enlightenment.

3.
Marrying Prince Suryagarbha

From then on the goddess known as Pandaravasini, she who had attained complete enlightenment in the Realm of Great Bliss, revealed herself in many different manifestations in order to tame beings in ongoing existence.

The aeon known as Bhaskara Sahasrakara was followed by the aeon known as Ratnavistirna, Covered with Jewels. During this aeon, the perfected Buddha Vajragarbha came into this world. In the country of Sukhavana, in the palace of Tamadu, the king was a holy man named Varunasena, and the queen was of royal caste. Her name was Anandashri, Glorious Joy, and she was in charge of the spiritual responsibilities of the kingdom. The name of the prince was Suryagarbha, Essence of the Sun.

When the time came for Prince Suryagarbha to take a queen, word spread throughout the kingdom. It was decided that the minister known as Ratnashri Bhadra would journey to many kingdoms in search of a suitable match. Unsuccessful in his initial attempts, he resolved to travel to the country of the sages, where the king's name was Shubha and the queen was Gyenlegma. They had seven sons and one daughter. The name of their superb palace was Samato, and their wealth and endowments were so extensive that all their subjects possessed great power.

Ratnashri Bhadra, curious to have a look for himself, approached the palace, at which time his attention was captured by a lovely flower garden nearby. Looking closer, he saw a bathing pool beside the garden where the king and queen had gathered with their sons and daughter. The daughter, bedecked in jewels, caught sight of him, approached, and said: "Kye! Minister of excellent virtue, glorious qualities, and pleasing appearance! Please tell me from which kingdom you have come and for what purpose you are here. Who are your father and mother? What is the name of your country, your caste, your clan, and what is your vocation? What is the name of your king? Is the name of his son Prince Suryagarbha? How large is the kingdom, how many provinces does it have, and what is the population? Honorable sir, kindly give me your reply." Thus did she inquire with her gentle beauty, smiling face, and melodious speech.

Minister Ratnashri Bhadra replied: "Kye! O Daughter of the king, please give heed! My country is called Sukhavana, and it is extremely pleasing. The name of my king is Varunasena, and the name of his consort, the queen, is Anandashri. Their son's name is indeed Suryagarbha. Fair princess, his status and intelligence are similar to yours with respect to caste, vocation, spirituality, strength, dominion, popularity, and so on. I am of royal caste, and my father's name is Devendrashri. My mother is the most beautiful Palmo Seldron, and my sister's name is Kshemadevi. My name is Ratnashri Bhadra, and I have come here on behalf of King Varunasena's son, Suryagarbha, who is preparing for enthronement and the responsibility of ruling the kingdom. But first, he must find the most suitable woman to take as his queen. I have come here in search of such a queen. Please bring this news to your father, mother, and brothers."

Accordingly, the princess went over to her mother and said: "Kye! O kind mother who gave me my very body, O guardian of love, dear mother, vessel of my birth—the minister of King Varunasena, named Ratnashri Bhadra, is here. He has come in search of a suitable queen for the occasion of Prince Suryagarbha's enthronement. Please present this message to the king." As she spoke, the minister marveled at what an excellent daughter she was and how exceptionally lovely to behold. He wondered how she knew about Suryagarbha and became convinced that she would be suitable and good for him. The minister then decided that she was the prime candidate for queenship.

The queen went before the king and respectfully said: "Kye! The king of the caste of holy men, Dharma King Varunasena, has sent his minister, Ratnashri Bhadra. The prince known as Suryagarbha is about to assume the throne, and they are searching for a suitable queen. He has asked that this message be presented to you, King Shubha, and that you may be so kind as to grant your response."

The king answered as follows: "The royal lineage of the sages is equal to the sky. Their line of royal ancestry has been similar in glory to the sun and the moon. Our daughter shall only wed a chakravartin. To wed her to another would be the greatest loss. What response shall I give to the minister who has come as an emissary of the great Dharma King Varunasena? It is important to take great care in the wording of our response."

Then the minister was brought before the king and spoke as follows: "Kye! King of the holy men Shubhamanidhara, please listen carefully to the essential point of my request. I am from the country known as Sukhavana, and my king's name is Varunasena. The name of his son is Prince Suryagarbha, who has a mind for spiritual affairs that is without equal. His appearance is so attractive that one cannot gaze upon him enough. His physical beauty rivals that of the god Brahma himself. His speech is both melodious and profound. He is in the prime of youth, about to assume his father's throne. I have come here to find a maiden who is suitable to become his queen. She must be compatible in caste, vocation, and ancestral heritage and be beautiful as well. King, you possess such a daughter, and I beseech you to allow your lovely daughter to come to our kingdom."

The king replied: "Kye! O minister of the great King Varuna, my daughter Natyendri, Lord of Dance, possesses signs that are inconceivably sublime. Her face is extremely beautiful, and her parents and siblings are all of good character. Since her qualities and knowledge are so excellent, it is difficult for me to give her to anyone." Hearing the king's words, the minister held them in his mind and quickly returned to his own country to meet with King Varunasena. In the presence of the queen and all the subjects, he made the following presentation: "Kye! Best of all gods, king and consort, I have journeyed to ten countries and was unable to find a suitable queen to join our future king for his enthronement. In the end, I went to the kingdom of King Shubha, whose palace is called Samato. When I arrived, the king, queen, and their children were bathing in a beautiful lotus pool. The king has seven sons and one daughter. The daughter, bedecked with jewels, saw me and approached to ask, 'Kye! Excellent minister Shri Bhadra of honorable character! For what reason have you come to this country? What is the name of your father, mother, your caste, country, and king?' She even asked about prince Suryagarbha by name. I carefully answered her, and she took that information to the queen, who took it to the king. Then I myself went before the king and repeated the purpose of my mission. When I asked the king for his daughter, the words he spoke in response were in poetic verse like that of the aryas."

The king and the minister decided that, whatever the case, the prince must be fully informed of this occurrence. The king went to meet his son face to face and, using gentle words, said: "Kye! Guardian of the Dharma, Suryagarbha, repayer of your parents' kindness! Hear the essence of your father's heartfelt wish. I sent Minister Ratnashri Bhadra to some ten countries on a search, and in the end he met the daughter of King Shubha, named Natyendri. She is exquisitely beautiful and possesses many wondrous signs. It is certain that she is the suitable woman to take as your queen. Please tell your father what you honestly feel we should do!" The Prince responded that it was necessary to check for auspicious signs.

On the full moon, abundant offerings were made to the Three Jewels, after which both king and son offered many prayers and fell asleep. Suryagarbha had an excellent dream. He dreamt that white light with a reddish hue arose from the east and dissolved into him. He, in turn, melted into light and became a *hum*. From the *hum*, a *hrih* emerged to encompass the three galaxies. The universe and contents became ablaze with five-colored light, and all was perceived as the essence of the two syllables. Boundless light rays proceeded to encompass the three galaxies, and wherever the light shone, seed syllables appeared. The king dreamt of a hollow crystal vessel that contained a white silken cloth. It appeared in the east, and he gave it to his son. When Suryagarbha had it in his hand, he draped his body with the cloth. Then Suryagarbha himself became the crystal vessel. The king dreamt that the news of this occurrence spread forth in the ten directions.

The following morning, both king and son felt that their dreams held auspicious indications. Assembling many precious jewels, riches, and other supporting objects, the king composed a letter, on behalf of his son, to King Shubhamanidhara. In the letter, written with gold ink, they said: "Kye! King of the holy men, Glorious Shubhamanidhara! Your exceptionally alluring daughter Natyendri holds the essence of great bliss. In order to maintain the throne of my kingdom, please grant her to me and accept this abundance of the most desirable precious substances. Please bring joy to the son of this fortunate king, and express your great kindness by recognizing the suitability of this union!"

The minister departed to deliver the letter by hand to King Shubhamanidhara. Arriving at the kingdom, he saw, to his surprise, King Sukhapala, King Shubhamanidhara with his son Bala Urdhi, King Khasarpana with the minister Hadzin, and many others. There were kings and representatives of some thirteen kingdoms with outer and inner ministers bearing countless varieties of wealth. They had all come with the intention of winning the princess for their own kingdoms. The minister Ratnashri Bhadra requested an audience with the king and presented him with the gifts and the letter composed in gold ink from King Varunasena. The king read the letter and conferred with his outer and inner ministers, the queen, and all his sons.

The King then said to his assembled subjects: "Kye! The kings from all directions have come here to try to win the hand of my exquisite daughter. If I promise to give her to one, it will surely offend another. Whatever I do will potentially bring great harm to our kingdom. Would it not be wise to give her to no one? With wisdom and intelligence, please consider the best way to deal with this problem."

After the king had spoken, there was much discussion. No one, however, was able to suggest a definitive solution. Then the queen spoke: "When our daughter Natyendri was born, her body was wrapped in white cloth, and she displayed the ability to dance. She moved her hand to bestow empowerment, so we named her Natyendri, Powerful Woman of Dance. She is an exquisitely beautiful consort, unequaled by any other who walks upon this earth. I cherish her as I do my own heart. So the thought of giving her away gives rise to great sadness. We are powerless not to act, since so many countries have gathered here to receive her. If great care is not taken in this decision, there is the danger that we could lose our very country. Now, by the force of karma, it is difficult to hold her back. We should allow her to decide her own future—but no matter who receives her, there will be others who will try to steal her. She will be forced to experience unbearable suffering. I feel as if my heart is being torn from my chest! Oh, what can be done?" After speaking, the queen shed tears and gazed sorrowfully at the king.

They all agreed that the princess herself should choose; so the king, queen, and her brothers went to her. With great care they lovingly spoke to her in this way: "Kye! Beautiful daughter, the heart of your parents and the eyes of your brothers, please listen. The kings, subjects, and messengers of many countries have gathered with much wealth and letters written in gold, all asking to take you to their kingdoms. There are so many of them that they fill the outer and inner regions of the kingdom. We cannot decide what to do. Although the thought of losing you brings us great sorrow, at the same time we fear for the safety of our kingdom. O daughter, wherever you go we intend to honor your decision, as we know it will be the right one. Please, O daughter of the gods, tell us what you wish to do." Hearing this, Natyendri addressed her parents and brothers, saying:

"Kye ho! Alas! O father, king of the gods of excellent lineage, kind mother who has given me the very body that I live in, and loving brothers of the same family, all of you look upon me with love and speak to me from your hearts. These troublesome questions and explanations that bring joy and sorrow do not affect me, for I have no intention of maintaining the worldly affairs or responsibilities of any kingdom. With the awakened mind of altruism as my motivating force, my actions must flow in accordance with the power of previous deeds.

"Before this life, I lived in Sukhavati paradise as the supreme consort and goddess Pandaravasini. Now I have manifested myself as the daughter of the king of the holy men. I have no other purpose than to fulfill the needs of sentient beings. By the force of previous prayers, Prince Suryagarbha, an emanation of Arya Avalokiteshvara, and I have generated bodhichitta. I shall never take an ordinary husband, whose body is the cause for leading others to lower rebirth. Forsaking this kingdom, I shall escape unnoticed to go to the palace of the future king Surya-garbha. Father, mother, and brothers, please practice Dharma well. In this place of samsara, unending suffering must be endured. My heart's advice to you is to achieve liberation from samsara. I have no attachment to samsara. Through the method of great compassion I shall work unceasingly for sentient beings. By accomplishing the commands of Buddha Amitabha, I have come to guide you all to the state of the aryas!"

Upon hearing her words, the king, queen, brothers, and ministers were moved with devotion and respect. Just as she had said she would, the princess escaped from the kingdom with her attendant. Seven days into the journey, the attendant suddenly fell ill and passed away. The princess performed the transference of consciousness for her, thus guiding her to the pure realm.

Seven days and nights passed. One morning, in the early hours of dawn, Prince Suryagarbha awoke and gazed up into the space before him. Suddenly, Arya Avalokiteshvara appeared, nearly unbearable to behold, blazing with one hundred thousand dazzling rays of light. Avalokiteshvara then spoke to him: "My son, now you must arise from your sleep. To the east of here, the daughter of the king of sages, Natyendri, by her clairvoyant powers has escaped from her kingdom, the blissful land of the gods, where many kings and princes still make aggressive overtures for her hand in marriage. Now she is coming to meet you and is presently en route quite a distance north of here. For the sake of maintaining the doctrine and benefiting beings, go find her!"

After receiving this prophecy, the prince assembled all his ministers and told them that they must make an important journey to the north and prepare for a very auspicious meeting. Accordingly, he gathered them into groups. Each member adorned in silk brocades and precious jewels, they traveled north to the banks of lake Pema Tsegpa. After seven days had passed, when the sun was well up in the sky, the future king addressed them. He said that the daughter of the king of sages, Natyendri, had escaped from her kingdom because the kings of many countries had gathered to ask for her hand in marriage. He informed them that she was about to arrive and that she would join him for the sake of benefiting beings. He urged them to celebrate with song, dance, and musical instruments so that everything would be as auspicious and cheerful as possible. Then, after greeting her in this way, they would all return with her to the kingdom. After he spoke, they all went to the edge of the lake to await her arrival. Then, from the eastern direction, they all craned their necks to witness a swirling mass of rainbow-colored light rays that appeared in space. A rain of flowers filled the sky with clouds of offerings suitable for gods, nagas, and humans alike. Natyendri herself, surrounded with blazing radiant light, then became visible. The prince and all the ministers gave her an extensive welcoming reception.

Meanwhile, the kings from the other countries began to suspect that the young princess was hiding somewhere in her kingdom. They looked for her in every direction. Some thought she might be hiding in a ravine or crevice; they even dug up the earth to look for her underground. Some thought she might be hiding in a treasure chest, so they searched treasuries everywhere. They also searched for her in the mountains. Wherever they looked, she was nowhere to be found. In the end, they were forced to return to their own kingdoms exhausted and empty-handed.

Suryagarbha sent the minister Mani Ratna ahead to tell the king and queen what was happening. The entire population of the kingdom then assembled. They played many different musical instruments and beat their drums. With incense bearers and the royal sons and daughters as their guides, the new couple arrived at the palace. The entire kingdom began a month long celebration. Extensive offerings were made to the Three Jewels of Refuge. The whole kingdom engaged in games, sports, and acts of pleasure. Minister Ratnashri Bhadra and the sage's son, Guna Indra, joined their respective assemblies and celebrated.

King Varunasena ruled the kingdom for three more years. One day he called a meeting with his son Suryagarbha, Natyendri, and the hosts of outer and inner ministers and their retinues. Suryagarbha and Natyendri were then formally enthroned to govern the kingdom. First they gave an abundance of alms to the poor and needy in the form of food and clothing. They introduced a new law that made the Buddhist doctrine the state religion and the dissemination of the Dharma the most important function of the new government. They made offerings to the king and queen, and everyone paid respect to them. All the fortunate people of their kingdom were brought to the path of Dharma, and

Natyendri gave teachings on the vehicle of secret mantra. In the end, the entire kingdom of one hundred thousand people attained enlightenment as one mandala!

Samaya

This completes the third chapter of
The Lives and Liberation
of the Princess of Zahor, Mandarava,
called *A Precious Garland,*

Describing how she manifested herself as
the daughter of the king of the sages,
married Prince Suryagarbha, brought the
entire kingdom to the Dharma, and
gradually led the entire population to the
state of perfect enlightenment.

4.

In the Kingdom of Kanaka

From then on, Dakini Pandaravasini, the consort of the conquerors, was empowered by the buddhas of the three times to manifest herself in order to bestow the empowerment of the five embodiments.[13] At that time, from the point between her eyebrows, a white *hrih* went forth into this world. From her throat a red *hrih* radiated eastward toward the continent of Potala. From her heart a clear blue *hrih* radiated into the upper regions of the realms of the gods. From her navel a luminous yellow *hrih* radiated into the lower regions of the supreme palace of the naga king. From her secret place a green *hrih* radiated into the demigod realm. From each of these syllables a billion emanations were produced through the power of her concentration.

All this occurred during the Age of Luminosity. This was the time of Buddha Kanakamuni,[14] one of the thousand buddhas to appear in this light aeon. In the land of East India, in the city of Kanika, there was a king named Kalasiddhi, whose virtuous queen was known as Pushpalamkara, Adorned with Flowers. The Buddha's doctrine was not being propagated that the kingdom, and the king had a strong intuition that the time had come to tame the minds of beings. He imposed the discipline of abstaining from killing, but when this law was ignored he became ill and passed from this world.

His queen, Pushpalamkara, suffered so greatly from the shock of his passing that she went to the shore of Lake Rayaya, where, on the verge of taking her own life by jumping in, a handsome young man suddenly appeared before her. With joyful confidence he approached her and asked why she was there. Pushpalamkara replied: "I am overwhelmed with great torment and sorrow. My husband was the great king Kalasiddhi, well-known for his powers throughout the world." Wailing with misery, she proclaimed her extreme misfortune at the sudden death of her beloved husband, the king.

The young man then spoke to her. "Although King Kalasiddhi has passed away, I am here now, and I have come to be your husband. Please do not despair! Come here, maiden, and let us return to the kingdom together." After he had spoken, Pushpalamkara experienced a change of heart and became attached to the young man. Together they returned to the kingdom, where all the people thought that the young man she had found was either a son of the gods or a prince. Everyone became infatuated with him. They offered him their wealth and possessions and enthroned him as their new king. The queen, feeling once again like a young maiden, fell deeply in love with him, experiencing much pleasure and happiness.

One night, Pushpalamkara thought to herself: "I wonder where this handsome young man came from? I did not even ask him where he was from, who his parents are, what his caste and family lineage are. Although he appears to be equal to the gods in beauty, I must inquire as to his background." She then approached him, saying:

"Kye! Wondrous and charming young man, turn your joyous attention to me and listen. In a state of unbearable sorrow, I was about to drown myself in Lake Rayaya when you suddenly appeared. Forgetting my sorrow, I have come to know such bliss with you. I feel that my merit is excellent, and I rejoice in my great fortune. Yet I am curious as to your background, your family heritage, your parents, and so on. Kindly tell me something about yourself."

The young man responded: "E ma! How wondrous! My father is the primordial Buddha Samantabhadra, my mother is the primordial wisdom of empty bliss, Samantabhadri. I am the manifestation of the great and powerful Hayagriva. In the paradise of discriminating primordial wisdom awareness, maiden Pushpalamkara, your lineage is that of the buddhas. Your sadness and depression came from nowhere and bring no benefit or result.

"Beings are tossed about in the ocean of samsara by the waves of previous karma. Living and remaining in this kingdom are like falling into a pit of fire. Don't you think that this jail-like existence of activities that leads to the lower realms is nothing other than the sowing of more seeds that lead to rebirth in the hell realms? The worldly activities with which the king was involved while alive were merely the cause for your unceasing accumulation of negative deeds. You should now develop renunciation toward this kingdom and know that the time has come for your voyage on the path to perfect awakening!"

The queen began crying: "E ma! Please, young man, let us never separate! I will do whatever you command of me." Having spoken, she suffered unceasingly throughout the day and night. After some time, the young man spoke to her again: "Maiden, you and I shall not leave this place. From now on, you must accomplish the Dharma as purely as possible." She then made her vow in accordance with his words. It was then that she met Buddha Kanakamuni, who was out begging for alms, and took the bodhisattva vow in his presence.

After that, the queen began to train on the path of the precious Dharma. One evening, a white *hrih* shimmering with light appeared in the air; descending, it multiplied so that one *hrih* dissolved into the young man, while she experienced the other dissolving into her heart. The next morning the young man commanded: "Arise, Pushpalamkara, and make offerings. By the force of past karma you shall give birth to a daughter." She said that she had nothing to give birth to. He replied that the experience of the previous evening meant that there was a child to be born.

For ten months the sound of *hrih* continued to resonate from her belly. Hearing this sound so repeatedly, she began to wonder what it was and felt that she was with child, though she felt no pain. She inquired of the young man, and he smilingly replied that it was as he had said. After ten months, she gave birth. At that moment rainbow light rays appeared in space and flowers fell like rain. From cloud formations came the sounds of musical instruments. Everyone was saying that the king and queen had given birth to a son.

On the child's first month's birthday, it became known that the son was in fact a daughter. At the moment of her birth, she had sat up and proclaimed "*Hrih*!" She possessed all the marvelous signs and indications, such that everyone accepted that the child was a daughter. The king gave her the name Özer Nangyen, Adorned with Light, by which she was known thereafter.

She studied the Dharma from her eighth month to sixteenth year under the supervision of her father. One day, when she saw her father, she said : "E ma! The miraculous activity of the conquerors, great powerful father! Although the ground dissolves into the baseless nature of original purity, the manifestations of the buddhas' incarnations are unceasing. I too am connected to the gods, as my nature is that of the aryas. I am a woman possessing profound and extensive previous aspirations." Shortly after she spoke, white rainbow light streamed down upon the palace, and the king ascended the rainbow as though it were a staircase. Nothing could stop him, and he dissolved into space. The princess succeeded in consoling her suffering mother and took over the administration of the kingdom and the establishment of its laws. Full sovereignty was given to the law of the Buddha's doctrine.

One day, when Özer Nangyen ventured outside for a stroll, she came across some five hundred nuns gathered in a lotus garden. In the garden there was a magnificent lotus flower of many petals, resembling a mandala. Radiant white light, so dazzling that it was difficult to gaze upon, arose from the tips of the petals of this flower. The entire gathering was compelled to watch this remarkable sight. Looking closer, they beheld, in the pollen heart of the center of the lotus, a sixteen-year-old youth. He was blazing with radiant light, smiling, and extremely attractive. Mesmerizing to behold, he possessed all the major and minor marks of perfection.

Then the youth spoke to them: "E ma! Amazing maiden of the gods, Özer Nangyen with your assembly of five hundred manifestations, it is most excellent that you have come here today. Your face is like a beautifully painted conch shell, and your teeth are like a string of white lotus flowers. Your tongue resembles a swathe of poppy-colored silk; your smiling lips are as attractive as luscious lotus petals. Your elongated eyes and eyebrows are fine and subtle, perfect in their design. Your arms and legs are perfectly proportioned, your skin soft and smooth like the fur of an antelope. The palms of your hands and the soles of your feet are fine and delicate, like the petals of the utpala lotus flower. Your breasts are voluptuous, your secret lotus enriched and essential. Your hair is blue-green and your forehead is like the white, shining moon. Your waist is slim, your manner is as seductive as a six-teen-year-old maiden. You are an emanation of the supreme consort of all the buddhas. I am an emanation of the sovereign of compassion, Avalokiteshvara. I was born miraculously from within a pure lotus. As the sole deity upholding the kingdom, you, fair maiden, have come here to meet me by the power of your karma. Dakini, you have brought your entire kingdom to the path of Dharma!"

Then the lady Özer Nangyen and her assembly of five hundred addressed him as follows: "E ma! Born from the heart of a lotus, amaz-ing youth of nobility, we are overjoyed to meet you. Seeing your face is like quenching our thirst. By your compassion please come with us to our palace."

They carefully examined him and determined that he was clearly an emanation of the Buddha in every possible way. His face appeared like a conch that had been painted with a fine brush; the palms of his hands and soles of his feet looked like the petals of the pali flower. His blue-green hair was wrapped like a silken scarf around his head. His nose was perfectly proportioned, his lips full, his eyes oblong, and his eye-brows appeared to be made of rainbow light rays. He wore precious jeweled ornaments. His smile radiated charm and happiness. He was a youth of about sixteen, in the very prime of health, a person so splen-did that one could not stop looking at him. He possessed the major and minor marks of physical perfection. His speech was so melodious that it sounded like the singing of the kalapanga song bird. "You are a great holy being and a true object of our devotion and offerings," they told him. "Please arise and come with us!"

He then arose in the midst of blazing light rays. Wherever he stepped, flowers spontaneously sprang forth. He was therefore known by the name of Padma, or Lotus. He was also known as Önang Pagme, Boundless Appearance of Light, Peme Gompar Shegpa, Lotuses Follow in His Wake, and Dakadhipati, Lord of the Dakinis.

He came with them to the kingdom, where he upheld and protected the Buddhist teachings. He gave secret mantra empowerments to Özer

Nangyen, and she practiced the stages of spiritual development until her merit ripened and she was liberated. The prince Önang Pagme, the princess Özer Nangyen, and their retinue brought all the people in the kingdom with them to the state of liberation in the rainbow body.[15] The kingdom was thereafter known as "The Power Place for Departure into the Rainbow Body."

Samaya

This completes the fourth chapter of
The Lives and Liberation
of the Princess of Zahor, Mandarava,
called *A Precious Garland,*

Which gives an account of her first
incarnation into the world of human
beings in the kingdom known as
Kanika, India, of how she brought that
kingdom to the Dharma, and of the
gradual stages of accomplishment that
lead to buddhahood.

5.

In the Kingdom of Damaru

From the throat center of Dakini Pandaravasini a *hrih* blazing with light shot directly into the palace of the eastern realm of Potala. In that realm, in the center of the great milky lake of the eight pure qualities, there are sixteen continents, each with sixteen surrounding subcontinents. The two continents to the east are Dhatrakosha and Mitrarashmi, where the two aryas, Drowa Dulwa and the excellent Khasarpani, teach the Dharma of infinite love to innumerable disciples. The two continents to the south are Katrokopa and Rinchenvyuha. There, Amoghapasha and Ratnajaya teach the Dharma of compassion to an assembly of countless disciples. The two continents to the west are Parardha and Palapatre Gyen. There, Arya Padma and Arya Ushnishavijaya teach the joyous Dharma to countless disciples.

The two continents to the north are Vajrapankti and Gyepepel. There Arya Avalokiteshvara and Padma Nateshvara teach the Dharma of equanimity to hosts of countless disciples. The two continents to the southeast are Maitrikanta and Ratnalamkara. There, Nilakanta and Özer Barwewang grant countless disciples the teachings on the action and conduct tantras. The two continents to the southwest are Mularasa and Aryakotra. There, the aryas Namkhe Gyalpo and Dongtrug Lha teach the doctrine of the highest vehicle to innumerable disciples. The two continents to the northwest are Dewe Tsalchen and Padmarashi. There, Ratnarchi and the arya Vikridita teach the doctrine of the three vehicles to countless scores of disciples. The two continents to the northeast are Padma Vikridita and Vajrakula. There, the aryas King Paltseg and Kuntuchang Wangpo teach the doctrine of the Ati vehicle[16] to countless disciples.

In the central pure palace of Potala, home of the mandala known as Powerful Lotus, resides Avalokiteshvara in the form of Gyalwa Gyatso, with one thousand arms and eyes. There he teaches the Dharma of unobstructed ultimate truth to a vast assembly of tenth-level bodhisattvas. Everything in this realm is splendid and luminously aglow. There are beautiful green meadows, pure pools of water, lotus gardens, and rivers of nectar. There are wish-granting trees whose branches and leaves are made of fine silken brocade. The branches are laden with fruits made of heaps of precious jewels that fall like rain. Divine birds melodiously chirp and sing the song of secret mantra. Gods and goddesses swirl in dance to the sound of the melodies. Clouds of offerings produce whatever is desired. The palaces are all studded with jewels of five varieties, and all the retinues are the color of crystals, blazing with light. There is no distinction between day or night; there is only the self-originating light of primordial wisdom. Food, clothing, and luxuries spontaneously appear as desired. There is no delusion, so suffering and illness are nonexistent. The very name of misery is unheard of in this realm of great bliss. In this perfectly arranged realm of the aryas, noble qualities are beyond imagination.

Below this paradise, to the north, is a country called Damaru. The substances found there are flesh, blood, and bones. This continent is shrouded in the darkness of killing and slaughter. There exists no mercy or compassion, and inhabitants have no faith in the realized ones. It is a dark land, where there are no buddhas to tame beings. All the female inhabitants find pleasure in taking the lives of others. Their faces are wild and ruddy, their manner is so barbaric that the mere sight of them incites fear and terror. They will even kill their own parents in order to make sacrificial offerings of blood and flesh.

In the center of this continent is Karmarupa,[17] a great palace with a circumference of many miles. There resides the nonvirtuous King Shinta, who gathers his ministers together daily and slaughters tens of thousands of inhabitants for their consumption. He has an assembly of three hundred thousand subjects, all of whom are strictly under his command. There is a lake called Ngampachen, swirling and swelling with waves of blood. In this lake is the palace of the demon king Black Yaksha. The lake is one thousand and one miles in circumference and fifty-three miles deep. All the people of this continent gather here each day to sacrifice beings and to offer their heads, hearts, and organs to the evil king. In turn, after the people themselves die, they take rebirth again in the king's retinue. In this hell realm, the blades of death circle unceasingly. The misery endured is quite unbearable. This continent is so dreadful that peaceful methods are utterly ineffective in pacifying it.

The great dakini understood that the time had come for this continent to be subdued. She transformed herself into a syllable *hrih* and manifested herself as blazing light before the aryas. By their blessings the syllable was transformed into a goddess. After she had made offerings to the aryas in all the sixteen continents, their intentions were fulfilled, and they knew that the time had indeed come to tame the minds of the inhabitants of Damaru.

She proclaimed that the time had come for all the buddhas to reveal their powerful abilities and that she herself was a female emanation of the buddhas. The great dakini implored the buddhas, as the unique protectors of beings, to display their wrathful enlightened activities. This request pleased all the buddhas, who then manifested themselves as the wrathful deity Hayagriva. In order to emanate in their five manifestations, the enlightened ones transferred the consciousness of five ministers from Damaru into space, entered their bodies, and became the retinue of Hayagriva. The dakini then descended into lake Ngampachen as a red *hrih* in order to slay and liberate the evil demon king Black Yaksha with her enlightened activity.

The lake then transformed into nectar, turning white in color. The naga king Rinchen Ö came and built a palace, summoning gods, nagas, and humans of this world as his friends. The lake no longer accepted offerings of flesh and blood. In retaliation the demon let forth a fury of torrential lightning and hail storms. Everyone noticed that the lake no longer accepted wrathful blood offerings and that its natural red color had been transformed into white. The subjects took this as an initial indication of the decline of the demons' doctrine.

It seemed certain that the religion of virtue would now flourish in this continent and that the banishing of the evil doctrine was close at hand. When nonvirtuous customs had nearly disappeared from the land, the ministers were commanded to gather. The king told them that it was the tradition of his royal lineage to support nonvirtuous actions and that he could not bring himself to maintain virtuous Dharma.

Then nine bad omens occurred at the demon lake Ngampachen, and the king himself experienced negative signs. In his dreams he heard the sound of neighing horses coming from the heads of the ministers. He heard the sound of a Dharma drum beating in the center of the lake. His supreme son, Yaksha Anandapala, was eaten by a red-colored girl. He dreamt that he lost all of his clothing. He also dreamt that the entire country became filled with white snow, that scriptures descended onto the top of the palace, and that white light penetrated his heart.

He took each of these signs as a negative omen and ordered his ministers to firmly enforce outer and inner laws of nonvirtue. If anyone was caught practicing Dharma, they were to be punished. No one in the kingdom was allowed to speak a word of Dharma. They were also told to make red offerings to the demon lake. All the ministers enforced the law according to these commands and maintained the policies of the great king. They then came to feel that the negative dreams were not a threat and that all was going well.

Yet, unknown to them, the dreams were excellent signs. The sound of neighing horses coming from the ministers' heads was an indication of respect for the king's life force sign, the horse. The sound of the drum in the lake was a sign of the birth of an amazing princess or the sign of finding a female nagini. The red-colored girl was an indication that the doctrine of Tsen[18] was to be propagated there. The country turning white was a sign of increasing endowments. The loss of his clothing was a sign of a great celebration. The descent of scriptures like rain was a sign of the great gods' prophecy. Light penetrating into the heart signified the king's excellent intelligence. The correct interpretation was explained to the king, and he believed it to be true. Then all the ministers felt very unsettled.

The time came for the king's son to wed and assume the throne. One day, during the search for a suitable bride among all the young women in the country and the surrounding areas, a ring of fire never before seen appeared around the edge of the lake. Everyone saw this ring of fire. It became the cause for much discussion among the ministers, and they decided to go to the lake to investigate. In the center of the lake, they saw a red flower blossoming in the shape of a shield, open in full bloom. In its center appeared a beautiful sixteen-year-old girl, dancing in a swaying motion. All the ministers were astonished, and they quickly returned to report this to the king.

"Kye! O meritorious king of the land of Damaru, it is just as the prophecy indicated. The lake became encircled by a ring of fire. Then, in its center, within the very pollen heart of a lotus in full bloom, a young woman was born. She is extremely beautiful to behold, white in color, about sixteen years of age, and is surely a female nagini. Indeed, she has appeared. She seems to be from the Black Heart race of nagas, who are very wealthy and possess many varieties of precious jewels. We feel that this amazing goddess must be the long-awaited bride of our future king!"

Then the king bedecked himself in fine brocade silk and made many offerings. He, the prince, and all the ministers set out for the lake while the king marveled again and again at his great fortune. At the very moment the prince laid eyes on the young woman, he was fully captivated by her beauty, and a great passion arose within him. The young woman said:

"Um! O king of Damaru, Shinta, the time has come for your son to wed and to prepare for his enthronement. Although you have been searching for a young woman within the human realm, my merit is much greater! Just by gazing at me, your son has become intoxicated with the bliss of Samantabadri. I am the daughter of the demon lord Yaksha. I have also been the daughter of the blue-clothed black lord of the nagas. There are eighteen classes of nagas in the subterranean continents, and nine of these classes slay sentient beings for their sustenance. The other nine classes use wish-fulfilling jewels for their food and drink. There is none whose wealth and endowments can surpass that of the nagas. At this time I am now ruled by the naga king. I have come to meet your son, Yaksha Anandapala. I pray this may be possible."

Upon hearing her words, the king and ministers convened. After much discussion, they came to an agreement and said: "Kye! O Black Yaksha! In the expanse of the terrifying life force lake, in the pollen heart of an astonishing lotus flower, the daughter of the naga king, Gö Ngön, so youthful and sublime, has come to wed the new king of this demonic race of black ones. How great is the fortune of the demons! We are overjoyed that such a nagini has come here among us."

After they spoke, the girl walked across the lake to reach them. Each step that she took left an imprint on the water. The king and his retinue made extensive offerings to her and escorted her back to the palace. All the subjects gathered, and a great celebration took place. She stayed with the prince at the top of the palace. After some time, she said to him: "O Yaksha Anandapala, please listen to me. I take no joy in remaining in this palace. Although I love you, I cannot remain here like this. Now I shall return to the lake of my origin. My country is countless miles from here. The palace of the naga king is exceptionally pleasant. There is no nonvirtue, only the increase of virtue. Merit is inexhaustible, and the holy Dharma thrives. All the ministers enforce the law to uphold virtue. In many ways, your country is inferior to mine. The king uses his power to uphold the ways of the demons. The outer and inner ministers are evil guardians of the land. This is a country of evil rulers obscured in the darkness of their own vice. I have no desire to remain in this place where the name of virtue is nonexistent and butchers prevail. My eyes cannot see my father, mother, brothers, and sisters. I cannot hear even a verse of the holy Dharma. My sorrow is immeasurable, O dear friend of mine. Your body that you cherish so dearly is produced from your parents. Having been born from a lotus, I shall now return to my country. We met this time by the force of our past karma. We cannot remain together for long. It is the nature of impermanence. Therefore please don't despair. Work hard to uphold your kingdom."

After she spoke, Yaksha Anandapala thought to himself that this young woman was a most remarkable nagini. There was no human in this world who could equal even a portion of her noble qualities. Having never seen anyone like her, he thought that it would be impossible to replace her. What a shame it was that they had not had a son during their time together! If there had been a son, she would hesitate to leave due to her love for her child. He resolved that he must discourage her from leaving, no matter what the cost.

He went to see the king and told him the following: "My only father the King! The astonishing nagini born from the lotus is planning to return to her own country. This demonic land only depresses her. No matter what she thinks or does, this amazing young woman, once lost, would be impossible to replace. I must find a method to convince her to stay." After he spoke, the king and all the ministers met to discuss the matter, but they could not think of a method to stop her from leaving. Then the five ministers who were emanations of Hayagriva caused the delusion in the mind of the great king to vanish through their enlightened powers. The king decided that the amazing young nagini born from the lotus should be allowed to take complete charge of running the secular affairs of the kingdom. None of the ministers thought that she should be allowed to leave, and the king proclaimed that they should do whatever she commanded. The king, prince, and everyone else agreed, so they all approached the young woman.

"E ma! Woman born from the lotus, even if one scoured the universe, it would be impossible to encounter a maiden as rare as you. You have decided to leave the prince, my son of honorable family. Please, I implore you, tell us what we have done to cause you to wish to leave us. Young woman, please take over the affairs of this kingdom. We will remain as your subjects under the order of whatever laws you establish and shall never transgress what you ask us to do. In return, we ask you to remain here among us."

To this request the young woman replied: "Would you rather be Dharma ministers or ministers of vice? Would you rather be a king of Dharma or a king of sin? Would you rather be on the side of good or the side of evil? If you would rather be on the side of Dharma, I will consent to stay and rule the kingdom. If you prefer to remain as an evil demon ruler, then I shall have to depart. If you decide to be a Dharma ruler, we can uphold the laws together. If you decide to be nonvirtuous ministers, then we shall have no further connection. If you do decide to be Dharma ministers, I will be able to join forces with you. I am a woman whose special talent is spreading the ways of virtue. You, the king and ministers, must now turn your attention and regard toward the path of virtue. Because you have failed to do so, we have been unable to live in harmony. The people of this land dwell mindlessly in darkness. I am a woman whose virtuous, noble qualities are complete. However you look at it, our points of view are different. The prince is following a path that leads nowhere. The evil ministers are heartless owls hooting in the dark. The hordes of insensate demons are caught in a vicious circle of negative actions. I will stay only if you totally abandon this futile mode of existence. If you do not give it up, I shall pray for the entire kingdom to vanish from existence, while I shall go straight ahead on the path that leads to liberation. If your minds are open, you will act with careful awareness. If you agree with these words of wisdom, approach me with strong remorse and sincerity, and become one with me. If you agree with me, take this advice into your hearts!"

After she spoke, the king and all the ministers embraced her every word and honored her as their queen. The young woman took control of the entire kingdom, and everyone gathered to accept her authority and honor her command.

Samaya

This completes the fifth chapter of
*The Lives and Liberation
of the Princess of Zahor, Mandarava,*
called *A Precious Garland,*

Explaining how her speech emanatation
manifested from the realm of Potala into
the kingdom of Damaru and how, born
from a lotus and mastering the successive
stages of development, she used her
enlightened activity to overpower the
kingdom.

6.

Enlightening the Kingdom of Damaru

Then the young woman, Lotus-born, intending to establish and enforce the law of Dharma in the kingdom, gathered together the king and the inner ministers, requesting them to pay heed. She spoke: "Listen closely, O king and faithful ministers. Turn inward and examine your own minds. All demonic hordes still inclined to nonvirtue must be brought to the path of goodness so that they can pass beyond sorrow. These beings must be led to the state of liberation. Whatever is done must be in accordance with Dharma activity. I am Lotus-born, and my intentions are extremely vast. Now it is no longer necessary for us to assemble and have discussions. The time has come to accomplish the aims of our previous agreement, to establish and enforce the law, to abandon the very root of negativity in this land!

"The ministers and their assemblies are to go to the banks of Lake Ngampachen on the excellent day of the waxing moon. They must put an end to unhappiness in the kingdom by offering the five varieties of precious jewels, grains, white and sweet substances, and silken cloth. Those whose Dharma efforts are supreme will be installed as ministers. Those who continue to conduct themselves nonvirtuously will be executed. On the eighth, fifteenth, and thirtieth days of the lunar calendar, the young women of the kingdom are to establish regular Dharma ceremonies. Those who are lazy and fail to practice Dharma will be severely punished."

Then the king and the ministers beat the great drum of the law. All who had gathered on this occasion at the banks of Lake Ngampachen heard the sound of musical instruments coming from within the lake. This was an indication that the nagas were pleased. A sweet smell permeated the entire country.

To the east of the lake a temple was erected. After consecrating it, the king and queen remained there. Yaksha Anandapala was instructed to train in the practice of sutrayana. They burned the evil books of the previous government so that even the name of the evil doctrine became obsolete. The five ministers who were blessed by Hayagriva enforced the law of Dharma throughout the land. All of the negative hordes were placed under the new system of virtue. Lotus-born had five female emanations: Kyema (Youthful), Dema (Blissful), Gama (Joyful), Chogzangma (Supreme Excellence), and Yangchenma (Melodious), who became the consorts of the five ministers. They turned the wheel of the Dharma of secret mantra on six occasions. Five hundred virtuous females congregated and became fully ordained.

One of the outer ministers, named Jihar, was the emanation of a demon. He was totally opposed to the Dharma and would stop at nothing to defeat it. He had a retinue of five hundred strong. One time, when the dakini Lotus-born was seated in equipoise, the great and glorious Hayagriva appeared in space and spoke to the young queen: "You, Lotus-born, are an emanation of wrathful enlightened activity. I shall assist you in slaying and liberating these hordes of demons. If they are not liberated, they will annihilate the doctrine of the Buddha. Do not hesitate, for the time has come!" As he predicted, hordes of demons holding many varieties of weapons approached Lotus-born, attempting to destroy her. At that moment she assumed her wrathful manifestation, with all the glorious protectors and guardians assisting her. Some wielded weapons, while others caused hail and lightning bolts to strike. Some screamed like warriors, while others shouted the sounds *hum*, *phat*, and *bhyo!*

The hordes of demons were liberated at once, and all of them without exception were led to the realm of Potala, where Avalokiteshvara resides. The doctrine of Lord Buddha spread in every direction, and Lotus-born became known thereafter as Heroine Victorious over the Maras. The common people all began training in Dharma so that throughout the day and night they remained in meditative concentration. All were taught the Dharma doctrine of the nine vehicles,[19] and seven hundred thousand were liberated as one mandala. Obtaining the rainbow body, they passed into the realm of the enlightened ones. Prince Yaksha Anandapala trained on the path and then began to give empowerments for secret mantra practice. Day and night he remained in meditative stabilization. Then one day his father, the king, passed from this world, and his mother, the queen, dissolved her body into space without leaving a trace. By the blessing of the queen, the king's body also dissolved into space without remains.

At that time Yaksha Anandapala proclaimed to Lotus-born: "Kye ma! Dear mother, wisdom dakini! Innermost deity-goddess! By the sun rays of your compassion, the classes of negative demons of the dark direction have completely been eliminated. Mother, you, by the hook of your moon-ray compassion, have led me and all others upon the path to liberation. May the essential nectar of the heart essence of the supreme path of secret mantra be fully accomplished, and may the stainless state of primordial wisdom be realized. Lamp of the world, one who gives vision to the three realms of existence, you are my extremely kind mother, and I am blessed with fortunate karma. As your follower, I bow down to you and place all my devotion in you. My venerable father, King Shinta, has passed from this world. Please tell me where he and the one who gave me my body, my birth mother Kala Yaksha, were reborn and when they shall achieve liberation. When will the end come to their suffering in the six realms of existence? Where will their next place of birth occur? In which country and continent shall they dwell? Please give me a clear answer by the power of your clairvoyance." Making this request, he pressed his palms together and bowed down to her with great devotion.

Then Lotus-born replied: "My dear companion Yaksha Anandapala, please listen. I am the consort Pandaravasini from the realm of Sukhavati. In the realm of Potala, I am the dakini born from the syllable *hrih*. Here in Damaru, I am well known as Lotus-born. Ultimately I am a primordial wisdom dakini. I manifest myself unceasingly in the three times and possess fifty-five powers of clairvoyance. I shall answer your questions in detail; please keep them in mind.

"From beginningless time your father King Shinta has possessed inconceivable blessings of body and speech. A thousand lifetimes ago, at the end of the doctrine of Buddha Vimala, there was a butcher's daughter named Ragamaha. She was so lovely that she was likened to the utpala flower. She became a servant of the king and was forced to tend many animals. She suffered tremendously. "In her delusion, she made a powerful negative prayer in the presence of five hundred shravakas. She prayed that all the animals she was then tending—as well as the king, queen, and all their ministers and assemblies—would come under her power so that she could force all of them to practice non-virtue. While she was making this deluded prayer, the five hundred shravakas prayed that the buddha who came to liberate beings during that time would be able to bring them all to enlightenment. After making her negative prayer, the servant woman died. She proceeded to take many rebirths in the three lower realms. After that, she was born in the eastern realm of the cannibals called Chamara under the rule of King Haling. During that life she was the king's mother, and her name was Kala. Now, in this life, she has become both the queen and the king, your parents. Due to the power of the prayers made by the shravakas, I am the one to bring her to spiritual maturation.

"Nonetheless, after this lifetime, she will be born as a daughter of the lowest caste in India in the city known as Gandhi. Her name will be Zangmo, and she will become a prostitute. It is then that I will be able to tame her mind and bring her to the path of Dharma. After that, both your mother and father will be born in the land of Zahor. Their names will be Ösema and Kunche. Born as craftsmen, they will be brother and sister, and I will bring them to liberation. Achieving the rainbow body, they will go to the land of Chamara."[20]

After she spoke, Yaksha Anandapala became filled with joy and vowed to follow her forever. A short time later, he died and, without leaving any remains behind, passed on to the realm of Potala. Then everyone in the entire country, along with Lotus-born and her assemblies, obtained the rainbow body and achieved perfect enlightenment.

Samaya

This completes the sixth chapter of
*The Lives and Liberation
of the Princess of Zahor, Mandarava,*
called *A Precious Garland,*

Explaining how she placed the entire
country of Damaru on the path of
Dharma and brought everyone to the
state of enlightenment.

7.
In the Realm of the Gods

Then, from the light rays of the manifestation of the great dakini, a mind emanation was sent forth as a clear blue *hrih*. Arriving in the upper regions of the gods' realm, she manifested herself in the palace of the great god Indra. There she became the daughter of the god Ratnadhara and the goddess Kunzig Önang. Known as Kangkari, she was beautiful beyond compare. The fame of her elegance spread throughout the country. Her companion's name was Dawa Özer, Moonlight, an emanation of the Buddha in the Brahmin class of the gods. Once, when they went to the peak of a mountain, they gave birth to the body emanation of the aryas, named Dampa Togkar.

In order to defeat the demigods[21] in the warring gods realm, Kangkari sent forth a wrathful manifestation. When the hordes of demigods were defeated, they abandoned their harmful intentions and paid homage to her. Thereafter she became known as the goddess Conqueror and Bestower of Bliss. All the gods of the powerful Brahmin class paid homage to her and requested that she turn the wheel of Dharma. Every one of them achieved the peaceful state of an arya.

Once, Dampa Togkar respectfully approached his honored mother to say: "Kye ma! Powerful Goddess Kangkari! You are known as the one who defeated the demigods, placing them in peaceful bliss. O mother, beautiful heroine, source of the Dharma, whose companion is Dawa Özer! In order to guide all the gods who remain in meditative stabilization, I am planning to go to the paradise of Tushita. Dakini of the profound Dharma of secret mantra who, without abandoning samsara, remains to guide sentient beings, please bestow this amazing and sublime doctrine upon me. By engaging on the swift path, I hope to bring this path of truth to the realm of Tushita and turn the wheel of the Prajnaparamita."

Kangkari replied: "Until this world system is empty, I shall not pass away to nirvana but shall undertake whatever activity is necessary for taming sentient beings. Son, when you go to the realm of Tushita, show the perfection of wisdom of the two truths[22] to your disciples. After this rebirth, you will be reborn in India as the son of King Shuddhodhana[23] and will achieve enlightenment. I shall emanate as the magically manifested mother who gives birth to you. With the karma of this rebirth, in the countries of gods, nagas, and human beings, you will become well known as a holder of the ancestral heritage of Shakyamuni, famous as the one who defeats the hordes of maras.[24] This will occur in accordance with the prophecy of the past Buddha Dipamkara. You will have countless nirmanakaya emanations. In order to bring five hundred thousand sons of the gods to the state of perfect awakening as one mandala, I shall reveal the profound Dharma to you in its entirety."

Then she gave all the teachings without exception to her supreme son, Dampa Togkar, whereupon he went to the realm of Tushita. Kangkari sent countless light rays from her body into the thirtieth level of the gods' realm. Whomever the light rays entered was brought before her and taught the causal doctrine, the four truths, and the paramitas.[25] She also turned the Dharma wheel of the resultant vehicle of secret mantra. Five hundred queens of the god realm were guided through the two stages of the path, and each of them achieved the state of perfect enlightenment. Dawa Özer emanated as a king of the demigod realm. Kangkari transformed into a syllable *hrih* and then dissolved into the god realm, where she left one hundred emanations. There they turned the wheel of Dharma for the sake of all beings.

Samaya

This completes the seventh chapter of
The Lives and Liberation
of the Princess of Zahor, Mandarava,
called *A Precious Garland,*

Explaining how she accomplished the
benefit of beings in the realm of the gods.

8.

In the Naga Realm of Black Chandala

An account of how she emanated her enlightened noble qualities.

Among the nine thousand realms and countries of the subterranean region of the nagas[26] was the realm known as Black
Chandala, where the naga emanation Nagalaru resided. This region was
twenty-one thousand miles in circumference, wherein hot sand poured
down like rain, bringing inconceivable suffering. All the inhabitants of
the land were of the Chandala race, and their minds were deluded with
hatred that raged like fire. They preyed on one another, experiencing
suffering greater than that in the hell realms. The main leader of these
Chandala, the lord of the nagas and nagis, was unbearably ugly, with a
dark black complexion. His body was covered with one hundred thousand varieties of open sores, and his head was afflicted with contagious
eruptions. The upper part of his body was that of a human, while the
lower was that of a snake. He was surrounded by scores of naga attendants, who wailed in perpetual pain. The stench of the vapor from their
mouths permeated the entire world. His son was the black naga
Kyabche Barwa, who was surrounded by countless demonic nagas, all
of whom were lost, without any object of refuge, protector, or beneficial companions. None of them knew anything other than the pain of
suffering. The dakini knew that the time had finally come for this country to be tamed.

Transforming into a golden *hrih*, the goddess entered the country of
the nagas by descending onto the peak of the wish-fulfilling jewel

mountain. Her radiance completely overcame the realms of the nagas without exception. Then she manifested herself as a female nagini replete with full ornamentation. Arriving in the place of the Black Chandala, she manifested white light rays that penetrated all the nagas. In one instant all illness and disease were completely dispelled by her blessings. Because of that, all the nagas became overwhelmingly grateful, and the naga king and his entire assembly paid homage to the consort. In a state of unspeakable joy, they managed to proclaim:

"E ma! Astonishing, self-originating, stainless dakini! We are the Black Chandala who must endure the pain of torrential sand and contagious disease. Our suffering has continued for what seems like eternity. Now that the light from your body has penetrated us to cleanse and purify our curse of illness, we implore you to remain as our permanent protector." All nagas whose nature was otherwise negative showed their pleasure in various ways: some looked at the earth, others stretched their backs, and some turned their backs, while still others ran away.

Then the dakini spoke: "Kings, ministers, and your assemblies, please do as I command! Kye ma! All classes of subterranean nagas, pay heed! I am the primordial wisdom dakini Dharmindra. My father is the Buddha Amitabha; my mother is the long-life goddess Pandaravasini. Our country is Sukhavati paradise, and the name of our palace is Pemaköpa. My assembly is a gathering of innumerable tenth-level bodhisattvas.

"I came here to serve as your protector. Each one of you must understand that the unbearable, unceasing suffering that you have all had to endure is only the result of past causes. Countless buddhas have manifested themselves in the realm of humans. Buddha Tubpa Namgyal came into the god realm, Buddha Padma Drodul into the naga realm, Buddha Dharmaraja into the hell realm, Buddha Nampar Nangwa into the animal realm, Buddha Padma Gyalwa into the hungry spirit realm, and Buddha Padma Tsegpa into the demigod realm. Each of them turned the wheel of Dharma inconceivably.

"Your land has become enshrouded in darkness, and not a single buddha has come here to tame the minds of beings. All this bad fortune is because you opposed morality in the past. Thus you have been reborn in the naga lake of the Black Chandala. As a result of your past harsh speech and angry demeanor, you must suffer unbearable torrential downpours of sand. The result of your past stinginess in making offerings is your present hunger and thirst, similar to that of the hungry spirit realm. Because you inflicted harm upon the bodies of others in the past, you now experience unbearable disease and suffering in this life. There is no suffering that occurs independently of karma. Therefore, rather than observing others, observe instead your own karma and understand clearly the fruition of past actions. Though I am beyond sorrow and death, there are many places to which I must travel to engage in beneficial activities for the sake of others.

"Now that you have met me, all your negative karma—without exception—is openly revealed and purified. Although your nature is habitually negative, this cannot possibly have a harmful effect upon me. It is only the poisons of desire, anger, delusion, pride, avarice, and jealousy that cause long-lasting harm. If you abandon these poisons, you will come to know happiness. These delusions and negative emotions are the root cause of samsara. If you liberate yourself from them, you will achieve permanent bliss."

Thus she gave these essential instructions to all the nagas, each of whom developed fervent regard for the Dharma. With deep remorse for their accumulated bad karma, they confessed all negative activities. They took the bodhisattva vow and persevered in practice. All the nagas purified their negative accumulations without exception and were thus placed upon the path to awakening. As one mandala, they all ascended to the realm of Tushita, achieved the power of the gods, and were well established on the path of Dharma. Dharmindra then dissolved back into the goddess Pandaravasini.

Samaya

This completes the eighth chapter of
The Lives and Liberation
of the Princess of Zahor, Mandarava,
called *A Precious Garland,*

Explaining how she sent forth her
enlightened noble qualities to the naga
realm of the Black Chandala and how she
led the nagas along the path to liberation.

9.
Daughter of the Demigod King

The syllable *hrih* went into the realm of the demigods, where the demigod king Gocha Zangpo reigned. He possessed power and strength like that of the gods and was engaged in constant battle with eighteen other realms. Because the demigods had to endure the inconceivable, constant suffering of defeat by the gods, they assembled to discuss a strategy. They sent for the worldly cannibal Düje Garab and the naga king Dolwa to come and befriend them. Then they gathered the demon, naga, and demigod armies together and decided to go to the god realm and meet with the king.

At that time in the most populous city of the demigod realm known as Gaumi, the ruling king was Rinchen Pung, an emanation of Dawa Özer, a son of the gods. His influence was vast, as he was the head of one hundred thousand disciples. The great dakini Samantabhadri appeared and captivated the king' senses, and she spoke to him as a friend.

"Kye ma! King of great power Rinchen Pung, in your past life you were Dawa Özer, the father of my husband Dampa Togkar, who later became a buddha. Now, in order to tame the demigods, you have emanated as their king. I am the one known as the Blissful Defeater of the Enemy, Kangkari. I have now come here in my emanation called Samantabhadri. In order to alleviate the suffering of the besieged demigod King Gocha Zangpo and his companions, we shall announce our intention to help them wage war on the gods. The time has come to tame the minds of beings with the help of the nagas, demons, and demigods. Go now and assemble all the demigods and their hosts. I shall emanate as the daughter of Gocha Zangpo, and we will overcome all the black demons and turn the profound wheel of the Dharma." Having thus spoken, she ejected the consciousness of King Gocha's daughter, Shintama, from her body, and projected her own consciousness into it. She then appeared before King Gocha Zangpo and his assembly. He thought she was his daughter, and they remained together as one.

The demigod army then appeared before the army of the gods. The war was waged, and the naga, demon, and demigod armies defeated their enemy. In one instant, all were led to the path of liberation. Following this battle, the demonic doctrine of darkness vanished. In order to establish the precious law of Dharma, Gocha Zangpo, Düje Garab, and their hosts of assemblies gathered together to seal their karmic connection with one another by receiving teachings on secret mantra. All their jealousy was pacified, and they remained together in a state of meditative stabilization. Achieving liberation, all the demigods attained a rainbow body, and the entire realm was emptied.

Samaya

This completes the ninth chapter of
The Lives and Liberation
of the Princess of Zahor, Mandarava,
called *A Precious Garland,*

Explaining how she manifested herself as
the daughter of the king of the demigods
to lead all the beings to the path of
Dharma, and how they all achieved
perfect awakening.

10.
Shri Sagara

When the life expectancy of human beings reached two hundred years, the perfect Buddha Kashyapa came into this world. When he was turning the Dharma wheel, King Dekyong Kungawo and Queen Getsoma, daughter of the sages, made many offerings to the Buddha as he begged for his daily alms. Until that time, the king and queen had been unable to bear a child. And so, in the presence of the great enlightened guide Kashyapa, King Dekyong Kungawo bowed down and offered a crystal vase filled to capacity with various grains. With palms pressed together, he made this humble request:

"E ma ho! O sun that clarifies the doctrine in this world, perfected Buddha, precious protector of all beings! I, the king, am a man of great merit, with wealth, endowments, and attendants beyond imagination. However, I am without a son, and as you—the victorious, omniscient one—know, this kingdom has enjoyed the benefits of our pure ancestral monarchy during the reign of some two hundred kings. Please look upon my state of childlessness with merciful compassion, for I am not solely concerned with political interests. My aim is that the royal heritage be untainted in its glory. Without the light of our royal monarchy, what will come to pass? Who will maintain the royal wealth, endowments, attendants, and subjects? Since it appears doubtful that we shall have a suitable successor, will the queen be blamed for this mishap? Please give us a clear indication of our karmic destiny."

Following his request, the Buddha replied: "O great King Dekyong

Kungawo! Do not despair. Your royal line will soon continue. Countless world systems beyond this one is a paradise known as Great Bliss,
where the Buddha Amitabha resides with his supreme consort, the goddess Pandaravasini. They unceasingly send forth manifestations into this
world of ours. For the benefit of sentient beings in this world, a daughter like a daughter of the sages will come to you. She will bear a son of
supreme birth who will become a chakravartin, and in the future he
will be King Shuddhodana, the father of the future Buddha Shakyamuni.
Have confidence, O king, for your karma is by no means exhausted.
Your daughter will become my follower. She will take the bodhisattva
vow and will have many disciples of her own." Upon hearing these
prophetic words, the king touched his head to the Buddha's holy feet
and returned to report everything to the queen.

After some time King Dekyong had a dream. There appeared a red
orb of light marked by a red *hrih*. This orb fell upon his his crown and
melted into his chest. The light radiated and disappeared into the
queen, from whose heart a red light then radiated. From the light emanating from the red *hrih* in the heart of the queen many deities
appeared, all holding vessels of longevity nectar. They proceeded to
bestow empowerment upon both king and queen.

When the king awoke in the morning, his body and mind were
filled with great exaltation. When he told the queen of his auspicious
dream, she replied that she had also received a special dream. In her
dream, she entered a red palace and found herself prostrating before the
spiritual master residing there. To his left was a pale red goddess whose
heart was marked by a red *hrih*. The *hrih* dissolved into the queen's
heart, and she awoke feeling very blissful. Due to that, both king and
queen felt certain that what the Buddha said would surely come to pass.
They were confident of their imminent good fortune, and after some
time the queen felt that she was with child. She carefully cleansed her
body and then heard a voice from her womb say, "I am free from the
suffering of this world, and I come from the land of the enlightened
ones." The voice spoke these astonishing words in poetic verse.

After ten months, a child was born in the upper chambers of the
palace. The mother experienced no pain during the birth. Rainbows
appeared in space, and musical instruments sounded throughout the

region. Flowers that had never bloomed before sprang forth, and the sweet smell of incense permeated the atmosphere. Rumors ran rampant that a son had been born to the kingdom. However, at the moment of birth, a daughter sat up and proclaimed that she was Shri Sagara, who had previously sat at the feet of the Buddha to receive the Dharma and was now here to benefit sentient beings. After she spoke, she gracefully danced in space. The news of her birth spread throughout the world, and gods appeared and bathed her sacred body. Close to the palace appeared an astonishingly large lake that had never been there before. In the center of the lake, the name Shri Sagara was written.

When Shri Sagara reached her eleventh year, kings from many countries came as suitors to bid for her hand in marriage. She was not promised to anyone. Instead she went before the king to take the bodhisattva vow. Maintaining strict discipline, she meditated on the path of the pure awareness holders. Perfecting her own purpose, she performed countless miraculous deeds for the benefit of others, bringing thousands of women in her country to the path of Dharma. As she revealed the path of the Four Noble Truths, all those who listened came to rest in the nature of reality. Everyone with whom she made contact generated the supreme awakened mind and obtained perfect enlightenment. She blessed the king, queen, their ministers, retinues, and the entire kingdom by teaching them the paramitas. Every single inhabitant was brought to the path of the aryas and liberated!

Samaya

This completes the tenth chapter of
*The Lives and Liberation
of the Princess of Zahor, Mandarava,*
called *A Precious Garland,*

Explaining how she emanated into the
royal family as Shri Sagara and brought
countless beings to maturity and liberation.

11.

The Twenty-Five Manifestations

During the time when Lord Buddha Shakyamuni propagated Dharma in the southern continent of Jambudvipa,[27] Pandaravasini sent forth the following manifestations:

In the presence of Shakyamuni she was Singmo Gangadevi. In the country of Bhaiti she was Zabmo Tashige. She was Prabhadhara, the daughter of Shonupel, and Shakyadevi's daughter, Kalpazang. She was the princess of Oddiyana, Palmo Ökyigyen, and the Shakya princess, the consort Getso Lhamo. She was the princess of Kashmir, the consort Kunga Zangmo, and Tsangchinma, the daughter of the supreme sage; as the wife of the king, she was known as Shrimati. In the land of Lanka she was Nyime Paldenma; in the country of Togar she was Vitanahuta. In the country of Rugma she was Menmo Rinchenzang; in the country of cannibals she was Dema Chogilha. In China she was Gangzang Umanti, and in the western country of Oddiyana she was born in the royal family as Gemapel. She was also known as Rigsum Kyegu Dagmo; in the country of Koshi she was Wangchen Pemakyi. In Dechetseg she was known as Roti Kirima; and in Shambhala she was Dronma Yeshema. In the country of Koli she was Karma Bhadriha; in the country of Hashi, she was Rigje Tsangnema. As the daughter of the king of Persia, she was Shrishti, and in the country of Rugma, she was Karkatamoha. In Malaya she was Kalpa Zangmo and the Great Yogini of Fearless Conduct. In Bhigche she was Chöma Wangmoche.

In brief, she sent forth some twenty-five manifestations, each of whom possessed the ability to benefit beings as numerous as the ocean is vast. Through the guise of enacting activities within the monarchy, she trained her followers on the path of secret mantra. Nearly every being who connected with her actualized the state of a pure awareness holder. An extensive account of her life stories was given to Nanam as an earth treasure called *A Beautiful Flower Rosary*, comprised of one hundred chapters. This is concealed at Tsangrong Dorje Drag. Here I have revealed the essence of the root text.

Samaya

This completes the eleventh chapter of
The Lives and Liberation
of the Princess of Zahor, Mandarava,
called *A Precious Garland,*

Revealing the names and places of her
twenty-five manifestations.

I2.
Blessings from the Dakinis

How the great dakini Mandarava came to be born in the country of Zahor.

In the western paradise of Great Bliss, from the heart of Buddha Amitabha, in the Realm of Lotus Light, surrounded by assemblies of deities beyond enumeration, Arya Avalokiteshvara radiated forth within boundless rays of light. From the arya's heart, countless emanations of the syllable *hrih* were sent forth to fill all the boundless pure realms in this world. In the one hundred million realms of Potala, one hundred million emanations of Avalokiteshvara were sent forth. In the one hundred million countries of India, one hundred million emanations of Shakyamuni were manifest. In the one hundred million manifested sambhogakaya paradises, one hundred million emanations of the protector of the Land of Snow, Avalokiteshvara, appeared. In the one hundred million nirmanakaya paradises, one hundred million emanations of Guru Padmasambhava were manifested. In the one hundred million paradises of Yonten Köpa, one hundred million emanations of Manjushri were sent forth. In the one hundred million paradises of Pemakö, one hundred million emanations of Padmoshnisha were manifested. In the one hundred million sacred realms of the gods, one hundred million chakravartins emanated. In the one hundred million countries of Tibet, one hundred million emanations of Songtsen Gampo were manifested. In the one hundred million lands of Kalinga, one hundred million great sages were made manifest. In this way, there arose boundless emanations of pure realms, each of which had its own sutras and tantras, its own unsurpassed teachers propagating the doctrine, and so forth. In addition, these teachers had inconceivable numbers of disciples with their followers, all of whom actively turned the wheel of the doctrine.

In particular, in the southern world system, the teacher of the doctrine of sutra was Shakyamuni, who, during the aeon called Dronme, when the life expectancy was one hundred years, taught an assembly of gods, nagas, humans, spirits, earthlords, ghouls, vampires, and so forth. He taught the shravakas, the bodhisattvas, and innumerable pure awareness holders, turning the great wheel of the Dharma in five stages. From this, there came to be nine distinct vehicles. To those of small capacity, he taught the Tripitika,[28] revealing the fundamental nature of reality in outer and inner distinctions. For those of moderate capacity, he revealed the entrance way to the three outer tantras of Kriya, Charya, and Yoga. For those of superior or excellent capability, he introduced the inner tantric methods of the highest tantric vehicles in the root tantra and accomplishment classes. Revealing the doctrine in three hundred and two thousand ways, he demonstrated the means through which nirvana is actualized.

At that time, the powerful shravaka Kashyapa directed his awareness and proclaimed: "In the future I, Padmasambhava, will be born in Dhanakosha. From the heart of the conqueror Amitabha, light rays will radiate, penetrating the heart of Avalokiteshvara. Then from Avalokiteshvara's heart, light rays will radiate into the pure realms of all the buddhas and their heirs. All the blessings of their enlightened body, speech, mind, noble qualities, and enlightened activities will gather to reabsorb into Arya Avalokiteshvara's heart. Then I, Padmasambhava, will myself manifest as a syllable *hrih* to envelop completely the one hundred million pure realms of the enlightened ones. Dissolving into the very core of a great udumbara flower in full bloom within lake Dhanakosha, I will emerge as Guru Padmasambhava on the tenth day of the monkey month. Acting as the son of King Indrabhuti, I shall wed the emanation Prabhadhara. Then, in accordance with the prophecies of Vajrasattva, I shall abandon worldly life to engage in uncontrived conduct. Relying upon the secret mantra mandala of the dakinis and in order to actualize activity to benefit beings, my mind and the enlightened mindstreams of all the buddhas will merge as one."

Through symbolic indication, all the buddha-deities[29] were then invoked, at which time the enlightened mindstream of the goddess of longevity, Pandaravasini, was inspired to manifest herself for the benefit of sentient beings. From her five places innumerable light rays issued forth and encompassed all paradises. White light radiated from her forehead into the eastern Paradise of Manifest Joy. There, the light made contact with the heart of Buddhalochana, the consort of the great conqueror Akshobya. Invoking her enlightened awareness, the blessing appeared as the syllable *lam*. Countless syllables then arose and reabsorbed into Pandaravasini's forehead. Similarly, countless red light rays radiated from the goddess Pandaravasini's throat into the Paradise of Manifold Array, where they merged into the consort of the primordial buddha Samantabhadra, invoking her enlightened mind, and the blessing arose as the syllable *mum*. Numberless *mum* syllables emanated to dissolve back into her throat. Then blue light rays issued from Pandaravasini's heart, radiating into the central pure realm of Buddha Vairochana. They dissolved into the heart of his supreme consort Dhateshvari; they invoked her enlightened awareness, which arose as blessings in the form of countless *mam* syllables, dissolving back into Pandaravasini's heart. Yellow light rays from the point in Pandaravasini's navel center radiated into the pure realm of the southern direction, the Realm of Glory. They dissolved into the heart of Mamaki, the supreme consort of Buddha Ratnasambhava, invoking her enlightened mind and emanating as the syllable *bam*. Countless emanations of this syllable then radiated back to dissolve into Pandaravasini's navel. Green light rays from the secret place of the goddess then proceeded to the northern Paradise known as Perfect Activity, dissolving into the heart of Samayatara, the supreme consort of Buddha Amoghasiddhi, invoking her enlightened awareness and appearing as the syllable *tam*. Unlimited seed syllables then reabsorbed into Pandaravasini's secret place. From her crown aperture red light rays emanated into the mandala of the deity Hayagriva, known as Wangdrag Rolpa. They dissolved into the heart of Hayagriva's supreme consort, Vajravarahi, and her blessings were invoked as the syllable *hrih*.

Countless syllables then dissolved into Pandaravasini's crown.

Light rays of the five colors then emerged from Pandaravasini's body to encompass all the buddha realms of the ten directions. All the consorts of the enlightened ones were invoked, and the very essence of the blessings of their body, speech, mind, noble qualities, and enlightened activities dissolved back into her body as boundless rays of radiant light. Then, from her two palms, green light rays radiated into the lower pure realm known as The Place of Glory, invoking the enlightened awareness of Sarasvati, the supreme consort of Manjushri. Here blessings appeared as a white *ah* that dissolved back into Pandaravasini. From the place of union between Amitayus, the Buddha of Longevity, and his consort, nectar and the syllables *mum, lam, mam, bam, tam,* and *ah* then emerged. Each syllable proceeded to dissolve one into the other, and finally into a white *hrih.* That syllable gave rise to one hundred million manifestations of *hrih.* It was as though a great rain of these syllables was descending simultaneously upon the world. In particular, an essential drop, a mixture of red and white, marked with *hrih,* descended into the country of Zahor like a shooting star. It fell upon the crown of King Viharadhara, and he was blessed by all the Sugatas and their heirs.

Samaya

This completes the twelfth chapter of
*The Lives and Liberation of the Princess of
Zahor, Mandarava,*
called *A Precious Garland,*

Explaining how blessings were received
from the dakinis of all the buddhas, how
the king, her father, was blessed, and how
she emanated for the benefit of beings.

13.
Seeing the Country of Her Birth

An explanation of how the dakini entered the womb and revealed the five types of omniscient seeing.

Of the ninety-four continents of this world system, the central continent is the sacred ground of the one thousand buddhas of this aeon, where Bodhgaya, India is located. To the east of Bodhgaya is the country Zahor, with a breadth of some one thousand miles. It is vast and pleasantly attractive, as colorful as the fine patterns on brocade silk, similar to the deva realms. Forty miles east is Kamaru,[30] a basin-like plain resembling a wheel. In the center of this plain is a round, deep lake known as Hasha Dhari, with waters of the eight pure qualities,[31] milky white and radiantly glowing. This deep, circular lake contains wish-fulfilling jewels. Encircling the lake, for about a mile's distance, are flower gardens and lovely pools, beautiful beyond imagination. Birds and geese of many varieties trumpet and warble in melodious song. In all directions there are caves and caverns of shiny blue slate. The inhabitants of the place are themselves exceedingly attractive. Some forty miles to the southeast is the great country Manika. Its mountainous peaks are extremely lofty and its forests abundant, while the ground is covered with flowers. In the middle of this country is the Great Lotus Palace. All those who reside there are brave, youthful, and healthy.

Some forty miles to the south lies the terrifying charnel ground known as The Great Play, where there is a stupa called Kotala, built by one hundred thousand dakinis; thus it is also known as the One Hundred Thousand of Kotala. In the daytime, it is enshrouded in darkness; in the evening, it blazes as though engulfed by fire. Wild animals, such as tigers, leopards, and wolves, roam about together with zombies and graveyard spirits. The trees there are called darusa, with green leaves that are large and thick enough to clothe a human body. The berries are the size of a human armspan and are bitter to the taste. The waters are turbulent, and the wind is chilly. Vultures converge on human corpses, and a holy man known as Meniha lives there. This charnel ground is identical to the famed Silwatsel. It is the residence of the protectors Mahakala, Ging, and Red Tsen.[32]

Some forty miles to the southwest is the country known as Glorious Red Palace. Its mountains and plains are both red in color. A river called Sitana runs through the middle of this country. The valleys are fully endowed with rich forests. The entire land is graced with happiness and bliss. Some forty miles to the west is the great country Dahina. The principal city is called Garden of Nectar, where there is an abundance of business, wealth, and material prosperity. All the inhabitants live happily and harmoniously. Some forty miles to the northwest is the continent known as Chatama, surrounded by many other land masses. In the midst of this region lives the great captain Lhawang Khorpa. He sails the seas gathering wish-fulfilling jewels, accompanied by five hundred merchant sailors. Some forty miles to the north is the great country Taluma. All its inhabitants wear beautiful ornaments and greatly value wealth, which they enjoy in abundance. There is no greed or strife, as everyone is honorable and harmonious. To the northeast is the region known as the Precious Jeweled Garden, where crops that need no harvest abound, and grains of many varieties grow. The forests are rich, and beautiful brocade silk is abundant.

In all of the above realms there are twenty separate kingdoms. The laws are fair and strictly enforced, so there are no butchers, prostitutes, or others of unclean behavior. Everything is very clean and pure. The eighteen surrounding countries outside the eight major continents are Kalinga, Nimsani Tsel, Rimahala, Beche, Nahuti, Dewata, Tang, Kumud Shepetsel, Kota Chungwa, Yampa Dihuta, Dombhi, Ngampa, Pemachen, Tanadug, Chandala, Shenpa, Drong, Kuluta, and others. Each of these countries has an honorable government.

In the middle of these major and minor countries lies the great region of Bengal. It is within this region that the great land of Zahor is located. The palace there is encircled by seven walls and has a nine-tiered roof. Beautiful beyond compare, it resembles a palace of the gods. Near the nine-tiered palace are four ponds, where many varieties of birds and flowers abound. There are parrots and swans that speak the language of human beings. All the different kinds of birds from the realms of the gods sing in their respective languages. In the surrounding places, there are one hundred outer ministers and fifty inner ministers with five hundred and ten leaders of the districts. This was by far the most sublime of all the lands in India, and was thus perceived as the best place to take rebirth for the purpose of guiding beings.

Now the entire land was blessed, and flowers that had never appeared there before began to bloom. Many varieties of birds began speaking the words of Dharma, and upon the roof of the palace rainbow light rays amassed. The land's king, queen, ministers, their subjects, and their attendants all began having auspicious dreams and indications of good fortune to come.

Samaya

This completes the thirteenth chapter of
The Lives and Liberation
of the Princess of Zahor, Mandarava,
called *A Precious Garland,*

Explaining how she saw the country of
her birth and blessed the entire kingdom.

14.
Choosing Her Mother and Father

It was then time for the dakini to choose her place of rebirth, her caste, and her mother. Of the twenty-five kingdoms in the land of India, Bodhgaya, Oddiyana, and Zahor were the most sublime in terms of size, shape, and beauty. They were most endowed with wealth and material resources. Their governments and judiciary systems were excellent, and the wealth and endowments of the people were incomparable. In addition, the people's beauty, charisma, and ability were sublime. The inhabitants of Zahor were endowed with the seven wealths of enlightened beings.[33]

During a previous time, the holy sage named Thubdzin had studied at the feet of the Buddha Kashyapa. In accordance with the Buddha's prophecies he gave rise to bodhichitta and took the basic, single vow of lay ordination to become a Buddhist. Having promised to keep this vow, he underwent the hardship of maintaining his discipline. In the center of the country of Zahor, he sat on the mountain Tangkar. After becoming a master of stainless meditative absorption, he returned to his teacher to receive the pointing-out instructions. Then, as his mind ripened through empowerment, the Buddha proclaimed the following prophetic statement in order for him to realize the path of secret mantra:

"Kye! You, the sage Thubdzin, accomplisher of the true path, must soon go to the place called Kapila, in India. In the previous aeon called Bhaskara Sahasrakara, this country was known as Kotamati. In the palace known as Samapatra, the king was named Tsugpudzin, and the queen's name was Rinchen Nangche Dronmed Ö. Their son's name was Bhaskarashri. After an unbroken reign of kings took one thousand rebirths in the royal line, the king took rebirth as the king of the Brahmins in the god realm. After that life, he was born here and is now known as the sage Thubdzin Wangpo. Before, he was the daughter of a sea captain whose mother was Queen Anananta. Now, in the city of Kapilavastu in the eastern direction, his father's name is Ratnapala, and his mother is Zangkye. Both are sages of the Shakya clan, and their beautiful daughter is Padma Shri Sagara. After she matures through secret empowerment, Padma Shri Sagara will carry forth your royal line by bearing your son Dawe Kyeu Drime. Over time many bodhisattvas will be born."

Upon hearing this prophecy, the holy man Thubdzin went to Kapilavastu. There he encountered an exceedingly lovely maiden bedecked with precious jewels and flowers. She was in a garden with an entourage of five and, upon observing the sage, addressed him with loving concern: "Kye! Attractive one whose gentle gait is like that of a swan, whose great presence indicates royalty, and who, by his medita- tive power, pacifies the minds of sentient beings! Your manner and style is that of a holy man, so attractive to the eye! Handsome one, please tell me who your parents are and to which caste you belong. Your conscientious manner indicates that you are a disciple of the Buddha. Please tell me: for what purpose have you come here?"

The holy man replied: "Kye! I am a lay disciple of the Buddha. My name is Thubdzin. My father is of the royal line of the great lineage of holy men. My mother is the sage Padma Yiongkyi, and my country is that of Zahor Sitana. What are the names of your parents, and what is the class of your birth?" She responded: "Kye! My country is the land of India, and my city is Kapilavastu. Our ancestry is that of the Shakya clan. My father's name is Ratnapala, and my mother's name is Zangkye. My name is Padma Shri Sagara, and these friends accompany- ing me are my attendants. You should come with me now to our home to beg for alms."

The sage accompanied her to her home, where he was shown great respect and hospitality. Then he told her mother and father that he was a lay disciple of the Buddha, named Thubdzin. He explained that the

Buddha had proclaimed a prophecy about their daughter, Padma Shri Sagara, which was why he had come to them. Upon hearing this, they offered him their daughter, upon whom he then bestowed empowerment. She returned with him to the country of Zahor, where their son, Dawe Kyeu Drime, was born. This prince was so sublime that he was unrivaled in ability. He assumed the throne and ruled over the entire kingdom of Zahor. He was succeeded by one thousand and two kings who ruled the land. As the son of Viharadhara, the final king in this royal line, he became a very powerful ruler. Under his great authority, the government of his kingdom increased in power. Then he took for his bride the lovely daughter of King Gache from Rajagriha, whose name was Princess Anandakara. They married and had two sons, Pawode and Norkyonglha, both of whom had been the king's father in past lives.

Viharadhara is now King Shuddhodana, and Queen Anandakara is the principal goddess of the twenty-four, Queen Ratna Dipamkara, of the race of dakinis. Now the interdependent karma of the union of method and wisdom is manifest in the maternal lineage and caste of the mother and father who were carefully chosen to meet the needs of beings to be tamed. Astonishing blessings were bestowed upon all.

Samaya

This completes the fourteenth chapter of
*The Lives and Liberation
of the Princess of Zahor, Mandarava,*
called *A Precious Garland,*

Explaining how she chose the class of
her mother and father and bestowed
blessings upon them.

15.
Entering Her Mother's Womb

Then, on the tenth day of the tenth month in the year of the horse, the dakini found a comfortable seat to rest upon atop the palace of the king and queen. The outer and inner ministers and all their subjects were singing melodious songs and playing various musical instruments. There was dancing, horse racing, feats of magic, and cannonades. In total, some eighteen different games and shows were displayed.

That day the space all around became filled with shimmering rainbow light. From between the clouds the sound of various instruments could be heard. All the subjects and servants were astounded and incessantly proclaimed their amazement. A great rainbow of five colors appeared above the king and queen, and in intermittent regions of space red lotus flowers and magnolias of gold, green, and other colors poured down like rain. Everyone could actually gather them up in their hands!

All these signs occurred directly before the ministers, subjects, and people of the kingdom, and everyone felt they were even more amazing than the signs that had occurred at the time of the birth of the great heroic bodhisattvas and wealth protector deities. With so many miracles appearing on this auspicious tenth day of the lunar calendar, everyone remarked that a son must have been born to the king, that a fully enlightened buddha had entered the world, or that a chakravartin had been born.

That very evening, the king and queen both saw many marvelous signs in their dreams. The king dreamt that a stupa made of white crystal, the tip of which reached into the sky, was born from his crown. In the vase-shaped center of the stupa countless dakinis were dancing and singing lovely songs. Surrounding them were many dakas making offerings. The light from the stupa encompassed the entire world. It was marked with the sun and moon at its peak, and it manifested light rays of extraordinary colors and patterns. Light completely filled the thirty-seven higher realms.

In turn, the queen dreamt that a rainbow filled with particles of light merged into her crown. Within each particle appeared a white dakini, eight years of age, glimmering in the beauty of a dance. Each dakini was chanting *om, hum, so, ah, ha* and *mum, lam, mam, bam, tam.* Vibrating in five colors with their inherent sounds, these syllables emerged and fell like rain, gently dissolving into the queen's five energy centers. She experienced physical bliss. Her body was filled by the light of the five colors and became stainless from without and within. All the dakinis dissolved into her crown, and the five colored lights—white, yellow, red, green, and blue—became the syllables *ah* and *bam.* Dissolving into her body, the syllables appeared as though on fire, light rays blazing forth incessantly.

When the queen awoke at dawn, the gentle sound of ringing bells could be heard from space. As she looked up, a beautiful white dakini appeared, sixteen years of age and adorned with white silk and bone ornaments. She was in the dancing posture, surrounded by sixteen other dakinis. The queen supplicated them with deep respect, her palms pressed together. Then the principal white dakini spoke the following words:

"*Kake tana ham eh!* O nature of all-pervasive air, with perfectly complete noble qualities, though the karmic gateways to buddhahood are infinite, you, Samayatara, are the mandala of the air that moves. Lady of great warmth, goddess consort Pandaravasini, do you know this is your element? Mandala of pure water, Mamaki, do you know this is your element? Mandala of the supporting earth, Buddhalochana, do you know this is your element? Do you know that this vast mandala of the space of consciousness is Dhateshvari Mandarava? O sole mother of the buddhas of the three times, O all-pervasive basis of everything, do you know that this abides as your body? The five primordial wisdoms[34] are the five natural light rays of five colors.[35] Mother, do you know that this is due to your blessing? The five empowerments[36] are the play of the dakas of the families. Do you know that the wisdom of the five consorts abides within you? The primordial wisdom bodhichitta dwells as the perfect purity of the eight fields of consciousness.[37] Do you know that the eight objects abide as this essential nature? The purified four dogmas[38] are the expanse of space with all attributes complete. Do you know that the dakinis of the four immeasurables[39] reside there? The actual daka consort is the Buddha of the three times. Do you know that this is the direct experience of the blessing of the four joys?[40] Without confusion, the passions[41] are self-liberated. Do you know that this remains as the primordial wisdom of great bliss? Mother, you are the palace of the three embodiments of the conquerors. Do you know that all five embodiments abide within you? Do you, in the blissful palace of the pure nature of the energy channels, know the dakini of the pure element of air? Do you, in the expanse of the pure nature of the ten airs,[42] the five lights of primordial wisdom, know the dakini of the pure nature of essential fluids? Do you, in the source of the Dharma palace of the essential fluid of great bliss, know the Buddha's goddess consort who resides there? O primordially pure Mother of natural wisdom, the absolute dakini of great bliss remains within you. Many dakinis have bestowed empowerment, and, free from habitual propensities, ripening instructions have been received. The consorts possess fully endowed merit, and the vajra family is endowed with good fortune. The mother of all the conquerors, with her fully endowed wisdom, and the lake-born lord of fully endowed method are inseparable. Through this light of the sun and moon, the darkness of wrong concepts is dispelled. May there be the splendid good fortune of the liberation of all beings!"

As she spoke, a rain of flowers and grains fell three times, and clear signs appeared. All the dakinis dissolved into space. In the outer, inner, upper, and lower regions of the palace many flowers were seen and felt. Varieties of grains that could be seen and felt were everywhere. The queen's perception became lucid and bliss blazed in her body. To the king she recounted her experience in great detail, and he explained his dream to the queen. Both were filled with joy and blazing bliss.

At the time of their union, they both saw the five buddhas and consorts appear before them in space. From the point of their union, the syllables *om, hum, so, ah, ha* and *mum, lam, mam, bam, tam*, as well as the vowels and consonants, appeared in the colors white and red. They both experienced them dissolving into their crowns, and the five buddhas naturally became the essence mantra of interdependent origination, which then dissolved into both of their bodies.

After one month, the queen experienced many dakas coming to anoint her body with a special perfume. She became far more beautiful than before. Everyone remarked that the queen was becoming more youthful and radiant as each month went by. "There is a dakini among us," they said.

Samaya

This completes the fifteenth chapter of
The Lives and Liberation
of the Princess of Zahor, Mandarava,
called *A Precious Garland*

Explaining how, through the five states of
omniscient seeing, she naturally entered the
womb of her mother and bestowed the
empowerment of the primordial wisdom of
the five families.

16.
Paying Homage to Her Father and Mother

After five months, the queen experienced an orb of light coming into her body. At nightfall everyone could see that her body was naturally luminous. The king said to her: "Your body is like an abode of light. In darkness it shines clear and resplendent like the light from a fire. This seems to be a sign that perhaps you are with child. Do you think so? Did you hear some profound esoteric instructions that have caused this to occur?"

The queen responded: "I feel absolutely no pain in my body. However, my breasts are swelling, and all of my physical movements seem to be propelled by vital energies. I continue to have excellent signs in my dreams, yet I have not received any pith instructions. If indeed I carry such a son of the gods, the signs that have occurred must have indicated this. Occasionally, however, I hear the sound of the vowels and consonants resounding from my belly. It is unlike any previous experience I have ever known. I am not sure if this means that I am pregnant or not."

The queen continued to maintain great care in cleanliness and bathing purification. As each month passed, the sounds grew clearer and clearer. The king and all the ministers voiced their certainty that the queen was with child. The sound of the vowels and consonants grew ever clearer, and her body resembled an orb of light both day and night. Everyone wondered if indeed a chakravartin was about to be born. Many special ceremonies were performed, and nine months passed with no additional signs.

In the year of the male wood horse, on the tenth day of the tenth month in the hours just before dawn, the sphere of space became filled with bursts of rainbow light in circular shapes; everyone was in disbelief. There was also yellow light in square shapes, red light in the shape of half moons, green light in the shape of triangles, and blue light of many different shapes. Sounds of musical instruments could be heard throughout the entire kingdom of Zahor. Scores of rainbow clouds amassed on the roof of the palace, and multitudes of white, red, and yellow flowers sprang forth all over the ground. A shower of multicolored flowers fell from the sky. Myriads of multicolored clouds and smoke surrounded all the mountains. The earth began to vibrate, and the birds began chirping the most melodious songs. Soft brocade silk spontaneously appeared, as did piles of grains and fruit ready to eat. These innumerable wonders were overwhelming to behold.

As the sun was shining, the queen gave birth to her child in bliss and without pain. The child was covered with cloth, its hair curly and azure blue. Its face was glowing with radiance, beaming with joy. The child was chanting *om, ah, hum,* and the vowels and consonants. Standing up, the child offered prostrations to the father and mother, then sang this pleasing song in honor of the parents:

"E ma ho! You of previous merit were known as King Indrabhuti, and now you have become my father of the family of Zahor. O learned one of great virtue, I prostrate to you! Powerful goddess of the class of royalty, mother of mine, I prostrate to you, mother of the bliss of the expanse of space! Although my births are free of defilement, you, parents of great kindness, created the fortunate circumstance for me to be born. Although I had no intention to take rebirth in a karmic body, I, the heroine, have come to benefit sentient beings. I have come to establish happiness and bliss in the kingdom of Zahor. Unaffected by the stain of the womb, I am never afraid of taking rebirth. I am the mother of the buddhas of the three times, the incarnate one known as Pandaravasini. There are millions of female bodhisattvas just like me who come into this world like rain pouring down. Not mired in samsara, they train on the path to liberation. I have come as the one who will bear the well-known name of Mandarava!"

Hearing these words, everyone was completely amazed. At that moment deities were actually present in the sky, and they bathed her body three times in ambrosia nectar. The nagas brought forth many varieties of wish-fulfilling jewels, which they piled around the palace in all directions. Many jeweled treasures spontaneously welled forth.

Then the queen spoke these words: "E ma! I am a woman of great merit—for a most astonishing daughter of the gods has been born, who bowed to me, her mother, and to her father, to acknowledge our kindness. Beautiful heroine with unrivaled noble qualities, at the moment of your birth you delighted us with melodious song and proclaimed that you are Mandarava. When you entered my body, I knew only bliss. Now we directly encounter an actual, astonishing, primordial wisdom dakini. You are free from the suffering of birth. Your mother's body experienced bliss. Precious treasures of outer and inner endowments have been revealed. Rainbow light and fragrant scents have permeated the kingdom of Zahor. Primordial wisdom deities bathed your body three times. Daughter, you have filled your mother with great exaltation!"

These words were received with a great smile by the Mother of Noble Qualities, who sang this song: "E ma! I, your daughter Pandaravasini, am a wisdom dakini! In absolute truth, my fundamental nature is the supreme wisdom of emptiness. I am the supreme consort of the deity of long life, Amitayus. I am the daughter who upholds enlightened noble qualities. The sole father of the one thousand buddhas is the protector Avalokiteshvara. By his blessings, I will care for all beings as my own. Until their karma is exhausted, I will lead all beings without exception to liberation. The manifestations of the infinite paradises are inconceivable. They are revealed here in whatever manner is necessary to tame the minds of beings. I am the daughter who reveals the various paths. The unelaborated ground is the originally pure, primordial father, Samantabhadra. This is all the sugatas and their heirs, as well as the basic nature of all sentient beings. Ultimately, 'above' and 'below' are nonexistent and, in nature, equal. All are primordially nondual, like the dharmakaya.

"I am the basis of everything. In the nondual, directionless expanse of space, with loving-kindness for all beings of the six realms who have been our parents, and with supreme joy like the sun that clarifies everything, I care for all beings with equanimity, just as a mother protects her child. This is your daughter's motivation.

"At no time should any living being be harmed. In particular, the cause of nonvirtue, negativity, must be fully abandoned! Nonvirtue accumulated physically should be arrested in its place, and all interdependent actions should be eliminated at the root. These are your daughter's vows of individual liberation.

"The Lord Guru is inseparable from the crown of my head, where I receive the vase, secret, wisdom, and absolute empowerments. Without grasping at the external tangible appearance of this form, I observe the actual, absolute deity of perfect awakening. This is your daughter's practice of the generation stage of secret mantra.

"In the twenty-one thousand six hundred channels, both gross and subtle vital energies are equally drawn into the central energy channel. The primordial wisdom fire blazes with luminous clarity, burning the aggregates and elements. Through the union of method and wisdom, sun and moon, the nectar of purification descends. The essential nature of the absolute embodiment of rapture is perfected. That is your daughter's completion stage practice.

"The vajra chain of awareness[43] of the pure sphere, empty and luminous, is a vortex of the five colors that displays the radiance of the five primordial wisdoms. Through the entrance way of the crucial point, arising and liberation are perfected. The four self-manifesting visions[44] are complete in the dharmakaya. Great confidence in the nondual single nature of the ground[45] is found. This is your daughter's view and meditation.

"Outwardly, the contaminated body is liberated as an embodiment of light. Inwardly, the mind's nature is perfected as the essential nature of the five enlightened embodiments. Secretly, the vase embodiment of the nature of phenomena is consummated. The confidence of the inseparable ground of the unique essence is discovered. That is your daughter's state of fruition.

"As the supreme state of original enlightenment is discovered, this all-encompassing dance becomes the magical display of the natural space of the five embodiments, where nothing is incomplete. With the method of great bliss and emptiness—male and female united—the enlightened embodiment of the major and minor marks is manifest. This is your daughter's mode of manifestation.

"Skillful methods will be employed to tame the minds of sentient beings in accordance with their faculties. All beings will be led impartially from the lower realms of existence to the supreme state of liberation, never to return from that place of permanent bliss. This is your daughter's commitment to sentient beings.

"The guru is the source of all empowerment and blessings of all the victorious ones. The key point is to keep pure words of honor and you will never be apart from the guru. O queen, do not ignore the crucial point of these words!" Thus these words were sealed with the imprint of the dakini.

When she had spoken, all the subjects of the kingdom, as well as the entire population in all directions, offered many varieties of precious jewels, and everyone celebrated the dakini's birth for three months. After three months, the girl's astonishing qualities became well-known throughout India. All the gods, nagas, nonhuman spirits, and the eight classes of spirits[46] marveled as her fame spread further. A holy sage expert in divination examined these signs, yet was unable to respond in any way at all. Then the great king spoke the following: "Kye! All holy diviners who possess clairvoyant abilities, please tell us why this daughter of ours displays such sublime enlightened qualities. Please indicate if there is anything negative that can be foreseen in her future without concealing anything."

After investigating in accordance with the command of the king, a holy man gave this response: "E ma! Revered father, King Lhayiwang! This daughter of the king and queen, named Mandarava, shows the physical mark of a dakini from the vajra family. Her speech indicates that she is a consort of the lotus class. The signs indicated by her mind make her an upholder of the five primordial wisdoms. Her wealth of noble qualities reveals her to be a powerful goddess of the dance, enacting inconceivable enlightened activities for the benefit of beings. She is the consort of the miraculously born prince who does not remain in samsara. Unfavorable events will occur, and the laws of the kingdom will be tested because of careless actions. The time will come when the revered father will know deep remorse, but in the end, everyone will be placed upon the path. How astonishing is this lotus-born one with her enlightened activities! The fame of her qualities will remain until this aeon is empty! In this world of existence, there are many who are of the flesh, but a wisdom dakini is like an udumbara flower. No one here has the ability to comprehend the potential of such a being."

After he spoke, both the king and queen were delighted, and they went to great expense to celebrate the occasion. The holy men then returned to their own places.

Samaya

This completes the sixteenth chapter of
The Lives and Liberation
of the Princess of Zahor, Mandarava,
called *A Precious Garland,*

Explaining her birth and how she payed
homage to her father and mother to
acknowledge their kindness.

17.
Aversion to Samsara

As time passed and Mandarava partook of the three white and the three sweet substances,[47] her body grew larger and she remained happily cloistered in the palace. When she was eight years of age, accompanied by her many attendants, she ventured to the palace roof, from which they gazed beyond the palace walls and beheld many throngs of people engaged in activities and games.

When the princess gazed to the east, she beheld a sow giving birth to seven piglets. If the suffering of birth is really so intense, she thought to herself, why not learn the methods that lead to liberation rather than remain in this unceasing round of rebirth? Then she heard a young girl crying out. Listening closely, she realized that the girl was giving birth. Then the princess thought, a female form is a basis for suffering in samsara. Even the mother of these piglets must endure the suffering of birth, yet due to her confusion she remains attached to the very cause of her suffering! Everything is determined by karma, yet few have the thought to repay the kindness of others.

Pondering this predicament, Princess Mandarava prayed with single-pointed devotion: "Namo! Homage to the Three Jewels: the Buddha, Dharma, and Sangha! Homage to the Three Roots: the Lama, Yidam,[48] and Dakini! Pay heed to me now and assist me in accomplishing this prayer! May I and all beings with whom I am connected—whose negative karma and confusion bind them to the endless rounds of rebirth in cyclic confusion—be swiftly liberated from this ocean of unbearable turmoil and obtain the unborn state of liberation! Please free us from this world of karma! May we never know suffering again!"

After making this prayer, the princess gazed to the south and saw an old man supporting himself with two canes. As he dragged himself along, his two knees were forced to slide through feces, which he inadvertently dragged along as well. With each motion, he moaned great sighs of despair, crying, "What have I done to deserve such suffering?" Those who passed by just looked at him with amusement and laughter.

The princess was distraught and overcome with compassion at this pitiful sight. Again she prayed: "Avalokiteshvara, Three Jewels, and Three Roots, pay heed! Alas! All parent sentient beings of the six classes cannot avoid the suffering of youth turning to old age. We are helpless: our limbs cripple up and cease to function. Alas, such a negative fate! May such suffering vanish forever!" Thus she prayed single-pointedly.

The princess then gazed to the west and saw many men and women afflicted with leprosy and other contagious diseases. She could even hear their cries of pain. Their skin was covered with open sores and eruptions. Even their internal organs were protruding, as blood spewed forth. Their veins bulged with pus and the stench permeated everywhere. The hair on their heads and eyebrows had fallen out so that their heads looked like copper ladles. Crippled and doubled over in pain, they were unable to die; yet they still maintained the hope that they might continue living in this way. Why was there no medicine to help them? Again she prayed: "By the blessing of the Three Precious Jewels and the aryas, may the negative karma that gives beings such illness be fully purified! Bestow the profound, supreme medicine of your compassion! May I and all other parent sentient beings, in all lifetimes, never know the fear of illness or disease. Place us in the state that is free from such suffering!"

Then she looked to the north and saw smoke billowing forth from a house. Wailing sounds could be clearly heard. Looking more closely, she was able to see an ailing man whose eyes were rolled back in his head. There was much whispering, and people were saying not to cry. The man gradually stopped breathing and died. Suddenly everyone who had been at his side left, while several others prepared to take the corpse to the burial ground. "Alas!" she exclaimed. "Such is the suffering of death! Unavoidable, it is the inevitable result of the negative karma of samsara. May I and all parent sentient beings equal to space exhaust our karma of transmigration and achieve the state of permanent freedom from death. May the state of stainless great bliss be obtained!" As she offered this prayer, her heart felt heavy, and when she went back inside the palace she broke down in tears.

Seeing this, the queen asked her daughter—who was as precious to her as her own heart—what had happened. Had she become ill? Had she fallen and hurt herself? Lovingly she caressed her, kissing her and wiping her tears. Then the dakini spoke: "Alas! O mother of great kindness! This mind has taken rebirth in this form of aggregates and elements! Today I ventured up to the palace roof and saw for the first time the suffering of the negative karma that is endured in this world. The suffering of birth, old age, sickness, and death is unavoidable! Alas! I can no longer bear the thought of it! Women in samsara are tied down, imprisoned, with no means to end their karma. It is like the relentless pounding of waves. All who are born in existence must experience such suffering as though they were a group of heartless fools! Now that I know such suffering exists, I cannot remain idle. However examined, samsara is something to seek liberation from. One cannot avoid the process of growing old. There is no way to prolong youth or prevent decrepitude. We are like grounded birds, unable to fly. We must struggle along like cripples, our limbs helplessly retracted. This suffering, however examined, is inescapable!

"Now I must find the path to freedom. By the power of previous karma, the pain of illness, like being pierced a hundred times by a sword, must be endured. Without believing in the reality of karmic cause and effect, one will continue to think that obstacles and suffering are imposed by some external force. I must free all beings from this deluded misconception! We who are born in this world must, with each passing day, month, and year, experience the exhaustion of our lives. No one is capable of postponing the miseries of death when its time arrives. Even though one is surrounded by relatives and dear friends, one must enter the narrow passageway of death alone when life is snatched away, like a candle flame that flickers and dies, like a strand of hair pulled out of butter. Even parents, relatives and friends cannot grant refuge or protection from our solitary journey down the narrow paths of the bardo.[49] Until karma is exhausted, all the suffering that must be endured is beyond comprehension. When death arrives, it is far too late to feel remorse. Our remorse and regret must then be laid bare before the Lord of Death[50] himself. I wonder when this unavoidable event will happen to me? I cannot help but weep uncontrollably at the futility of our condition. As we fail to appreciate this opportunity, life passes by like a burst of wind. I shall ponder this until I cannot even stay at rest in my own bed due to the intensity of my fear and anticipation. Now my only thought is to go as quickly as possible to where I can practice the sacred Dharma. O parents of great kindness, please grant me your permission!"

Hearing her words, the queen was filled with fear and anxiety. "Daughter," she replied, "you are like your mother's eyes and heart. It is not easy to consider sending you elsewhere to practice Dharma. You are young, inexperienced, and extremely attractive. If you meet the wrong person it may become difficult for you to pursue the Dharma. Would it not be better to stay here in the palace to practice?"

Mandarava replied: "Mother, please listen. I am not interested in the ordinary phenomena of this world. I wish to meet a spiritual guide who can give me the essential instructions. Once I have received them, I will strive to accomplish them until I am liberated. It is difficult for me to imagine how I can accomplish and realize the inner meaning of the practice if I remain in the palace—the phenomena of samsara are deceptive! If I am alone, I shall be free to be happy or sad as I please. O father and mother, if you look upon me with loving-kindness and compassion, then grant me your permission!"

The distraught queen went immediately to the king and told him all that had transpired. The king replied: "Our daughter is young and impressionable. What could have made her have such thoughts? She is so young and immature. It will be difficult for her to accomplish the Dharma. I cannot possibly allow her to go off alone like this. On the other hand, if I send her away with attendants, it will be hard for her to accomplish her goal. No matter what, our daughter must stay in the palace! She will not dwell on this idea for long. Her young, impressionable mind will change like clouds passing over the sun. Her enthusiasm, though great at first, like the head of a guppy, will diminish in the end, like a guppy's narrow tail. However, according to the holy man's true words, if she meets a spiritual teacher she will engage upon the path of Dharma."

The queen returned to her daughter and said: "O Mandarava, the only concern of this mother of yours, listen to what your father has to say, and you will be pleased! We cannot send you away to a place where we are unable to see you or look after you. But as long as your intention remains the same, you may stay in the palace and practice the Dharma to your heart's content. Daughter, I, your mother, shall serve your every need!" Upon hearing this, Mandarava thought, "My very existence is due to the kindness of my parents," and therefore replied that she would obey.

Samaya

This completes the seventeenth chapter of
*The Lives and Liberation
of the Princess of Zahor, Mandarava,*
called *A Precious Garland,*

Explaining her sadness and strong aversion
for the condition of samsara and her request
to her father and mother to be allowed to
pursue the path of Dharma.

18.
Perfecting the Outer Sciences

From then on the princess stayed in the upper chambers of the palace, immersing herself in all aspects of literature and composition under the guidance of the excellent sage Kamalashri. She studied until she thoroughly understood the five major, eight minor, and one hundred branch and auxiliary texts. Then she mastered the languages of eastern and western India, Oddiyana, Maruta, Nepal, Raksasa, Dakini, all the border lands, Singhala, and Yangchen Üpa, plus the language and written script of the kingdom of Shambhala and many others. Not only did she master these languages, but she also learned the local dialects perfectly. She became a scholar without rival.

The heretic Atashi entered the Buddhist path and became a spiritual teacher himself. He was invited to the palace. The princess studied the ten non-Buddhist subjects of learning, such as poetics, logic, and grammar. She studied the great sutras such as the *King of Samadhi* and others. She received all the teachings and transmissions of the Buddha's spoken teachings and contemplated them thoroughly. At that time, she developed perfect comprehension of twenty-five sutras. She also studied all there was to know about the subject of chanting and spiritual melodies.

One day, as the princess was looking out from the window of the palace, she saw a large gathering of women by the southern fence. A beautiful woman sat at their head, addressing the group. She held an arura sprig and was explaining the many qualities of the plant. A woman seated upon a tree refuted her, saying that except for its bitter flavor the arura possessed no significant qualities. The beautiful woman replied: "The arura is the seed of origination, and, as the golden precious jewel of plants, it was blessed by the Buddha. *A* is the unborn jewel of perfect purity. *Ru* is the unobstructed explanation of the illnesses that affect beings. *Ra* is the fruition of compassion. The eight edges of the plant symbolize the eight-fold path of the aryas. The eight facets symbolize the cleansing of the eight passions. The fine root symbolizes that the phenomena of existence can be extinguished! The broad top indicates expansive noble qualities. The outer bark, astringent and bitter, eliminates all types of poisonous properties. The inner bark is sour, eliminating all illness. This is a substance that delights the minds of all the victorious ones. The innermost trunk of the plant is hollow, indicating that the absolute meaning of all relative dharmas is emptiness. The trunk of the plant is wide and the bark is layered, indicating that the dharmas of samsara must be gradually eliminated. The ample blooms symbolize the fact that wisdom permeates all dharmas. In these many ways, the arura plant embodies sublime, noble qualities, and has many medicinal properties!"

Asked about the worth of the plant, she replied that, if sold, it would be as valuable as gold—yet, if one possesses gold without cherishing it as wealth, this is a sign of small-minded ignorance. Upon hearing this, Mandarava knew that it was time for her to study the science of medicine. She began at once. The doctor Ratna was invited to the palace to become her teacher. First, she made a thorough investigation of the medical tantras. Then she studied the four seasons, the eleven changes in the five elements, the twenty-one thousand six hundred vital energies, and all corresponding root and branch texts, including the *Four Cycles of Mother and Son*, the extraordinary *Seven Roots*, and so on. Her studies were extensive and thorough. With regard to the science of weather, she studied light, clouds, moisture, atomic particles, colors, and the cycle of tides. She studied some eighteen tantras in all dealing with this subject. She also studied the causes, conditions for, and process of fetal development in the womb. The *Katitsa* and other texts explaining the solid and hollow organs were investigated. She thoroughly comprehended all one hundred chapters of the root tantra. Then she learned the tantras on pointing-out instructions concerning the corresponding accomplishment practices. Other scriptures on the subject of medicine that she studied included the five hundred *Auxilliary Scriptures of the Sages*, the *Ajita* medical scripture in one hundred chapters, and the five texts on abandonment. She became a great scholar of the science of medicine.

Early one morning, when she went to the top of the palace, she saw people of many cultures gathered in the western garden. Among them was a poorly dressed monk holding a staff. His name was Arnapa. Many people began asking him questions. Some could not figure out what he was saying; others clearly understood him. The discussions kept leading to more confusion, and clarification was not forthcoming.

A young girl asked the monk where he had trained to develop his knowledge. He replied that he had studied almost every subject, but in particular he showed her many pages of an astrological text, explaining that he had studied this subject in particular detail. He told the girl that if she was intelligent, she should also study in this way. The girl replied that this was something she already knew. She had thoroughly studied the cycle of the four seasons, the correspondence of the twelve months to the male and female genders, the twenty-four hour cycle of the day, the dissolution of time, and how the cycle of the twenty-one thousand six hundred breaths is complete. She went on to say that she had also studied the white and black cycles of astrology[51] in their entirety.

All this displeased the monk. He denounced the girl for rambling like a magpie. He accused her of falsifying her comprehension and blasted her for speaking too much, which was proof that she could not possibly have mastered such topics. To his verbal abuse, the young girl responded, "The esoteric instructions on astrology are just like a wish-fulfilling treasury. How could someone like you—with no qualifications at all—claim to know anything about it? Within the wisdom text of Sarasvati, there are the extraordinary instructions on astrology, which clarify the karmic results of relative truth, while the Kalachakra tantra discusses the subject of unchanging absolute truth. This wisdom text of Sarasvati is as melodious as the sound of the vina. The composition is as beautiful as a dance of art upon paper. This great treatise clarifies both the excellent and the negative and is famous in a thousand ways. It is an ornament of the most fortunate minds; if one is without protection, wandering vulnerably in the state of delusion, to simply make contact with this great wealth of scriptures is to perfect transcendent primordial wisdom. After all, isn't this the precious doctrine of the Buddha?" After she thus spoke, the monk became infuriated and replied, "Who knows if the doctrine of the Buddha would be given to someone like you?" Then he quickly went on his way.

Mandarava then told the queen what she had seen and heard. "In the garden to the west of the palace, many people were gathered. Among them was a youthful maiden. Her qualities are so astonishing that I feel a strong need to meet her." The queen gave her permission, and Mandarava went immediately to find the girl. Upon meeting her, Mandarava said, "You are a girl of great intelligence. Who are your parents, what is your caste, and why have you come here?" The girl replied, "My father's name is Rigche Dawalha. My mother is Lhamo Yukye. My lineage is that of the Mingpo Dawa gods. I am sixteen years of age, and my name is Palmo Shonu. When I turn seventeen I will live in the western region of Zahor, near the city of the Nectar Garden."

Mandarava asked the girl to teach her everything she knew. The girl replied: "Although my training in Dharma is weak, I have had an opportunity to study the sacred literature on the subject of astrology from my father. I have achieved a strong sense of confidence in my studies. But, aside from that, I know very little. Goddess, it is doubtful that I am a suitable candidate to be your teacher. If you insist, however, I will do my best to offer you what I can."

Mandarava returned to the queen. "O daughter of my heart," said the queen, "with whom have you been speaking?" Mandarava answered: "Mother, there is an amazing girl who is the daughter of Rigche Dawalha, of divine lineage. Her name is Palmo Shonu. She debated with a monk on the subject of astrology and defeated him. She has previous training in the scriptures and is highly learned in astrology. I requested her to be my teacher in that subject." The queen replied that she thought the king would never allow a common person to instruct his daughter, and it might be better to invite a scholar of astrology to come to the palace instead. Mandarava replied, "The male teachers are so strict and overbearing, it is difficult to learn from them. I prefer a female teacher, who would be more gentle."

Then the queen went off to speak to the king. She told him how Mandarava desired to study astrology and wished to have permission to invite this young woman to be her teacher. Indeed, the king felt strongly that the princess' teacher must be equal to her in status and caste. He decided to invite a holy man to the palace for consultation. After carefully examining the situation, the holy man proclaimed that the daughter of Rigche Dawalha was a manifestation of a dakini and that it would be good for her to remain permanently with the princess Mandarava. She was destined to eventually become Manda-rava's main disciple. After this prophecy, the girl Palmo Shonu was invited to the palace. She became a member of Mandarava's entourage and taught the princess everything she knew about astrology. After some time, Palmo took the vows of ordination and remained close to Mandarava thereafter.

At this time, there were many heretics in the land of India, so the king ordered Mandarava to study the art of logic. He requested her previous teacher, Atashi, to return to teach dialectics to both Mandarava and Palmo. He was a master of both the outer and inner teachings on the five sciences. Mandarava studied until her noble qualities were unsurpassed by any other. She also studied arts and crafts and sorcery. Mastering every science that existed in India at that time, she became a scholar without rival.

Samaya

This completes the eighteenth chapter of
*The Lives and Liberation
of the Princess of Zahor, Mandarava,*
called *A Precious Garland,*

Explaining how she perfected her studies
of the outer sciences.

19.
Liberating the Heretic Kyabsal Nagpo

Then one of the most famous heretical teachers traveled to the Indian country of Gautala. He was so skilled in the art of debate that not a single Buddhist scholar could defeat him. The Buddhist king of that country, King Charje, became disturbed by his presence in the kingdom. He was overjoyed, however, when the great master Drime Yeshe revealed an important prophecy of Dorje Pagmo.

The prophecy stated that, as a result of negative prayers, the famous heretical teacher, known as Kyabsel Nagpo, was in fact an emanation of a demon. The force of his negative prayers was so powerful that no one could defeat him in dialectics. His miraculous powers were so developed that others were no match for him. According to the prophecy, only one person had the strength to break this spell of negative karmic aspirations. That person was to be found in the eastern country of Bengal, and she was the honorable Princess of Zahor, the primordial wisdom dakini Mandarava. By age thirteen, Mandarava had trained in and thoroughly mastered all the sciences—she was a dakini incarnate, unstained by the effect of the womb. The prophecy stated that she was a revealer of great miraculous abilities and that whoever wished to receive the blessings of Dorje Pagmo should make contact with her.

Upon hearing this prophecy, King Charje and his ministers convened and immediately prepared a letter of invitation to be sent to the king of Zahor. The letter said: "O king of Zahor, possessed of great strength, wealth, and power, the activities of the heretic Kyabsel Nagpo have become like a poisonous fire. His negative view has incinerated the Dharma teachings of the five masters from Gautala. His conduct is like a blazing mass of negativity. According to the dakini's prophecy, the only antidote powerful enough to extinguish his flames is the potent nectar of princess Mandarava, your daughter. Please, by your great kindness, send her to us as quickly as possible!"

This letter was delivered to the king of Zahor, and the king, queen, and ministers all gathered to discuss it. Then they informed Mandarava of the letter's contents. She agreed that she must leave immediately for the land of Gautala. Bedecked in her finest attire, Mandarava departed with her entourage of attendants.

Upon her arrival, King Charje, his ministers, attendants, and the entire kingdom greeted her with great respect and honor. The five most prominent heretics assembled to debate with Mandarava. She easily defeated them, and her victory was proclaimed.

Then the powerful Kyabsel Nagpo himself approached and challenged her to debate the inner meaning of the six treatises teaching wrong views. She accepted his challenge and proceeded to defeat him easily. Then he mockingly referred to her as a woman with a clever mouth, who mistakenly wears the garments of one with noble attributes. He said, furthermore, that if the rumors of her miraculous abilities were true, he thereby challenged her to display them.

She accepted the challenge, and, when he suddenly flew off into space, Mandarava made the threatening mudra with her hand, and he dropped from the sky like a stone. Still convinced that he could defeat her, he created a great storm of hail and meteorites, with nine meteorite tormas.[52] The dakini made a mudra and the hail and showers of thunderbolts dissolved in their own place. Still convinced that he was her match, he set out walking across the river Ganges as light as a bird. The dakini clapped her hands, and he sank in the water as though he were a stone. After he emerged, he persisted, enticing her to compete with him by claiming that he had many other miraculous abilities. Suddenly six heretics manifested themselves as eight snow lions, flames shooting from their mouths and violent, red wind blasting from their nostrils. The snow lion roared, "We will annihilate you, woman of magic." They all jumped in front of Mandarava, causing the king and all his attendants to gasp in fear. At that moment the dakini shouted a single *hum*. The eight snow lions were reduced to dog skins. Once again, the six heretics appeared.

Suddenly, a torrential rain of poison descended upon the king and his retinue. The dakini performed the breathing purification practice, immediately reversing the poison rain, so that it eliminated three countries of heretics. Still the teacher of the heretics persisted to taunt the dakini, telling her it was not enough to show her powers by just sitting there—if she were truly a magician, she had to prove that she could fly. Saying this, he manifested a threatening spear from which a rain of arrows emerged. The dakini elevated into space, caught the arrows in her hands and, blessing them, sent them back toward the demon, where they penetrated the heretics. Crying out in pain, they fell from the sky and, as they hit the ground, lost consciousness and expired. With that final miraculous deed, the heretics were completely defeated, and all the remaining followers were brought to the path of Dharma.

Thereafter the dakini became renowned as "the heroine who miraculously tamed the heretics," and the king and all his subjects made extensive offerings to her. Remaining for some time in their kingdom, Mandarava studied the Four Noble Truths and took the bodhisattva vow with the master Drime Yeshe. Eventually she returned to her own kingdom of Zahor and continued her Dharma studies under the supervision of her noble parents.

Samaya

This completes the nineteenth chapter of
The Lives and Liberation
of the Princess of Zahor, Mandarava,
called *A Precious Garland,*

Explaining how Mandarava defeated and
liberated the heretic Kyabsel Nagpo and
his followers.

20.

Leading Three Hundred
Noble Women to the Dharma

Once a day, the king of Zahor went to the top of the palace, where he observed the activities taking place outside the gates. He often watched the various competitions taking place and evaluated each sport. If he fancied the sport he would praise it, and if he disliked it he would disparage it. All the subjects of the kingdom were obliged to observe strict discipline under his watchful eye. During this time the queen, with her family and attendants, bathed and then ventured outside the boundaries of the palace, adorned in beautiful clothing and ornaments.

One day, Mandarava wanted to go out for a stroll. She asked the group of maidens attending her if they would like to go along. They replied in the affirmative, and all set out together for a long walk. Having passed through a dense forest, they arrived at a large lake between a mountain and a valley. Mandarava proceeded to walk directly across the top of the lake. Then she addressed the group of women as follows: "Young women who have decided to accompany me here, please listen to what I have to say. What in this world of ours brings you pleasure? What do you truly wish to accomplish? Please answer."

The women replied: "Our greatest wish is to become like you, goddess Mandarava. We wish to be of noble caste, class, wealth, and royalty. If we marry, we wish to wed only a prince of the royal family and to live happily ever after in the great palace of the nine-tiered roof!"

After hearing this, Mandarava asked them to listen with great care: "Each of you should examine your own mind, to see how you have squandered your lives on your needs and desires. Thoughtless maidens, get hold of your minds! We women establish the seeds of samsara with such hankering after ordinary pleasures. No matter how beautiful you may be, your beauty and youth are illusory. By even the smallest condition you can fall to a lower status. Your minds and eyes are both so spoiled that you cannot even see the need for the precious Dharma! You could easily be persuaded and enticed by negative companions who would lead you into the hells. You would give up your body and even your life for your husband, yet after some time you would lose control and start to bicker and quarrel incessantly, and you would experience even greater suffering than the inhabitants of the jealous god realm. The suffering of birth and death is beyond your imagination.

"Consider the ways in which karma bears fruit. All the endowments, wealth, and possessions of this world are like an illusion or a dream, with no true existence. Beauty and endowments are like a rainbow vanishing in space. Even though they are present now, they can never be permanent. A wonderful nine-tiered palace adorned with the five precious jewels is itself an illusion and a cause for downfall. Youth and beauty are like a summertime flower, unable to endure the onset of aging and destroyed by the first frost. Expensive silks and jewels are like dewdrops on the grass. Though present now, they vanish in an instant with the first strong wind. All gatherings of relatives, friends, and attendants are like visitors in a marketplace. One instant they gather, in the next they inevitably part. Your own life essence is like a candle attempting to endure a strong wind: there is no way to determine when it will be extinguished, and it must be protected with great care. Power and fame are like a roar of thunder in the sky: heard for a moment, they become a pointless echo. However you look at it, all this has less essence than a pile of crumbs.

"The cause of the mind's destruction is the futile pursuit of meaningless, confused perception. The suffering of being born into this world is like being forced to stay within an iron-fenced prison. Taking unceasing rebirth in the realms of existence is worse than remaining in the eighteen states of hell. The suffering of old age is like a great old bird that has lost its feathers: youth, dignity, and strength inevitably decline. You cannot even escape with a needle's worth of pleasure. The suffering of illness and disease is like falling into a pit of fire. There is not even a chance for a moment of happiness when it feels as though your flesh and bones are being pulled apart. The suffering of death is like a great meteor falling from the sky: no one can benefit you, and there is absolutely no way to escape. The suffering in the bardo is like being surrounded by a hostile army.

"There is no method to employ, except to accumulate virtue. Alas! Young maidens, you must think carefully! Your dwelling place and endowments are only the deception of Mara, leading you to further delusion. Your relatives and friends are maras who come to escort you. All these attachments are the handcuffs that bind you to samsara. Your temporary pleasures, your fleeting moments of happiness, are ultimately the cause for the executioner's celebration. Even your cherished body is merely a vessel full of unclean substances. If you do not persevere in making offerings to the victorious ones, then to adorn and anoint this unclean vessel is only an act of delusion. The impure body is the product of confusion, which cannot transcend this karmic predicament. This is the result of cherishing and grasping one's own body and self. The body you possess will decay and dissolve. In whatever way you examine it, nothing about it is real or true. Everything that is of this world is cause for confusion.

"By thinking in this way, you will turn to the precious Dharma as your path. Unconfused, you will persevere with clarity, through the use of your three doors,[53] to accomplish that which is wholesome. Young maidens, consider your future life! Then enter this spiritual tradition, which is the path of Mandarava."

After receiving her personal instruction, they all took the bodhisattva vow in order to be liberated. Thereafter, each and every one of them maintained the path of virtue, bringing virtue and goodness to the kingdom. Now on the path of Dharma, they gradually erected a temple, and Mandarava taught them the three baskets of scripture.

Samaya

This completes the twentieth chapter of
The Lives and Liberation
of the Princess of Zahor, Mandarava,
called *A Precious Garland,*

Explaining how she led three hundred
maidens of nobility to the path of
Dharma.

21.

The Death of Prince Pawode

Mandarava, the daughter of the gods, continued to dedicate herself only to the welfare of sentient beings and to accomplish their benefit according to her enlightened intention. She expressed generosity toward the weak and needy by giving alms and whatever else was required. She never conducted herself inappropriately. Her speech was always pleasing, her conduct always in harmony with whomever she encountered. Her countenance was always peaceful and attentive; she constantly showed loving-kindness toward those whose position was below hers. She looked upon the negative activities of others with compassionate concern. She had unfailing faith and tremendous regard and devotion for her spiritual teachers. In addition, she showed great respect for her parents, the king and queen, and always praised those who accumulated excellent merit and virtue. Even her weakest attributes she utilized to their fullest potential. She was truly impartial in her attitude toward everyone, whether high or low, and always cheerful and mindful in whatever she did. With skillful discernment, she always showed great respect to the venerable and worthy objects of offering, while she herself was nothing less than a treasure of glorious, sublime qualities. She had fully abandoned the mind of attachment and desire, and even if a virtuous quality was small or minor in weight, she would embrace it, praise its value, and rejoice in its accumulation. Her personal conviction and confidence were unfaltering as well as uncommon. She always pursued the pure path and—depending on her strength and capability—trained upon it. Her enthusiastic effort remained unfailing as she dedicated herself to practice. In this way, her noble qualities became inconceivably sublime. In fact, no one could rival her virtue.

One day she approached her father, the king, requesting him to listen to the words of respect she had to offer. "Kye ma! Astonishingly supreme father of great kindness, your strength and power is equal to that of a chakravartin. The activity of the heirs of the buddhas is the excellent conduct that is praised by all the enlightened ones. Thinking of such virtue, I yearn to engage in the conduct of the holy ones. I will never remain in the mire of samsara. My only wish is to become ordained—to shave my head and wear the robes of the Sangha. By maintaining the discipline of the vows of moral conduct, I intend to enter the door of the ever-turning wheel of Dharma and live within the confines of a monastery."

After hearing these words spoken from her heart, the king still did not give her permission to pursue her true path. Instead, he told her to spend the daytime serving and attending to the needs of her mother. She did as he requested and became a servant in this way. At night she would refrain from sleeping in order to persevere in her Dharma practice.

Then, one day, the only son of the royal family Prince Pawode unexpectedly passed away. The king and queen were devastated and plunged into a state of intense mourning. Overcome with grief, the king touched his head to the corpse of his son, lamenting: "Alas! How unbearable to lose my only son! Before this I was a king of great merit! I possessed great wealth and endowments, and had one son and three daughters. I loved and cherished them all more than my own eyes and heart. The karma of samsara brings such misfortune, such hardship! How could this have happened to me? Now we parents must suffer the most. I feel as though my heart has been ripped out and thrown on the earth. Alas! What shall I do with this body—an empty ribcage with its essence torn out? I feel as though my very eyes have fallen to the ground. With my most essential organs missing, how can I go on? When a sharp sword severs the arms from the body, what is there left to do with the aggregate of form? Without my two legs, how shall I walk? Although this palace has nine tiers and is splendid beyond compare, what is the use of such a dwelling when there is no son inside?

All the wealth, endowments, and objects of enjoyment have been gathered but, without a successor, to whom shall I pass all of this? There are many attendants and subjects to rule and sustain but, without a successor, what will become of this country? My son, who was just like my own heart, is lost. What shall this mother and father do now without him? Alas, I am grief-stricken beyond belief!" Having thus lamented, he broke down and wept uncontrollably.

Then the queen cried out in anguish: "Alas! The pain and sorrow I feel is unbearable! It is as though the heart within my chest has been split apart. What could possibly be the cause of such karmic ripening as this? How could our son have become such an object of pity? Is this terrible consequence our karma, or is some other negative force at work here? Our son, like my own eyes, has vanished before me like a rainbow dissolving into space. What am I to think, having been abandoned in such a way? My son—the pure essence of my heart— has left me, his old mother, with an empty, torn-out chest. There is nothing to do but end my own life!" Crying out these words of great pain, she fainted.

Mandarava went to her and revived her by blowing upon her. When she was conscious again, Mandarava asked both the king and queen to listen to what their daughter had to say:

"In this world of ours, nothing is permanent and stable. Eventually, all created things will disintegrate. Even the external vessel itself, the universe, will be destroyed. All beings born in this world must eventually die, and all gatherings must disperse, just as all accumulations must become exhausted. In the end, all youth will decay, and all that is created will be destroyed. Even the vajra body of the Buddha, unable to remain in this world, demonstrated the need to pass into nirvana.

"No matter how great the merit of the king, when he dies, he dies alone. You must have unfailing confidence in the ripening of karmic causes, since this is the very nature of everything, without exception, and indicates to us the interdependency of all phenomena. Please see that your pain and lament is of no benefit at all. O father and mother, please understand the illusory nature of compounded phenomena! Understand and trust that it is impossible for oneself or another to do anything about a human being's death. Therefore you must transcend the object of your suffering. Please, my parents of great kindness, accept these words of advice offered to you by your daughter."

After hearing this, the king and queen both found some comfort and relief from their torment. They replied that they would do their best to take the meaning of her words to heart.

Samaya

This completes the twenty-first chapter of
The Lives and Liberation
of the Princess of Zahor, Mandarava,
called *A Precious Garland,*

Explaining how Mandarava consoled her
father and mother, the king and queen,
at the death of their only son, Prince
Pawode, and dispelled their suffering
through the use of the Dharma.

22.
Setting Five Hundred Women
on the Path to Liberation

In the year that followed, the kingdom of Zahor fell under hard times as the great river swelled to the bursting point, unable to contain the unceasing torrential monsoons. The river was so swollen that the people could not even travel upon it in boats or cross its bridges. The land became flooded. All the fish were washed ashore. As the flood-water stagnated, it became polluted to the point that even getting enough clean water for a cup of tea was difficult. Salty water inundated the entire land. In addition, the weather patterns became disturbed, such that lightning and hail storms predominated. New diseases gradually arose, and the people suffered from various illnesses.

Frustration and anger intensified, giving way to petty borderland squabbles that erupted into war. King Anga of Bheta and the king of Zahor began warring against each other. Fierce battles ensued. They waged war at the borders of their two countries by hurling bombs and pursuing one another with powerful weapons. The battles became so nasty that they spread forth like fire through every valley and region of the two lands. This, of course, intensified the already existing anger and aggression, and people began to slaughter one another mercilessly.

When rancor between the two countries had escalated to the extreme, the sister of the gods, Mandarava, interceded by speaking to her father the king as follows: "Kye ma! O king of great, expansive wealth and power! You are well skilled in maintaining a government in accordance with the law of the precious Dharma. Therefore I would like to know if the dishonorable activities occurring have been ordered by your command or that of your ministers? Who is responsible for the weighty negative karma being accrued? Who can patiently endure the ripening effect of the karma of taking the lives of others? How completely confused are those who could accrue karma that is heavy beyond compare. Can you not take a moment to see that such karma will ensure your continued circling in the round of birth and death? O king, please consider now a way to reverse this negative karma. As your daughter, I will do whatever you command of me."

Upon hearing her words, the king knew he must employ a method to make peace with the king of Bheta. He decided to compose a letter that Mandarava wrote in golden ink. His messengers delivered it, along with many precious jewels and offerings, to the king. Receiving the letter, the king of Bheta read as follows: "Great king who upholds and maintains all that is fully endowed! The war between Bheta and Zahor is like experiencing the suffering of the lower realms right here in the human realm. May the cooling white light rays of the moon swiftly illuminate the darkness of hatred in these two lands."

When the king of Bheta had read his letter, he instructed his minister Kari and his attendants to deliver a letter that he wrote to the troops on the battlefield. Its contents were as follows: "The king of Zahor, his ministers, and his entire army turn in compassion from this futile battle and celebrate the victory of upholding the precious Dharma. Gather your weapons and return with them to your own countries. Raise the victory banner of the stainless mind of equanimity for one another, and may peace and happiness prevail! This is the command of the king." When this proclamation had been read, good will prevailed among everyone.

Then the king of Bheta read aloud from another golden letter that had been sent to him: "Golden, courageous king of Bheta with your ministers, retinue, and assemblies, powerful and wealthy ruler of a great kingdom of subjects! Showing tremendous forbearance, your mind has turned from the thought of war, and the pure, white light rays of your miraculous activities are luminously displayed. By your command, the weapons that could have destroyed your own people have been gathered up, and bliss prevails in all directions!"

Hearing the contents of this letter, everyone agreed, feeling deep respect. The army disarmed, and peace became the law of the land. Gradually the two countries renewed their strength on the path of profound truth, and words of mutual goodwill prevailed.

The sister of the gods, Mandarava, said that the opportunity for true happiness had now arrived. From that time onward, Mandarava was responsible for leading countless beings upon the path of virtue by causing them to turn from taking lives or accumulating any of the ten nonvirtues.[54]

One day, accompanied by a group of virtuous companions, Mandarava went outside to stroll in a lovely flower garden. Suddenly an intoxicatingly beautiful goddess approached them and asked who they were.

Mandarava responded:

"Kye ma! Daughter of the gods, whose beautiful smile illuminates this garden, who is adorned with splendid jewels that blaze with radiant light! Like a lotus your complexion is rosy and clear. Like the sun and moon, your eyes glance enticingly to and fro. Your breasts are as voluptuous as those of a sixteen-year-old maiden, while the palms of your hands are as soft as the petals of the utpala flower. Your waist is refined and your demeanor seductive. The soles of your feet are pliant and smooth, like lotus petals. Your face is like a stainless, self-originating mandala of the major and minor marks. Now that this astonishing mandala of your enlightened form has actually appeared here before us, please tell us: where have you come from, to which caste do you belong, and who are your parents? Why have you suddenly appeared here? Please quench the thirst of our curiosity by causing the great rain shower of your ambrosial speech to descend upon us."

The dakini then responded: "E ma ho! Great Dakini, daughter of the king of Zahor! Mandarava of supreme caste, please listen well. I am without father, having been born from a lotus. My mother is the keeper of bliss, Dhateshvari, of the sphere of truth. I, this girl, am the supreme consort Pandaravasini. As the consort from the Western Paradise of Sukhavati, I am naturally a dakini of the lotus family. My family is of the class of the primordial wisdom of discriminating awareness. I have come here to give you some pith instructions and to reveal to you a chapter of the prophecy about your life. I am a dakini emanating from the same ground as yourself. In the nature of ultimate truth there are no characteristics of coming and going."

Mandarava then made prostrations to her and, in a melody of devotional respect, offered the following supplication: "E ma ho! Primordial wisdom dakini, please pay heed to me. I have been born from an earthly womb. I possess a remarkable storehouse of excellent common and primordial wisdom merit. My caste is that of the royal family of Zahor. I was born in the country of Bengal in female form. Powerless, I am a lowly creature, led along in the realm of samsaric activity. Having fallen under the power of the confusion of deluded perceptions, I must continue empty-handed on this meaningless journey, acquiring the fully ripened results of the three poisons.[55] O primordial wisdom dakini, please hold me fast with your loving-kindness and compassion! Grant refuge to me, Mandarava, who is otherwise without protection! Bestow upon me the revelation contained in your enlightened speech. Protect me from falling onto the treacherous path of wrong views. Swiftly lead me across this ocean of samsara. Never allow me to fall into the hands of the executioner of deluded perceptions. You, goddess, are a true follower of the conquerors and their heirs. I have no source of refuge and protection other than you. Please turn the mind of Mandarava to the pure path of Dharma. Clarify all outer, inner, and secret obstacles. Revered mother, hold me constantly with your precious, pure compassion." All the maidens in Mandarava's company requested to be included in this supplication prayer.

Then the melodious sound of the dakini's speech could be heard: "Kye ma ho! Woman of great fortune among human beings, Mandarava, I shall give you the blessing of my three avenues of body, speech, and mind so that your mind can persevere in the practice of pure Dharma. The king will search the four principal and eight cardinal directions to find a suitable man for you to wed. But you must realize that if you consider only the wishes of your father and mother, this will merely bring you the karma to remain in samsara. You must wear the armor of patience. Although your parents are forcing you to wed, you must always be aware of the law of cause and result. All you maidens gathered here as harmonious companions must enter and travel upon the path of the truth, which leads to certain liberation. The great primordial wisdom manifestation of the second Buddha is the spiritual teacher to whom you must listen and follow by the force of previous aspirations. When the disturbing, restless wind of distorted thoughts and negative karma blows, pray single-pointedly with faith and devotion to the enlightened form of the buddhas. Demonic obstacles will be instantly reversed in their place. Obtaining the empowerment of immortality and achieving liberation from the fear of birth and death, you will make excellent, enlightened connections in seven great continents. You will obtain all the noble enlightened qualities of the buddhas. With the exhaustion of your karma, which propels you, you will be led to the realm of the nirmanakaya. Ultimately, you will mingle indivisibly in the space of the great mother."

Having spoken, the goddess dissolved into space. Mandarava thought to herself how very fortunate she was to have the great merit to have directly met with such a dakini. She knew that her aggregates and elements had been purified such that she had the great merit to receive such pointing-out instructions. She realized that Mara, the obstacle of deluded perceptions, was the real executioner. She vowed that if this deceiver ever came to seduce her, she would never fall prey to it. She felt as though she had encountered the actual Buddha, and she committed herself to accomplishing enlightenment in that very lifetime.

Then she taught the Dharma to the group of women who were gathered there: "Kye! Friends of mine, please listen attentively! The chances of knowing true happiness in this world are extremely rare. The enjoyments of samsara are like honey to the honeybee: because of attachment and compulsive attraction to the honey, the bee may eventually lose its life. When thoughtlessly utilized, the objects of desire in samsara, an ocean of poisons, are the cause for one's own failure and unhappiness. Like an undiscerning child, one's body is literally destroyed in the depth of the fire pit of negative karmic accumulations. Those who are foolish will enter this pit and fall into its depths, from which liberation cannot occur. In this ocean of samsaric enjoyments that cannot bring satisfaction, one is constantly distracted by the powerful, turbulent waves of negative accumulations. The activities of samsara are like being lost in a great forest of sharp razors: if one moves without looking, one's body is instantly destroyed! Within the iron-fenced enclosure of samsara, one is heartlessly encouraged to continue fooling oneself. In samsara, an unceasing wheel of various weapons, one is constantly suppressed in a state of lethargy where time is wasted and one's true purpose is never accomplished!

"When you are directly pursuing this karmic condition, you are like a blind person who wishes his sight organs would function. What purpose, however, does this desire serve when it cannot come to pass? Rather, you must consider what methods will allow you to persevere in the pursuit of your goals and to achieve freedom from this predicament. Do not expose this dakini's prophecies to others. Recognize that if you do speak of them, unfortunate consequences will arise, due to the breaking of the dakini's command. Do not befriend mindless companions, and instead strive only to accomplish the Dharma. O friends of mine, in the end you will obtain final absolute bliss!"

Thus she advised them, and all the young women rejoiced. They committed themselves to the path of Dharma, and they went off to accomplish their goal.

Samaya

This completes the twenty-second chapter of
The Lives and Liberation
of the Princess of Zahor, Mandarava,
called *A Precious Garland,*

Explaining how Mandarava interceded to
end a war and established five hundred
fortunate women on the path to liberation.

23.

The Sacred Flesh of a Bodhisattva

From then on, the fame of Princess Mandarava spread in the four directions and throughout all the surrounding kingdoms. Everyone regarded her with admiration, and their expectations were high. One day King Viharadhara said to the queen: "Kye! This amazingly supreme daughter of ours shows great loving-kindness toward her parents. With her excellent qualities, character, and beauty, merely to gaze upon her is not enough. The kingdoms of the ten directions all want her for their queen. If we give her to one, we will incur the wrath of another. If we give her away, it will bring obstacles to her Dharma practice. No matter which way we turn, there is a conflict. Perhaps it would be most appropriate if our daughter took the vows of ordination."

After listening carefully, the queen spoke her mind. "Kye! O great King, son of the gods, I think that is an excellent idea. Our daughter is interested in nothing but Dharma. With loving thoughts and the kindness of her heart, she considers only how she can help lead all beings to the path of Dharma and the state of liberation. I myself have already promised to follow her advice. It is better to keep her close to us, no matter what!"

Both king and queen decided that no matter what the offer, they would not send her away into the hands of another. No matter how they examined her, she was only interested in the Dharma. The king decided to appease the kings of the many directions by giving them much wealth, for once they were satisfied, Mandarava would enjoy more personal freedom. In this way, even if Mandarava did not take vows of ordination, she could continue to pursue her Dharma practice and no one would blame them. The king and queen felt that if they also were to accomplish the Dharma—difficult as it was for them—others would, in time, follow their example. Their decision was final, and things settled down for some time.

One day, as the king was about to partake of his meal, he discovered that no meat had been offered to him. It was hard to catch fish in the great river, and meat was not available in the marketplace. So the queen sent Mandarava out in search of some meat for her father. Mandarava searched unsuccessfully throughout the village. While returning home empty-handed, she came across a human corpse, pale and swollen, on the top of a hill. She cut the limbs off this corpse and brought them home with her. She told the queen that she had found some meat, and the queen was quite delighted.

The queen carefully prepared the meat, skimming the broth so that it became clear and rich. Adding some tenderizing herbs, she then presented it as an offering to the king. The king partook of the meat and broth, and his body became so light and blissful that he spontaneously levitated. Alarmed, he called out to the queen to come at once. When she arrived before him, the king suddenly became so angry that he seized her, and, holding a sharp knife, threatened to stab her. The queen was terrified. In his rage, the king said: "Where did you get this meat you just fed me? Answer truthfully. Did you try to poison me or just do something horrible? Answer me! My body has become lighter than ever before! If you do not tell me the truth, I will cast you out among the servants!"

The queen replied, "These pieces of meat were brought back from town by our daughter, whom I had sent out for that purpose. I have no idea where she got it, so you will have to ask her." The king commanded the servants to bring Mandarava to him immediately. When she arrived, he accused her of giving him meat that was either poisoned or impure, since his body felt so unusually strange. Yelling at her, he insisted that she tell him the truth. He grabbed her by the neck, threw her down, and waved his knife in her face.

Petrified, Mandarava replied that the meat was not poisoned. Her mother had sent her to town to get some, and on her way home, after she had failed to find any meat or fish for sale in the marketplace, she came across a pale and swollen human corpse that had been out in the rain. She took just enough from the limbs of the body and gave it, together with some tenderizing herbs, to the queen to cook. Suddenly she burst into tears, saying that she had harmed her father and lamenting that her actions had truly spoiled everything.

At that moment, the king knew that this was the flesh of a sage successively reincarnated seven times. He commanded that the rest of the corpse be brought to him immediately. Mandarava went there in an instant. Quickly wrapping the remains of the corpse in her silken garments, she set off for the palace. On the way, she was confronted by several of the villagers, who recognized her and inquired as to her reason for journeying outside of the palace. She replied that she had been out shopping for food.

Mandarava offered all the remains of the corpse to her father the king, and he was amazed that his remarkable daughter had truly made no mistake. There was no doubt that this was indeed the flesh of a sage of seven successive rebirths. Then, in accordance with the king's instructions, Mandarava dried the flesh and all the body parts, purifying them with incense and the like. The precious substance was then placed within a jeweled vessel, where it was kept and honored with great reverence.

Samaya

This completes the twenty-third chapter of
*The Lives and Liberation
of the Princess of Zahor, Mandarava,*
called *A Precious Garland,*

Explaining how she discovered the sacred
flesh of a bodhisattva, seven times successively
reincarnated, and how, through her efforts,
this sacred substance became a basis for
offering and devotion.

24.
A Vision of Vajrasattva

Unwilling to wait any longer, kings and ministers from all the surrounding countries gathered in force, attempting to win Princess Mandarava as their own queen. The arriving kings were: King Bhitota of Oddiyana; King Trigna Trighata of Kashmir; King Shanka Kotali of Bheta; the King Dharmavata of Murum; King Singha Sutitra of Charje; King Indradam of Kuluta; King Sukhahi of Yangpachen; King Hasabid of Mangadha; King Udughi of Shambhala; King Gagana of Togar; King Mudra Bhudani of Ngatug; King Dhahimune of Sinpo; King Sartasumtibha of Nepal; King Bhatato of Shang Shung; King Thalihangti of Persia; King Trushangden of Gesar; King Mokyau Ching of China; King Dharmakosala of India; King Shangtsen Mayi of Tibet, and others.

Each king arrived accompanied by his chief ministers and their assemblies. Bearing riches and delicacies, they congregated in the country of Zahor. Each was bedecked in the costume of his native country, their displays magnificent as they filled the country with their numbers and presence. Each envoy respectfully inquired about Princess Mandarava and presented the king of Zahor with a letter written in gold, asking for his daughter. They were so anxious to receive her that the riches they presented were glorious beyond compare.

The king, queen, and ministers of Zahor convened to discuss the sublime nature of Princess Mandarava. In spiritual accomplishment, no one could surpass her qualities. She was a supreme ornament among ordinary women of the world. Though young and beautiful, she was unrivaled in skill and power and extremely knowledgeable. At her birth, astonishing signs had occurred that were utterly inexpressible: no one of ordinary birth could compare to her. She had great respect for her parents, always honoring their word above all others. She had the beauty and excellent rebirth of a dakini. The fame of her nobility had already encompassed the ten directions. Even the blind and crippled inquired about the well-being of this princess. So great was her past virtue that her present virtue was stainless. So cherished was she by her father, the king, that the thought of sending her away to another would be his greatest defeat. So precious was she to her mother, the queen, that losing her would be comparable to the loss of her own eyes or heart. Yet so many kings from so many kingdoms had gathered here at one time. To give her to one would only infuriate the others. To appease them by promising them another young maiden would be difficult indeed. Knowing that whatever he did would be a source of conflict, the king fell into a deep depression. On three occasions he met with the emissaries to discuss this dilemma; finally, he requested them to express their own opinions.

Then the queen spoke: "O great king of ours! Sometimes putting thoughts into words does not help to resolve such a problem. Nor does it always bring us to a proper decision. Too much contemplation of such a quandary can bring us to a deeper state of confusion and turmoil. Do you agree that it is not useful to be too forceful or to push too hard? Let us withdraw from this excessive talk, conceptualizing, and visual contact. You will not be able to decide under such circumstances. O king, remove yourself from this problem. Do not acquire more debts than can be repaid. Do not accept gifts from other kingdoms just to appease them. If you enforce strict rules, all your problems will be solved. If you treat all the emissaries equally and with respect, they will eventually be satisfied. Do not make many promises that are difficult to keep, or hardship will befall you. Let us ask our excellent daughter of exalted birth what she prefers to do. If she chooses samsara, let us allow her to go where she pleases. If she chooses the Dharma, she will be on the path of Dharma as a queen. Perhaps it is wise to consult the deities or a diviner as well. Whatever the holy sages advise, we should act accordingly."

After she spoke, the minister Trignadzin said, "What do you propose to do about these other countries? You should compare each of their proposals and offer her to the most suitable candidate."

Then the minister of Oddiyana declared: "I have come here by the command of my king. Much wealth has been gathered to acquire the daughter of the gods. Many letters have already been submitted, stating the amount each king is willing to offer. Now the king and his ministers must decide what to do. If your decision is decisive, it will be respected accordingly. If you deceive us with too much discussion, I will not believe your words. The king and ministers of Zahor are advised to remain open and attentive."

Then the minister from China took his turn: "Too many words get carried away by the wind. Regardless of what is said, the noble qualities of the king are inexpressible. It is difficult to make such a decision whether to give the princess Mandarava to one and not to another. In my opinion, O Queen, it is up to you to ask the king of Zahor to make a firm decision and to accept whatever that may be."

Then the minister of Bheta, named Karshita, said, "Although the king of Zahor has profound knowledge about the Dharma of virtue and nonvirtue, when it comes to secular matters our kingdom can defeat his political system. Mandarava's path is clearly that of Dharma."

Then Palasiddhi, the minister representing the king of Gesar, said, "In my opinion, the princess of Zahor, Mandarava, does have some political interests, but no amount of jewels or riches could possibly measure her worth. The king of Zahor is deceptive in his protection of her. Otherwise he would simply give Mandarava to our kingdom!"

Then Nidzu, the minister of Kashmir, said, "King of great physical signs of nobility, if you think that the princess is capable of running a kingdom, then make your decision based on the best offer. If you do not wish to send her away, do not accept any offerings of wealth. There is nothing more to say."

Then the minister Kartrari of Persia spoke: "In order for us to remain on good terms with you, O king, you must be decisive. If you cannot decide, then it is time to prepare our armies for battle. Having confronted such a king as you, possessed of great wealth, nobility and power, I am unable now to return to the kingdom of Persia empty-handed."

Then Simha, the minister of Maru, declared: "To allow her mother to make the decision is to entertain uncertainty and confusion. The decision made by the king is firm and stable. There is no need to continue to listen to this baseless rhetoric. Let us ask the princess herself what she prefers to do. If we allow this indecisiveness to continue, everything will turn to disaster in the end. It is far better to make a decision based upon what she herself wishes, so that the situation is favorable and pleasant."

Then Yagantha, the minister from Tibet, spoke up: "O king of Zahor, who follows the words of a woman! With so many ideas available, you must know that we will hold you responsible in the end. The king of Tibet is extremely shrewd in politics, and great is his desire to possess this princess of noble qualities. In fact, if you do not send her to him, my own life will be in danger. It rests in your hands."

Then the minister of Yangpachen said, "Only the king should be consulted on this matter. The king should confer with the princess, and they should make the choice together." Everyone agreed to this, and they explained their feelings to the king, queen, and ministers of Zahor, who gathered all the people of the kingdom together. The king asked the queen to summon Princess Mandarava so that she could be asked what she preferred to do. Everyone agreed that the princess should choose the place to which she would go. Mandarava was brought before her parents, and the entire situation was carefully explained to her. When they told her that they would give her to whomever she wanted, they also explained that all possessions, wealth, attendants, and companions would accompany her as she wished.

She was told that in the land of India, the Dharma prevailed. In the land of China, entertainment and pleasure abounded. In the land of Gesar, companionship was supreme, while in the land of Oddiyana, ancestral heritage was excellent and sublime. In the land of Shambhala, the Dharma, wealth, and prosperity were enjoyed. In the land of Bheto, there was great might; in Persia, great wealth. The country of Tibet was known for its excellence in archery, the country of Kashmir for the beauty of its people. Finally, they requested her to tell them to which place she preferred to go.

Mandarava pondered for a while, concluding that if she lived the life

of a laywoman she would never be happy. Realizing that all of this was
due to previous karmic causes, she resolved that—even at the cost of
her life—she must pursue only the path of Dharma. Placing all her confidence in the prediction given by the dakini, she gave the following
response: "Kye ma! My only father, who has fallen under the power of
others, please listen to me! Although I aspire to do only as you ask of
me, this time I shall not go to another land with anyone. I will dedicate
my life solely to the path of Dharma. Without the freedom to practice
the Dharma, I shall put an end to this life, offering fervent prayers to be
born in a land where I can practice the Dharma without interruption."

Then the king replied: "No matter which kingdom or family you
choose, it is clear that you will not stay there. Let me think for three
days. Then I shall give you my reply." Even though the king had
already spoken, Mandarava declared:

"No matter how long you say that you will ponder, my mind is
made up. I shall pursue only the path of Dharma. Due to the merit you
have accrued in your previous lives, I have been born as your daughter.
Now that I have the opportunity, if I do not accomplish the precious
Dharma, the essence of this rebirth will be spoiled and lost. The
Dharma has been propagated in India, but the opportunity to practice is
rare. I shall never marry for the sake of caste or class. In any case, the
life of an ordinary householder is only a cause for rebirth in the lower
realms. I am like a wounded deer who hopes only to die, so as to be
released from its misery. O father, understand my final wish."

Although Mandarava had made her intentions extremely clear, the
king still tried to suppress her. He ordered the servants not to let her
venture outside the palace walls. After some time, the princess broke
down in anguish, and in her moment of utter despair, Buddha Vajrasattva suddenly appeared in the space before her. He spoke: "Kye ma!
Maiden Mandarava, without the stain of fault! Be without attachment
to samsara. Be free from despair. Never turn back! Arouse confidence
and courage in your conviction! As one who must accomplish the two
great benefits, you are a woman who is an ocean of noble qualities!"
After she received this advice, Mandarava's commitment to the Dharma
never left her heart.

Samaya

This completes the twenty-fourth chapter of
The Lives and Liberation
of the Princess of Zahor, Mandarava,
called *A Precious Garland,*

Explaining how Mandarava was sought by
the countries of each direction, how she
displayed no attachment to samsara, and how
she had a vision of Vajrasattva, who reminded
her of the prophecy she held.

25.
Taking Vows and Training in the Dharma

Mandarava escaped from the palace. For a period of time she sought shelter in a nearby garden of red flowers. Her attendant Semshogma remained with her, while the other attendants were positioned in the surrounding area to watch for spies.

One day, Mandarava discarded all her jewelry and, shredding her silken garments with a knife, made prayers to be free of such unnecessary adornments in the future. The servant Semshogma went to the king to report this news. The king was not pleased. He felt that if his daughter did not follow his rules, future difficulties could arise with her pursuit of the Dharma. Realizing there was nothing he could do, the king gathered all the kings and their emissaries. He distributed great amounts of wealth to them and sent them on their way, assuring them that the princess had vowed to follow only the path of the holy Dharma.

The following morning, the princess went to see a bodhisattva and, with single-pointed faith, offered this prayer: "E ma! Great bodhisattva, regent of the buddhas! Though I have not cut my ties to samsara, my faith in the Dharma has endured. Kings from every direction gathered to win my hand in marriage. My father the king was deceived and enticed by their offerings of great wealth. Forbidden to pursue the path of Dharma, I had no choice but to escape to this forest and discard all my wealth. My servant, observing this, returned to report my decision to the king. I have heard that the news of this finally satisfied the suitors of the many directions. Now it is my request that you bestow the vows of ordination upon me."

The bodhisattva replied: "Excellent! Princess Mandarava, your sublime intentions are the result of the awakening of past aspirations. In the past, you listened to the holy Dharma in the presence of the Buddha. At that time, your name was Singmo Gangadevi, and I was one of the five principal arhats in the Buddha's assembly. You perfected the path of the thirty-seven branches,[56] so that now you have been reborn as the daughter of the king of Zahor. Do not be attached to samsara. Recall your Dharma connections of the past! Come forward, and I shall ordain you. By receiving and purely maintaining the vows of the individual liberation and bodhisattva training, you will soon become a disciple of the second Buddha, Padmasambhava. Your merit is such that you shall be a precious protector of all beings." Having made this prediction, he ordained her, and she received the name Bodhisattva Yeshe Zangmo.

At the same time, the king told his ministers to determine Princess Mandarava's whereabouts and her activities. They went to the forest, where they saw that she had indeed been ordained. They hastily returned to report this news to the king. When they told him that his daughter had taken vows of ordination in the presence of the great abbot, the king felt it would be difficult for his daughter to maintain her commitments while surrounded by only a few attendants. He then ordered that all of her five hundred servants receive ordination as well. He told his ministers to check on the princess, inform her and the others of his command, and see to it that his wishes were accomplished expediently.

The ministers gathered all the servants together, informing them of the king's command that those in attendance to Mandarava must become ordained on the same path that she had embraced. The king also warned them that if they broke their vows there would be retribution. The servants then went before the great abbot and preceptor and supplicated: "E ma! Great abbot who is like the Buddha! We are the attendants of Princess Mandarava, and it is the command of our king that we come to you to receive the vows of ordination. By your loving compassion, please bestow the blessing of ordination upon us." So it happened that the five hundred servants all received ordination and new Dharma names.

Mandarava's new palace was built within a lovely garden enclosure about a mile from the king's palace. A statue of the Buddha was erected, and the Abbot Bodhisattva came three times to perform the appropriate consecrations. Five encircling enclosures protected the innermost quarters where the princess resided. Each enclosure housed one hundred attendants. The eastern and southern entrances were placed under heavy guard, and the remaining directions were closed off. Twenty attendants were assigned to guard the entrance ways, and the inhabitants were not allowed to venture outside the gates.

Each day from then on, Mandarava diligently studied the scriptures of individual liberation. She inaugurated the tradition of spending the three winter months practicing mantra in retreat; the three months of spring meditating on the meaning of the sutras and teaching; the three summer months in meditative equipoise; and the three months of fall performing the daily practices for generating bodhichitta. Her practice of the holy Dharma proceeded throughout the day and night.

Samaya

This completes the twenty-fifth chapter of
The Lives and Liberation
of the Princess of Zahor, Mandarava,
called *A Precious Garland,*

Explaining her commitment to the Dharma,
which caused her to take the vows of
ordination and to train in the Dharma of
the Sutra Vehicle.

26.
Meeting Master Padmasambhava

The time arrived for Vajra Guru Padmasambhava to tame the kingdom of Zahor, including Princess Mandarava and her assembly. Light radiated from his heart and entered the three doors of Mandarava and her assembly, bestowing profound blessings.

That night she had the following dream: In the space before her, within an expanse of five-colored light rays, there appeared a golden flower with a red stamen. Upon the flower appeared a nirmanakaya manifestation of a buddha. She prostrated and supplicated with devotion. Then this buddha spoke: "O maiden of perfect noble qualities, Princess Mandarava, I am an emanation of Avalokiteshvara. Tomorrow, on the tenth day of the monkey month, come to the top of the grassy hill to meet me. I shall bestow upon you the pointing-out instructions that bring about liberation in one lifetime." After thus speaking, he dissolved into space.

Mandarava awoke from her dream ecstatic at the prospect of meeting such a sublime manifestation. The next morning, while giving her Dharma discourse, she said to the five hundred attendants who had gathered: "E ma! Last evening I had a most remarkable dream. Today we shall go out for a stroll and meet an enlightened being who will bestow upon us the pointing-out instructions that bring liberation in one lifetime." Mandarava and her virtuous attendants went to the grassy hill that was adorned with flowers fragrant as incense. Suddenly, in the space before them, appeared the great Vajra Guru Padmasambhava, radiating wondrous rainbow-colored light. At the moment they beheld him, Mandarava and her assembly were overcome with irreversible faith. The princess spoke: "E ma ho! Crown jewel heart son of the buddhas of the three times! Having fulfilled your destiny, you work only for the welfare of others. With your hook of loving compassion, you constantly gaze upon all sentient beings, nourishing everyone with the medicine of your boundless love. Display your joyful, radiant countenance and deliver us all to the shore of liberation upon the vessel of equanimity. Look upon those of us who are blind and lost, unable to find the way! We implore you to come to our palace and turn the wheel of Dharma!"

The guru promised to come. Mandarava and her assembly quickly returned to the palace to prepare for his imminent arrival. Some prepared the outside, others the inside. Some arranged his teaching cushion, while others prepared the food. Some held up offerings of incense. When all the preparations were complete, the guru arrived. They closed and sealed the doors, and the guru took his teaching seat. They offered the five precious jewels, various dry substances, grains, liquor, wine, and beverages to quench his thirst. Presenting all these substances as a mandala offering to the guru, Mandarava supplicated: "E ma! One like you, whose face represents the buddhas of the three times, where could you possibly have been born? What could be your caste and the class of your parents? O precious one, please bestow upon us the nectar of your sacred words!"

Then the guru replied: "E ma! Amazingly beautiful maiden Mandarava, captivator of the mind's attention! I am fatherless—as my birthplace is the empty nature of truth. The womb of my mother is the wisdom of emptiness. I arose from within a lotus in the center of lake Dhanakosha. I am from the family that is free from the limitation of both existence and quiescence. I myself represent the spiritual attainment of self-originating bliss.

"In the sublime realm where the minds of sentient beings are tamed, a buddha appears who meets the needs of each and every being. Although these emanations have different names and modes of appearance throughout the three times, ultimately they are nondual. In the past, the Buddha of Boundless Light, Amitabha, created Mount Potala, the paradise of Avalokiteshvara. Avalokiteshvara then manifested as

Padmasambhava in Lake Dhanakosha. In the sphere of truth, he is the primordial buddha Samantabhadra; in the Realm of Dense Array, he is the buddha Vajradhara; and in the vajra seat Bodhgaya, he is the enlightened one, Lord Buddha.

I too am this spontaneous presence, appearing indivisible as the Lotus-born, Padmasambhava. The inconceivable blessings that arise in response to the needs of sentient beings further emanate as the eight male buddhas and their eight consorts, the eight places and eight supreme power spots, the eight great charnel ground practice places, and the eight manifestations of the guru, which are the pure display of the eight groups of consciousness. In addition there are the manifestations of the eight vajra masters and the eight emanations, the eight glorious ones and the eight accomplishment herukas, the eight great accomplishments of perfected union and liberation, the eight tantras of the approaching stage, as well as the eight aspects of miraculous enlightened activity. These eight buddhas have perfected the two accumulations and all noble qualities in the past, present, and future. With supreme heirs manifesting themselves from this base, inconceivable emanations are present throughout the past, present, and future, always raising the victory banner of the doctrine in the ten directions."

Hearing his words, Mandarava and her assembly were overcome with joy. Under the guru's guidance they began training day and night in the Dharma of secret mantra. They were taught the three outer tantras of Kriya, Charya, and Yoga, and the three highest tantras of father, mother, and nondual. They also studied the one hundred classes of secret mantra vehicles. In accordance with these classifications of inner tantra, they received teachings on the generation stage with elaboration, as well as on the thousands of major tantras dealing with the energy channels, essential winds, and fluids. They received all the principal teachings in their entirety on the path of secret mantra.

Samaya

This completes the twenty-sixth chapter of
*The Lives and Liberation
of the Princess of Zahor, Mandarava,*
called *A Precious Garland,*

Explaining how, according to the
prophecy, Mandarava met Vajra Guru
Padmasambhava and how she received
the stages of spiritual transmission.

27.
Subduing the King with Miracles

Then, just as the vajra master was extremely pleased with the progress of the teachings being given to the princess and her retinue, an ominous sign occurred. A very unsavory, antagonistic cowherd caught sight of them while they were in a state of complete joy, receiving teachings from Guru Padmasambhava and celebrating the occasion. While the cowherd was returning home he heard many of the villagers praising Princess Mandarava and her female followers. Then he began gossiping slanderously about what he had witnessed, which of course gave rise to more gossip. The rumor spread, eventually reaching the ears of the outer ministers of the king's palace. Then it passed to the inner ministers who, in turn, mentioned it to the queen. The youngest queen then went to the king and said, "Your daughter Mandarava is now living with an ordinary layman with a shaved head."

Upon hearing this, the king became very angry and scolded the younger queen for her slanderous words: "What you have said is idiotic and crazy. Your mouth is like a storehouse of negativity. A woman like you, who yearns to whisper such deceitful rhetoric, is nothing less than a demoness. My daughter, Princess Mandarava, was ordained in the presence of the great abbot. She had no attachment to any of the kings who came for her hand from every direction. It is impossible that she would care to stay in the company of an ordinary man. This talk is incredible! Even if it were a consideration, it is physically impossible because she lives in the center of a five-winged enclosure with five rings of five hundred attendants residing there. Who could pass by them without being noticed? Even if one of them kept such an intrusion a secret, surely not all of the many attendants would be able to remain silent! I demand to know who started this rumor! See to it that this person is brought to me!"

The queen returned to the seven inner ministers. They went to the outer ministers from whom they had heard the rumor. In vain they sought the source of this vicious slander. The principal ministers then returned to the king, unable to fulfill his wish. The king was furious. He reprimanded them and cautioned them to keep their thoughts silent in the future. Reminding them that many important people had great desire for the princess and that the kings of the surrounding directions would become upset, he threw them all behind bars.

Gathering together much wealth, he ordered all the people of the kingdom of Zahor to congregate. Then, in the presence of all the subjects, he made the following announcement: "Kye ho! Inhabitants of the kingdom of Zahor, listen closely! Princess Mandarava has abandoned ordinary life to pursue the path of Dharma. It has been said that she is staying with a young monk. Whoever claims to have witnessed this should come forward, and this bounty of gathered wealth will be his or her reward." Despite this amazing offer, not a single person came forward to claim the reward. News of this public announcement spread far and wide. The kings of the surrounding countries sent spies to find out if it was true, each inquiring as to the whereabouts of the princess. Unable to discover anything unusual, they eventually returned to their own countries.

Then the wives of the imprisoned men went to the cowherd and offered him a great deal of money to speak up. Offering to tend his herd, they encouraged him to tell the king immediately that he was the one who had seen the young man with the princess. The cowherd set out for town. Along the way, he encountered nine unpleasant signs. Upon arriving in the marketplace, he loudly addressed the townsfolk, "Kye! Listen to me, all you citizens of the kingdom! I am the one who will receive the reward offered by our king! I am the one who saw Mandarava in the company of a young man. You may check and see for yourselves if my words are true or false." With that, he collected his reward and returned home to his herd.

Hearing the news, the king ordered his ministers to go to Mandarava's palace and investigate. The queen, however, insisted that she should go instead—and so it was decided. When the queen arrived, she was refused entrance and fainted on the spot. News of this was then taken to the king. Outraged, he ordered that the queen return to him and that they break down the door to Mandarava's quarters and bring the man in her presence to him immediately.

The ministers complied, yet when they entered the inner chambers, much to their amazement, they saw a magnificent young man seated upon a jeweled throne. His body was the very picture of dignity, blazing with luminous light. Princess Mandarava and her assembly were all seated on the floor before him, their palms pressed together in reverence as they carefully absorbed his every word. Unable to accomplish the king's command, the minsters returned to report what they had seen: "Kye ma! The bhikshu man in the company of the princess and her assembly is not of the ranks of ordinary men! Either he is a son of the god of wealth or the son of the god Brahma, the king of the gods. Otherwise, he must be a buddha who has emanated into the world of human beings. When we saw that he was the spiritual teacher of the princess, we were unable to disturb them. It is important to examine him carefully before reacting. It is possible that if a mistake is made concerning this being, irreversible negative karma may be accrued. Such an accumulation could be difficult to purify or confess."

Hearing their words, the king was outraged. He jumped up unexpectedly from his throne. "You ministers are willing to break the law that I have enforced! Any ordinary man who would dishonor my daughter like this must be punished accordingly. Seize this lowly vagabond, bind him, and burn him alive in a pyre of tala wood. As for Mandarava, she refused to go into a family of honor according to my wishes, and now she stays with a common vagrant. Throw her into a dark pit of thorns, where she shall remain for twenty-five human years without seeing the light of day. Place her two main attendants in darkness and the remaining five hundred servants in confinement! Make certain that they never even hear the sound of a male voice." After this command, the ministers who had been put behind bars were released.

News of all this spread to the bordering countries. They were angry that the king of Zahor had deceived them and began to prepare their armies for battle. Princess Mandarava and her two main attendants were captured and punished according to the king's command. The princess was so distraught over what the ministers were doing to the precious guru that she shamed them in front of all her servants: "Are you not afraid of such intensely negative karmic accumulations, which cause unlimited rebirths in the lowest hell realms?" But there was nothing that they could do.

Meanwhile, the vajra master displayed his enlightened miraculous powers. Numerous deities appeared in space, and rain showers suddenly fell. The pyre became a lake of sesame oil. In its center bloomed a marvelous, huge lotus flower surrounded by rainbows and lofty, massing clouds. The king, ministers, and all the people in the kingdom could clearly hear auspicious words and songs resounding throughout space. The entire lake and its flower were now surrounded by a ring of fire. Seated on the very center of the lotus was the Vajra Guru Padmasambhava as an eight-year-old youth, with all the marks of perfection. A normal fire would have burned out in seven days, leaving no trace of smoke. But what a display of fire remained! The air was filled with rainbows, the sound of instruments, and the scent of pure incense.

Everyone then knew beyond a trace of doubt that this young man was indeed a nirmanakaya buddha. The king met with all his ministers. Then he sent the head minister Chöden to the scene, where this minister astonishingly beheld the transformed fire and the magnificent lake with its lotus in full bloom. Upon it sat the great vajra master, whose amazing, sublime appearance was like Buddha Amitabha. Sur-rounding him were five maidens, each as beautiful as Mandarava, holding the five offerings. Imbued with profound faith, the minister ran back to report all of this to the king.

The king went immediately with his entourage to see for himself. Wherever he gazed in the four directions, all he could see was clear light. His astonishment left him speechless. At that moment, the amazing youth, Padmasambhava, spoke to him: "Has the negative king finally come? He who attempts to burn alive the guru who is the nature of the buddhas of the three times? Has the king with tremendous attachment to the deceptions of this world, who imposes laws that are based on meaningless delusion, finally arrived? Has the king with the greatest sense of inflated pride, who wages war on his innocent daughter, finally joined us? The root of the five passions is ignorance. Has the negative king who lacks recognition now and in the future finally come? Has the king with the intention to deceive sentient beings, the king of nonvirtue—the evil king and his minister of non-virtue—finally come?"

After the guru had thus spoken, the king was so distraught with remorse that he fell to the ground unconscious. Then, coming to his senses, he lamented: "How could I have thought of accumulating such negative karma as this? Although my daughter has found a living buddha, I perceived this with such wrong view! Oh, how could I think to be so negative? Kye ma! Kye hu!" He cried in despair and began pulling his hair out, scratching and marring his face while rolling and thrashing on the ground in an emotional uproar.

The principal ministers were filled with remorse and began proclaiming their deep regret. In their duress, they supplicated their leader, the king: "Listen, great king, lord of men! Although we cautioned you to examine this young man more closely, it was to no avail. Now you must offer confession, offerings, and supplication prayers." This time, the king took their advice to heart. The people of Zahor were asked to assemble, regardless of race, class, age, or creed. Countless in number, they arrived to bear witness. The king stood up among them and began offering many full-length prostrations to Guru Padmasambhava. With the sound of strong remorse in his trembling voice, he offered this supplication prayer:

"Kye ma! O buddha of the three times, please listen to me! The remorse I now feel in my heart is unbearable. When I attempted to burn one such as you in the hottest of fires, you transformed the flames into a lake of sesame seed oil. Then, in the center of this magnificent lake, you appeared in full glory, seated upon the stamen of a lotus flower in full bloom. O faultlessly pure one, master of transformation, I prostrate and render praise to you, the self-originating immortal Padmasambhava! I openly confess with deep remorse and regret any harm that I have brought upon your sacred, enlightened body, and I beg your forbearance for my misdeeds! I humbly offer you my kingdom, and I pray that you will accept it now. I, King Indra Viharadhara, will remain as your follower, and I pray that you will dispel the ignorance in the minds of beings! Please come now to take your seat in the palace."

As the king made this offering and request, everyone present could see the gods, nagas, dakinis, emanations of the guru, and buddhas within the massing clouds and rainbows. Then the lovely sound of a fine vina could be heard, accompanying these verses of praise: "*Hrih*! Praise to the body of the great Padmasambhava, unattached and untainted by impurity!" Many such verses of praise could be clearly heard. Then everything dissolved into space, and the people of the kingdom were overcome with devotion and faith.

The great vajra master himself spoke again: "E ma ho! O great king and your hosts of subjects, please pay heed! I am the nature of the buddhas of the three times! Unstained by the womb, I have self-originated from a lotus. My background is like the nature of space, unaffected by happiness or displeasure. My body, stainless in nature, cannot be harmed by the element of fire. The workings of positive and negative karmic accumulations do not affect me in the slightest, but sentient beings will surely make mistakes because of confused perception. Your noble qualities, O king, are like the greatest of mountains, Mount Meru. All of this has occurred in order to guide you to the path of the Buddha. O king, do not despair; I accept your offer. Now I shall go to the palace as you have requested."

The king was overwhelmed with joy. He ordered all the ministers to depart at once for the palace and to bring his newest and finest brocade silk cloak, articles of clothing, and crown. He also ordered that they return with seven of the finest carriages, adorned with various flags and victory banners. They quickly departed to accomplish his wishes. When they returned, a silk brocade throne was prepared on the most splendid carriage, and the vajra master took his seat, surrounded by silken flags and banners of victory and good fortune. The king then offered each of his royal articles of brocade clothing to the master, who carefully put on each one. He also donned the crown and boots of the king. Then the king himself hung the yoke of the carriage around his own neck and, replacing the horses, began pulling the carriage to the palace. This was witnessed by all the people of the kingdom, who surrounded the carriage in a great parade, offering unceasing prostrations and prayers with fervent faith and devotion. Upon arriving at the palace, the great vajra master entered the inner chambers and took his seat upon the throne of seven precious jewels.

Samaya

This completes the twenty-seventh[57] chapter of
*The Lives and Liberation
of the Princess of Zahor, Mandarava,*
called *A Precious Garland,*

Explaining how she met Guru
Padmasambhava, received Dharma
teachings, and how, due to slanderous
words of malicious gossip, the king had
to be subdued through miraculous means.

28.
Freed from Imprisonment

Then the king asked that Princess Mandarava be brought to him. When the ministers went to open the pit into which she had been thrown, they told her of the miracles that the great vajra master had performed. Showing her the king's golden parchment letter requesting her to come to the palace, they begged her over and over to respond. She remained silent.

When the ministers returned without success, the king then told the queen to go and convince Mandarava to come and join them. The queen gathered the silken garments of the princess, hoping that she would wear them and return. When she met her daughter and begged her to reconsider, Mandarava replied: "No matter what happens, I intend to remain here for the duration of twenty-five human years. I shall never disobey the command of my father the king. However, you and my father have only one daughter like me. How could you do what you did to my guru, who is the actual buddha of the three times?" Mandarava then broke down in tears and fell into the arms of her mother. They both wept uncontrollably.

In a short time, all the women in the country of Zahor began to weep, and the king feared that the princess had passed away. He rushed to the pit. To his relief, he found her still alive, and he begged her to return to the palace to see for herself what had transpired. Breaking down in tears, he said: "O daughter, I never intended to create such an obstacle to your Dharma. This father of yours feels deep regret for what he has done. Thinking of myself as so high, I have now fallen so low. My meaningless behavior has brought you such grief. Please forgive me." Then he took her hands and kissed her, and her mother caressed her.

As she consented to join them and return to the palace, both the king and queen were crying. Mandarava was reunited with the vajra master, to whom she prostrated as he wiped away her tears. She praised him with this song of heartfelt devotion:

"You, the enlightened one, came to this continent of nonvirtue. Fearlessly powerful, you came with neither expectation nor apprehension. Embodiment of miraculous enlightened activities, may there be the good fortune of the unceasing radiance of your enlightened display! Born from the lotus, your body is a radiant hue of white and red. You are adorned with the sublime marks of excellence, and your thirty-two major marks are resplendent to behold. The noble qualities of the lotus-born buddha of the three times are beyond the limits of the mind. With faith I bow down to you, the embodiment who is one with the buddhas of the three times. As the embodiment of rapture with the major and minor marks, your form is as great and perfectly proportioned as Mount Meru. Shaped like the king of all mountains, you have a head round as a vase; your hair is lovely as the blooming udumbara flower. Your nose is perfectly proportioned; your upper and lower lips are like the petals of a lotus flower. Your tongue is long, thick, and red like a lotus. Your array of fifty-eight teeth glow white, like a range of snow mountains. Your face is peaceful. Your neck and chin are endowed with the richness of youth. The sound of your voice is as resplendent as the kalapanga bird. Your black mustache and beard are like the fur of a magnificent black bear. Your coloring is like a white conch shell that has been delicately painted with vermillion. Your perfect neck is shaped like a lovely vase. Praise to your presence! You are like a grand snow lion poised in full glory. Your shoulders are broad and arched in perfect proportion. Your toes and fingers are long and webbed. Your nails are the color of a copper-red crystal, your navel attractive, like the stem of the lotus. Your male organ is drawn in and contracted, completely concealed like that of an elephant or horse. Your calves are like the legs of a deer, and your lotus feet are rich and fleshy. You pass through space in the flash of an instant, like a rainbow.

Your ever-youthful presence supports limbs that are full and strong. When you smile, you are so attractive that not a fault can be found. Your presence is so pleasing that one cannot gaze upon you enough. Your radiance blazes like an orb of light. To touch your skin brings unique vajra-bliss to everyone. You, Padmasambhava, are the one who displays these marks of sublime excellence. Praise to the body of the buddha that displays the thirty-two major marks." Thus she offered prostrations and rendered praise with great devotion.

The vajra master was very pleased, and he offered the princess this response: "E ma! Your present relatives cannot be called loving relatives. The truly loving relative is the precious spiritual guide who leads one upon the true path, revealing the virtous path and causing one to turn from the harmful path. Your present blood relatives are now objects of compassion and mercy, and ordinary relatives will only encourage you to pursue that which is other than the spiritual path. Count the many examples of this, and you will clearly see that this is indeed the cycle of existence.

"Unable to satisfy their endless needs and desires, beings suffer unceasingly. This is not the meaning of wealth and endowment at all. What you have finally found is the treasure of true wealth. The seven-fold wealth of the aryas is wealth that cannot be found externally. Except for that, all other attempts to acquire and maintain ordinary wealth are the cause of suffering. That which we call wealth is not found in existence or quiescence—it is instead your indwelling precious buddha nature. This is not widely recognized, and not recognizing it causes it to be wasted. Even if it *is* recognized, it is wasted if it is not sustained. The time has come to understand that negative circumstances can be transformed into spiritual power and attainment, and to make use of this truth. Utilize adversities and obstacles as the path!" Just by hearing his words, Princess Mandarava was naturally liberated.

King Viharadhara then offered to his daughter the flesh of a holy man, a wish-fulfilling jewel, and the wealth of the kingdom without exception. He supplicated the guru to transmit his noble qualities to him until the end of his life. He requested the vajra master to stay in the land of Zahor until all the people were led to fruition. For the next three years the vajra master turned the wheel of the vast ocean of the Buddha's teachings.

When the kings of all directions heard the news that Mandarava had been offered to the vajra master, they felt deceived and angrily prepared their armies for war, aggressively advancing on the kingdom of Zahor from the four directions. The general Mahabala entered Zahor through a narrow ravine and captured some small villages. The vajra master intervened, using his miraculous powers against the enemies. In particular, he released the mandalas of the eight herukas, turning the aggressors back so that they all returned to their own countries.

The vajra master gathered together the three hundred and sixty ministers of the king, the five queens, the five hundred servants of Mandarava, and one hundred and eight monks in his assembly, and turned the Dharma wheel for them. He taught the eight volumes on the sacred utterance and guardians, the five tantras on the condensed utterance of the Great Perfection, four volumes on the Heart Essence doctrine, five other titles, twenty tantras, and forty-two volumes of esoteric instructions.

Each and every one of his disciples was brought to fruition, and twelve became mahasiddhas.[58] All were established irreversibly on the spiritual path. The doctrine of Avalokiteshvara spread throughout the land of Zahor, and all its inhabitants were brought to fruition. The king eliminated all heretics from the kingdom, and his heir, the Vajra Guru Padmasambhava, took his seat on the throne to govern the entire kingdom thereafter.

Samaya

This completes the twenty-eighth chapter of
*The Lives and Liberation
of the Princess of Zahor, Mandarava,*
called *A Precious Garland,*

Explaining how Mandarava was freed from
imprisonment and how Guru Padmasambhava
turned the Dharma wheel, thus placing the
entire kingdom of Zahor on the path of Dharma
and on higher levels of accomplishment.

29.
Abandoning Samsara

The vajra master was preparing to depart for the cave known as Maratika in order to accomplish immortality. Everyone begged him not to go, but to no avail. Then he sang this vajra song to Mandarava: "E ma ho! Amazing young maiden whose body blazes with light! Your beautiful form is graceful, supple, and utterly sublime. Lovely one of radiant smiles, unstained by any fault, your vajra body resembles a lovely lotus. As I gaze upon you, young maiden with all the perfect marks, so luminous is your relaxed, youthful form that you captivate my mind with your incredible beauty.

"This flower Mandarava is youthful only once. Listen to me closely, O princess of noble qualities. In this limitless ocean of suffering existence, the obsession with samsara that occurred before can only bring more pointless obsession. Now the time has come to prepare for a meaningful future. Accomplish the sacred Dharma, youthful princess! Worldly activity is endless. The meaningless bustle of activity from the past is all that can be expected in the future. Now it is time to free yourself from activity. Youthful princess, watch your own mind! When one is overpowered by anger, the enemy is mistakenly held to be external. This has caused self and others to fail in the past, and it is all that can be expected in the future. The time has come to tame your own mental delusions. Youthful princess, take charge of yourself! Overpowered by delusions, unashamed of the causes of samsara and unable to distinguish them, what else can you expect in the future? The time has come to realize the fallacy of all this and to proceed on the path of Dharma without further distraction.

"Youthful princess, arouse your wisdom! Being overpowered by pride, holding to the ways of a queen, and giving orders to others, you will always remain the same. The time has come to examine yourself and give orders to yourself. Youthful maiden, recognize your shortcomings! When you are overpowered by jealousy, you disparage and belittle others. The competition for position and power will always be just as it has been. The time has come to follow the way of the victorious ones.

"Youthful princess, train in pure perception! In this swirling ocean of negative karmic accumulations, unwholesome rebirths will always be just as they have been. The time has come to meditate upon the empty, radiant form of the deity. Youthful princess, be diligent on the path of the generation stage! Engaging in confusion-based conversations is the cause for increased delusions. The endless idle words of the past will only be the same in the future. The time has come to recite the essence of empty sound.

"Youthful princess, generate the deity! Youthful princess, meditate on the generation and completion stages, the profound path of method, which is the secret path of the pure awareness holders. I wonder if you have the good fortune to enter upon this path. The time has come to meditate upon impartial, pure perception. Youthful princess, develop single-pointed faith!"

When Mandrava heard these words she was overcome with emotion and responded as follows: "E ma ho! Youthful male, so pleasing to behold! Your body is perfectly proportioned in every way. You possess the supreme form of the major and minor marks of perfection. No matter how much I gaze upon you, it is still not enough. No matter how much I hear your vajra speech of melodious and meaningful words, I still long to hear more. No matter how much I feel the bounty of your unceasing loving-kindness and compassion, my mind cannot bear to be apart from you.

"From now on, throughout all future lifetimes, sublime one, please hold me always in your compassionate, loving care. Whomever I see, wherever I go, whether the country is excellent or not, all such experiences are like being in a vast city of spirit dwellers.

"When this girl dies, I shall be without my country. In which direction or place can the true motherland be found? This jeweled palace may be supreme, but like a bubble about to burst, it cannot endure.

"When this girl dies, she will no longer have a home full of relatives. Where can a permanent palace be found? Although the king of Zahor, my father, is of excellent caste, he, like the clouds passing in the sky, will not remain forever.

"When this girl dies, there will no longer remain even the name of my father. Where can a permanent place of my ancestors be found? Although my mother, the queen, was born of highest family caste, this status, like a seat for temporary rest, cannot remain firm.

"When this girl dies, there will be no friend with whom she can truly share the sorrow of that experience. In which direction can a permanent friend be found? Although the wish-fulfilling jewel is the best of all jewels, it cannot remain forever.

"When this girl dies, like the frost upon grass, no amount of wealth can be taken with her. Where can the good fortune of permanent wealth be found? In this place of samsara, one is constantly distracted by the activities of the world. One is bound by the constricting forces of the five passions based on attachment and aversion. By acquiring an unwholesome form, more attachment develops for relatives. Occupied with lying, slandering, and uttering trivial words, one has no time to remember the Dharma. Please, with your limitless loving-kindness protect me from this negative karma. So that we may never be apart, I beg you to take me with you on this journey. Reveal to me now the precious path of the secret doctrine."

Then the vajra master replied: "Fair maiden, although you possess fortunate karma, in order to practice the secret path you must have the diligence to practice through whatever hardships present themselves and to persevere even at the cost of your life! With a mind that thinks of the future and is ready to endure hardships in the present, one must be willing to discard this body of flesh and blood, if that is deemed necessary, to accomplish the secret path!"

Mandarava replied: "I have unceasing great faith, pure view, and fervent devotion. I request you to bring me with you on this journey. Even if I must eat earth and stones to sustain myself, I will!"

Then the master said, "Alas! Then I shall depart to the East. You, young maiden, should turn and face the East. Remain in your present position. Until we meet again, no matter how frightened you may become, maintain the courageous dignity of pure perception."

Having said this, he ascended into space. All the dakinis from the realm of Khechari came to escort him. The king of Zahor, his ministers, subjects, and assemblies were overcome with sorrow. Consumed with grief and sobbing uncontrollably, they supplicated the guru.

The next day, at the crack of dawn, as they all looked on, Mandarava went away without the slightest attachment to the king, her relatives, attendants, wealth, or endowments. She remained, however, in her posture of equipoise, seated within the protective net of Guru Padmasambhava of Oddiyana's loving-kindness and compassion. She traversed not one, but two or three valleys and countries, and suddenly found herself in an uninhabited land that was frightful, wrathful, and rugged beyond belief.

For three long days, she remained trapped in a craggy ravine without food, drink, or shelter. She was famished and chilled to the bone. All she could hear were the eerie sounds of many tropical birds and wild animals. Finally, she managed to climb over a peak, only to find herself forced to descend into yet another frightening valley of doom. Then she lost heart and, in a state of disturbed sorrow, went into the depth of her soul, where her spontaneous, fervent devotion remained unaffected. She cried out in urgent despair: "Kye ma! Kye hu! Lord Guru of Oddiyana! Guru who reveals the path to liberation! Please look upon me now with your merciful compassion! First, I arrived here in this country to the north. Second, I was engulfed by a dense jungle full of wild animals. Third, the sound of water crashing in craggy ravines is piercing my ears. I fear I am in a barbaric country possessed by demons and cannibals! O young man of grace, where can I find you now? Without you my mind is unstable and weak!

"First, I am here in an uninhabited land where the grass is so wild that the wind makes it dance. Second, there is the unceasing sound of ravens crying in the forest. Third, the sun is obscured by the darkness of night. I wonder if I have entered the bardo between this life and the next? Where is the one whose melodious speech is like music to my ears? That you cannot see me now, at this time, fills my mind with chilling sorrow.

"First, I am alone in this country, without a single companion. Second, it resembles a haunted charnel ground. Third, there is the constant eerie din of jungle creatures. It seems that I have arrived in the city of the lord of death! Be quick to look upon me now with your compassionate mercy! Hold me in your heart, O perfect Lord of Dharma!" Then she fell to the ground in tears.

Through his omniscience, the lotus guru knew of her duress and went to her. Mandarava wept in his presence, so overcome with gratitude that she grabbed him and held him tight. He then spoke these words to her: "What has become of your fearless pledge of courage now that you are confronted by such a malevolent and unruly land? A frightful environment such as this is the catalyst for a practitioner's true practice to emerge. Adverse conditions are the true wealth of a practitioner. Such a supreme place of practice is the most exalted spot for accomplishing the innermost profound Dharma. A frightening, uncomfortable place is the knife that severs discursive thought. The wrathful charnel ground is the environment through which the deceptive view of eternalism is exposed. To discover the illusory nature of the barren, frightening land is to discover the innermost sacred Dharma. The sound of the jungle is the introduction to the bardo. Sadness and elation, truth and deception—these are nonexistent. The true practice of guru devotion is the cultivation of undiminishing fervent faithfulness. This is the resting ground where relief from the bardo is sought. In the bardo the terrifying sounds that resemble a thousand roaring dragons are like the sound of the approaching messengers of the lord of death. Such a storehouse of darkness cannot be illuminated in an aeon of light. It is like being trapped in a thick forest where sharp weapons abound, with the eight terrifying narrow passageways and the four wrathful sounds. The suffering is unbearable beyond imagination!"

Instantly, Mandarava's negativities and obscurations were purified. All the noble qualities that develop on the path arose in her mind.

Samaya

This completes the twenty-ninth chapter of
*The Lives and Liberation
of the Princess of Zahor, Manadarava,*
called *A Precious Garland,*

Explaining how, through the liberating
instructions of the master, the signs of her
abandonment of samsara appeared, and the
path of true Dharma was found.

30.
Accomplishing Longevity in Maratika Cave

Then they went together to the Maratika cave, the sacred power spot where the outer, inner, and secret mandalas were complete. In terms of perfect noble attributes, this place was like a wish-fulfilling jewel that surpasses any other sacred place in India for the practice of spiritual attainment. Guru and consort both gave rise to the mandala of the deity, and the princess made this offering to the vajra master: "In order to enter the secret path of the vajra mandala, I offer my own body of great fortune as the mandala offering."

Thus offering her own body and life, Mandarava sang this song of supplication to the guru: "Kye! O great pure awareness holder Padmasambhava, on this precious occasion, when you are about to bestow the empowerment of the precious secret path of the pure awareness holders, by your kindness please confer the outer, inner, and secret empowerments that ripen and mature."

Then, from the warmth of the great vajra master's forehead emerged the blessings that bestowed the vase empowerment. In successive order, he bestowed the secret speech empowerment that gives rise to the development of all noble qualities, the crystal mind empowerment that arouses the essential fluids, and, in order to reveal the essential nature of reality as it is, the absolute indication empowerment of the mind. He bestowed the empowerment of great bliss to purify the energy channels, the empowerment of empty ambrosia to purify the essential vital energies, the vajra mandala empowerment of the path of union practice, and the great secret empowerment of pure union practice. He bestowed the empowerment of the five primordial wisdoms to liberate the five passions. He bestowed the vajra master empowerment to perfect the state of becoming a pure awareness holder. Finally, he bestowed the initiation that reveals the pure path of empowerment.

Having thus ripened from all the transmissions, Mandarava obtained the noble qualities necessary to perform the generation and completion stage practices. After practicing for three months, they received a clear vision of the Buddha of Long Life, Amitayus, and accomplished the state of an immortal pure awareness holder. The guru proclaimed that she was a fortunate upholder of pure awareness and that in order to eliminate any obstacles to their accomplishment, they both should practice the deity Hayagriva. They practiced the Hayagriva Mechar cycle from the tantra known as the Great Play of the Quintessential Lotus and the Treasury of One Thousand Essential Instructions, a tantra on the union of Hayagriva and Vajravarahi. Following this, both guru and consort had clear visions of Hayagriva, whose neighing and sounding of *hum* could be clearly heard around them thereafter. At this point, all possible demonic and obstructing forces had been banished. Mandarava compiled a treasury of more than a thousand extensive and concise longevity methods, including essential pointing-out instructions. Both guru and consort became free from the process of birth, old age, sickness, and death, until the end of this age of ongoing existence. They appeared in the embodiment of rapture, from which they went on to accomplish the secret practice of union.

When the vajra master manifested himself in the form of the slightly wrathful guru of the Buddha family, the princess followed accordingly. By engaging in the perfectly pure mandala of primordial wisdom, they discovered the primordial awareness of stainless miraculous display. They gained the ability to transcend the ordinary elements, with powers that included leaving impressions on solid matter, rainbow light displays, and so forth. Their enlightened union naturally caused flowers to descend from the sky and captivated and summoned those who were oath-bound guardians of the secret doctrine. These guardians were then given the task of ensuring that the lineage of accomplishing longevity was secure. Even the gods, nagas, and the gods among humans and their assemblies offered the essence of their life without hesitation. The vajra master became known as the Immortal Padmasambhava, and Mandarava as the dakini pure awareness holder of immortality Dungmen Karmo, Maiden of the White Conch.

Samaya

This completes the thirtieth chapter of
The Lives and Liberation
of the Princess of Zahor, Mandarava,
called *A Precious Garland,*

Explaining how she received the instructions on accomplishing longevity in the Maratika Cave and how she accomplished the state of an immortal pure awareness holder.

31.
Subjugating Heretics in the Kingdom of Kotala

Then the vajra master knew that the time had come to tame the minds of the beings who inhabited the country of Kotala. When he arrived there, King Ratnashri of Kotala and five of his close attendants were taking a rest in a cool garden near the palace.

The vajra master then asked Mandarava to sing a song, and so she sang: "E ma! Here in the middle of Kotala in this pleasure garden, where you, the king, ministers, and five attendants of good merit have gathered, I request you to pay close attention to the words of this song that I, this wandering vagrant, will now sing. By the force of your excellent karmic accumulations of the past, you enjoy a king's rebirth in the present life. As a man of great wealth and bounty, what do you propose to do to alleviate the suffering of the poverty-stricken, who are weak and helpless? If more law enforcement and control is the solution, then how do you make the distinction between that which is beneficial and that which is harmful? With all your power, attendants, land, and wealth, where have you established and propagated the doctrine of the ten virtuous deeds? With all your entertainment, special events, and musical instrumentation, how much has your mind been able to recognize the law of cause and result? Although this beautifully pleasing palace is visible to all, where are the spiritual teachers and masters residing? Although your political interests are broad and expansive, who is serving or propagating the Buddha's doctrine? Since the Second Buddha has now come to your kingdom, do you, the king and ministers, have the merit to receive him?"

It was not until she had finished singing that the king and ministers could see her. They could then also see the vajra master, who appeared as a lay practitioner. The youngest minister stepped away and, turning back to face them, spoke these words: "Kye ma ho! O nirmamakaya embodiment, you are adorned with sublime noble qualities. The brilliance of your presence is so pleasing to behold. You are accompanied by a female Dharma practitioner whom we have never seen before. Begging your pardon, please tell me from which country you have come. What do you intend to do here? From here, where will you be travelling to next? Please give me a truthful answer to my queries."

Mandarava replied: " E ma ho! This great spiritual teacher has been born from Lake Dhanakosha. He is a fully enlightened being with all the astonishing attributes! He is well known as Guru Padmasambhava. His essential nature is that of the buddhas of the three times. I am Princess Mandarava from the land of Zahor. Just now we have returned from the Maratika cave. We are about to proceed to an isolated mountain cave to resume our retreat."

The king and his attendants quickly returned home, where they called together their family members to say: "Kye! The spiritual teacher of the land of Zahor has come to our kingdom. He is known as the great Guru Padmasambhava, the Lotus-born. We have heard that even the four elements cannot harm him and that his miraculous abilities are sublime. Today he has arrived in our kingdom, accompanied by the Princess Mandarava. They told us that they plan to go to a high mountain cave for retreat. Let us prepare the palace and a teaching throne and fill the space with silken banners of victory, the sound of instruments, incense, and the like." The outer and inner ministers and their assemblies rushed to make the appropriate preparations. When everything was ready, they all went together with the king to invite and escort the guru to the palace. The vajra master took his seat upon a magnificent snow lion throne, and Mandarava was seated at his side upon a seat of brocade silk.

Then the sage Karmadhani, a venerable holy man who was a spiritual mentor to the king, addressed the guru: "Kye! You, who are known as the great scholar of Oddiyana, a nirmanakaya emanation unaffected by the element of fire, we have heard that you are an emanation free from

attachment, yet you are in the company of the princess, who has chosen the unworthy position of acting as your servant. We also know that
the kings of the many directions have tried to win her favor, yet she
has rejected them all, deciding to pursue the path of Dharma. What is it
that allows you to qualify to win her company? It is my opinion that it
would be wise for you to either give her to this kingdom or else allow
her to remain on her own. O nirmanakaya emanation, this girl is the
cause for many to have doubt in you." After the holy man spoke, the
king asked the guru to remain as his object of refuge and for Mandarava
to return to her own country. Then the guru spoke to them:

"Kye ma! O holy man of virtue, Karmadhani, I am the nature of the
buddhas of the three times. Just as the arrangement of space cannot
change, it is difficult to for me think childishly, with many preconcep-
tions. The princess is a dakini of the vajra family who has accomplished
the state of immortality. No matter how excellent the situation may be
in any kingdom, these are still places of worldly entanglements. She
could never live in such a way, so she left it all behind to pursue the
path of Dharma. Deserting all kingdoms, she is absorbed in the task of
taming the minds of sentient beings.

"Your speech is the result of deluded confusion. The Lotus-born
Guru, who is like a snow lion, has the capacity to live at the peak of a
snow mountain. Fully confident, he will never be weak and think of
ice as the enemy. The Lotus-born Guru is like a magnificent peacock.
Although his diet consists of poison, it enhances the brilliance of his
complexion. Fully confident, he will never be weak and consider his
poisonous food harmful. The Lotus-born Guru is like a turquoise dragon
who remains in space as the sovereign of the four elements. Fully confident, he will never be weak and fall to the ground from hearing a
loud sound. The Lotus-born Guru is like the ocean. His patience prevails over all that is clean or impure. With full confidence he knows the
nature of all speech to be like an echo. The Lotus-born Guru is like the
foundation of the earth. Accepting of all, he is impartial toward good
and bad. Fully confident, he sees that all conflicting concepts are the
real opposition. The Lotus-born Guru is like the great garuda, whose
nature is primordially perfected with the six displays of excellence. Fully
confident, among any breed of bird he is never weakened by their

power. The Lotus-born Guru is like the element of wind, constantly mobile in space. Fully confident, he is never intimidated by the obstructions of those with limited perception. The Lotus-born Guru is the keeper of the secret mantra on the path of the union of wisdom and method. Fully confident, he is never intimidated by the tenets of the lower vehicles. The maiden Mandarava is the consort of primordial wisdom. Her physical presence transforms into whatever is deemed necessary. Fully confident, she is never weakened by wrong views. Your incorrect, mistaken words of confused perception are shocking to my ears and those of Mandarava."

Then the holy man Karmadhani became angry. He addressed the king and his ministers with this retort: "Kye ma! O king and honorable ministers! This negative vagrant named Padmasambhava is nothing more than a clever magician! He is playing with, and deceiving the minds of, sentient beings. Furthermore, he brings with him this girl of no qualities from Zahor, who is herself a disgrace to the path of Dharma. I completely disagree that we should allow them to remain here in our kingdom. You must strongly consider immediately sending them back to their own country."

After listening to the holy man, the king and his ministers had a change of heart. Feeling now that the guru had deceived them, they decided to send him away, and they asked the holy man to forgive them if they had brought harm to him in any way. They promised to have nothing to do with the guru in the future, and that everything would go back to normal. Then the vajra master spoke:

"The time has arrived for Mandarava to emanate a special manifestation. Since they have decided to exile us because of the pride of this so-called holy man, we shall now quickly depart for the high mountain cave of our destination. From there, various manifestations will come to tame this kingdom and place everyone upon the Dharma path." After thus speaking, they left by speed-walking[59] and immediately arrived in the high mountain cave.

The king and his ministers returned to the palace. They could not determine where the vajra master and his consort had gone so suddenly and secretly. They began asking everyone if they had any knowledge of where the two had gone. After investigating, they all felt certain that the two were in the high mountain cave. The king, his ministers, and the holy man convened. They agreed that the high mountain was at the center of their kingdom, and that it was not a suitable place for inhabitants. They decided to insist that the guru and his consort depart from there immediately and that, if they failed to obey this command, they would remove them by force. A messenger was dispatched, and they began to prepare the army for battle. Meanwhile, from the top of the mountain the guru and his consort heard this news.

The vajra master then requested Mandarava to reveal her miraculous abilities. Mandarava transformed herself into a nine-headed wrathful dakini. In her hands she wielded weapons and a lasso of human entrails. Her two feet were securely placed on the peaks of two mountains. As she swung her fire lasso, the sound of scorching, roaring flames resounded everywhere. From her mouth came the proclamation that she was Mandarava, embodiment of the Buddha, and that she would devour all enemies of the doctrine. This caused all the soldiers to immediately retreat and bring the amazing news of her transformation and her threat to the king and his assembly. The king was infuriated. He gathered his army and gave strict orders to annihilate these enemies into dust particles by dropping bombs—like a rain of hailstones—upon them. Then the army, together with the heretic Kotashri and nine attendants, went to wage war upon them.

As the army came close and began to hurl bombs, the guru manifested himself as Simhanada, the Lion's Roar, while Mandarava emanated as Simhamukha, the Lion-headed Dakini. As the heretics wielded their weapons and began waging war, the dakini roared like a lion. This sound dispersed the bombs and caused all the soldiers to faint. Then all the heretics chanted their nefarious incantations, which produced a rain of arrows like shooting stars. As the arrows approached, the dakini transformed them into a rain of flowers. Nothing could affect the guru and his consort.

The guru approached them and spoke: "O powerful heretic of wrathful incantations! Two humble practitioners, male and female, are hardly a match for your powers. Let us put an end to this by deciding that the winner of our competition will take charge of the entire kingdom." The king and his ministers agreed to this plan. The heretics began chanting their powerful black magic. Nine great hailstorms descended to flatten the mountains to the right and left. The vajra master then flashed the threatening mudra, which caused such a powerful hailstorm to descend that the heretics were put to death. The holy man vomited blood and, close to death, he called out in desperation to the king and his ministers, asking them what method they had in mind to save his life. Meanwhile, the dakini restored the mountains to their original form.

Once again, the king and his ministers convened. Then the great minister Ajivaija addressed Guru Padmasambhava: "Illuminator of the sacred Dharma in many kingdoms, controller of the four elements! There is no need to compete with one such as you, who imbued this kingdom with faith at the moment of your arrival. The holy man should be exiled from the kingdom for what he has done, and all heretics should be eliminated so that not even a name remains. The kingdom needs a suitable object of refuge, and it is far too late for the holy man to suffice. Except for the loving-kindness and compassion of the second Buddha, what hope is there? The time has come for this kingdom to be protected by a true object of refuge." The king and all his ministers agreed. Then the minister Ajivaija recommended that the king go to the guru and his consort to offer confession and request them to protect the kingdom. In addition, they decided to ask them to spare the life of the holy man.

Arriving before the guru and his consort, the minister respectfully supplicated: "Kye ma ho! O great vajra master and consort, sovereign of enlightened miraculous activity! Please hold this king and his ministers, who are ignorant sentient beings, with the hook of your merciful compassion. We take refuge in you and beg your forbearance. Please bestow upon us the gift of the precious holy Dharma. Following the incorrect advice of our previous guide, we have made a grave mistake."

The vajra master replied: "The faultless Padmasambhava and consort were afflicted by you, the king, and your assembly of ministers. Overcome by confused perception, you followed your karma accordingly. This negative, ruthless so-called holy man turned all of you against us. Although such harmful intentions do not have an adverse effect upon me, he is the one who has lost in the end. Now he must save himself.

The time has come to place the entire kingdom on the path of the holy Dharma." The king and minister quickly confessed their negativities and begged the guru to have mercy for their deluded confusion. Then one of the ministers returned to find that the holy man had passed away.

Thereafter the king followed every word that the vajra master said. He gathered all his subjects, and in the presence of the great vajra teacher, they received the teachings on the causal vehicle. Through the explanations then given by Mandarava, the king and his ministers were liberated. One thousand female practitioners in the kingdom took the vows of ordination with Mandarava as their spiritual head, and several thousand women began practicing the Dharma day and night. The vajra master then taught the secret mantra to the king and all his ministers. He took the princess Ratnashri as his consort and brought the disciples into the mandala of Hayagriva of the lotus family. For three successive years, he turned the Dharma wheel, and over one hundred people in the kingdom achieved liberation. Three thousand male and female practitioners became fully accomplished.

Samaya

This completes the thirty-first chapter of
The Lives and Liberation
of the Princess of Zahor, Mandarava,
called *A Precious Garland,*

Explaining how she placed the kingdom
of Kotala on the path of Dharma and
how she subjugated the heretics.

32.
Conquering Elementals at the Charnel Ground

Guru and consort went to the charnel grounds known as Kalinga and Simhavana, where the wrathful dakinis Shrigani, Pratima, Sukama, and others convened with five hundred and ten followers. In the daytime they remained in the semi-dark shadows of the trees. In the evening the guru engaged in the practice of union with the charnel ground demonesses in the Garden of Blazing Fire. Then, he turned the wheel of Dharma for all the wrathful dakinis.

During that time Mandarava went to the northern charnel ground called Yongdutsal, where she displayed many magical powers to the terrifying demon spirits and their assemblies. Some of these wretched beings screeched in horror and whistled shrilly, while others called out to their demon gods in despair. Some dragged dismembered corpses, while others beat the flayed skin. Some sobbed hysterically, and some sang melodiously. Some held weapons; others yelled, "Kill, kill!" Some caused the mountains to collapse, while others pushed back the ocean. Some built fires, others cut wood. Some pushed rocks, creating land-slides, and some tried to harm Mandarava physically. They displayed their magical powers in many ways.

The dakini supplicated the guru, and in one instant he was at her side. "These malevolent charnel ground demons are yours to tame. In the past, in the kingdom of Damaru, there were many ministers who, along with the king, never developed faith. At that time, you emanated as Pemakye and became the powerful companion of the prince. Many demonic ministers and their retinues made perverse prayers, and they have since been reborn as these demonic elementals. You are the dakini who, from a previous time, holds the aspiration to tame their minds. In doing so, tame them with the compassionate method of union and liberation and reveal the doctrine to them for five years. I shall overcome the son Dhaha and others and place them on the secret mantra path of fruition and liberation." Having thus prophesied, he returned to his own place.

Mandarava now knew that it was time for her to bring these irascible demons to the Dharma. Intending to do whatever necessary to bring them to enlightenment, she went to the cave in the charnel ground known as Hematsal. There she performed enlightened miraculous activities even greater than before.

Then the dakini sang this song to all the elementals: "Kye! Listen, all you gathered here! In order to cross this great ocean of samsara, you need to carefully rely upon the ship of nonattachment. I am a girl who has crossed over this great ocean. May all of you elementals achieve what I have accomplished! To cross over the great vast plain of delusion, you must mount the horse of diligence. I am a girl who has crossed this great plain. May all of you elementals achieve the same! To cross the great river of passions, you must construct the bridge of nonattachment. I am a girl who knows the great bliss of nonattachment! I shall reveal this to all of you elementals. From the frightening narrow passageway of the suffering of death, the unborn companion can grant freedom. I am a girl who has obtained the state of the nirmanakaya. I shall reveal this way to all of you elementals. To escape from the prison of the suffering of death, one must know the method through which to cross over to the state beyond sorrow. I am a girl who has obtained immortality, and I shall reveal to all you elementals the path that I have tread. All the buddhas of the past have transcended this burning firepit of negativity in samsara to arrive in the state beyond. I am a girl who has accomplished buddhahood, and you elementals, the forms of confusion who are opposing me, are objects of my loving-kindness."

Even though she spoke in this way, the elementals continued displaying their magical feats. She chided them, saying, "Your miracles are as mighty as a girl's jewelery!" Then they let loose an uproarious din, and some of the cruelest demon leaders began dragging the dakini's body here and there. Some of them began to beat her, some to rape her, and some to stretch open her secret place. Others were busy lighting fires, carrying water, and displaying their own inconceivable powers.

During this time, the dakini remained in the meditative absorption upon compassion without wavering. Then, entering into wrathful meditative absorption, she arose as a blazing, fierce female of wrath. She transformed the demons' rain, hail, and thunderbolts into coal and pieces of burnt wood. She cried, "Hum bhyoh! I am the consort of the buddhas of the three times! All of you and your attendants are subservient to me! I am the blazing, fierce female of wrath! I am the executioner of all elemental demons who cannot be tamed through loving-kindness! I shall make you surrender your life essence, and you will promise to take the oath!"

Immediately the demons were overwhelmed. Some lost consciousness, while others, in their fear, tried to flee. Some were rendered crazy, yet all were unable to escape her command. By the light rays of the dakini's body, each one of them swore loyalty and awoke to the path of virtue. Then the dakini bestowed secret empowerment upon them, and her secret name became Kalaraksha Marajita. She gave each of them a Dharma name and water that conferred the words of honor. She herself continued to send forth many manifestations, all of which continued to liberate the demons through secret means, thus exclusively revealing the secret mantra doctrine. They all accomplished the secret mantra, and so she further entrusted them with the essential secrets and conferred upon them the cycle of accomplishment called Wrathful Demon Tamer, including all pointing-out instructions and supplementary practices. She then commanded them to pass the entrustments on to future incarnate teachers in the land of Tibet, and further predicted that all of the elementals would eventually achieve buddhahood.

Samaya

This completes the thirty-second chapter of
The Lives and Liberation
of the Princess of Zahor, Mandarava,
called *A Precious Garland,*

Explaining how, according to the prophecy
of the vajra master, Mandarava conquered
the eight hundred and seven elementals of
the Yongdutsal charnel ground, turned the
wheel of the Dharma, and established them
as guardians of the treasures.

33.
Bringing the Cannibals of Chamara to the Dharma

Then the great guru spoke: "Kye! Listen closely, Princess Mandarava! In the copper-colored continent of Chamara, there are many cannibals who are still untamed. Their king is named Zakhaha Ling and their queen, Bhumahing. The time has come for you to tame their minds. Travel by speed-walking to the center of the kingdom. In the pinnacle of the palace called Hatakin, you will be eaten by the cannibal queen who resides there. At that time, transfer your consciousness and possess her body, pretending you are she. Then, overcoming the king, you will lead them all to the path of Dharma. For three years, you will teach them all the secret mantra. I, Padmasambhava, will be in another kingdom, turning the wheel of Dharma. Together we will then travel to the land of Oddiyana to establish the Dharma there."

Receiving his prophecy, the dakini accomplished the practice of speed-walking in three months' time. Then she went to the land of Chamara, directly to the pinnacle of the palace. There she found Queen Bhumahing, who was red in color with orange hair standing straight up. Her fangs were so large that they touched her breasts, and she wore a flayed human skin. Her brow was a mass of wrinkles. From her mouth resounded a shrill whistle, and she devoured the dakini in a single instant. The dakini shouted "*Phat!*" and transferred her consciousness so that the queen's body collapsed and fell apart. The cannibal's abdomen split open, and the princess emerged. At this time, the other male and female cannibals converged to see that their queen had collapsed and that another girl had emerged from her body. They felt amazed that their queen had offered her own body. Although the queen was no more, they felt that this girl was her daughter, and accepted her as such.

King Zakhaha Ling said that this girl did not resemble him and could not be his daughter, so he decided to take her as his queen, and they went off together to his palace. That night, when the king fell asleep, the dakini transferred the king's consciousness to a paradise. The daka of activity, an emanation of Akshobhyavajra, dissolved into the king and possessed his body. From that time onward the entire kingdom was kept under control, and everyone was told to practice the Dharma. Still, no one would comply, and the people of the kingdom blamed the queen. They declared that they would kill her and set out with that intention, weapons in hand.

Then Mandarava manifested herself as a wrathful lion-headed dakini, while King Akshobyavajra appeared as wrathful Heruka deities. Just by their utterance of *hum*, all the cannibals were paralyzed with fear. Stunned and dumbfounded, they were rendered powerless. By clapping their hands, the Herukas began slaying the cannibals one by one. Gradually, the cannibals promised to accomplish whatever was asked of them, and their spiritual practice began. Those who were inclined toward virtue were brought to the path of the secret mantra. Those who remained nonvirtuous were punished and liberated through wrathful means. The dakini bestowed the ripening empowerments like a flowing river.

In turn, the king bestowed the liberating commentaries. Through both day and night, they trained in the practice of the holy Dharma so that all were liberated in one united experience of understanding and realization. For three years they turned the wheel of Dharma, and, in the end, every single inhabitant achieved a body of light, and the land of Chamara was emptied.

Samaya

This completes the thirty-third chapter of
The Lives and Liberation
of the Princess of Zahor, Mandarava,
called *A Precious Garland,*

Explaining how Mandarava brought the male
and female cannibals of Chamara to the path
of Dharma, how they achieved a rainbow
body, and how the land was emptied.

34.
Eight Miracles in Eight Countries

Then the guru and his consort Mandarava went to live in the eight major and minor charnel grounds, including Ngampa Tsalchen and Kailadrog. During this time, the great vajra master turned the Dharma wheel for the wrathful dakinis, gods, and cannibals. Also during this time, Mandarava displayed eight great miraculous deeds.

First, in the charnel ground of wrathful sounds called the Garden of Nectar, while eight wrathful dakinis were displaying their magic, Mandarava sent forth five manifestations, who sat in empty space in the full lotus position. Ambrosia nectar descended from the palms of their hands, becoming eight great swirling lakes of nectar in the eight directions. In the center of each lake, a thousand-petaled lotus flower appeared, and seated upon the pollen stem of the lotus was an emanation of herself. Each manifestation was surrounded by a host of identical emanations. Some were making offerings, others circumambulating, while still others played vinas. Some were prostrating, some singing praises, and some tossing flowers.

This amazing display imbued all the wrathful dakinis with faith, and they proclaimed: "Kye ma! Princess among humans, Mandarava! You are a consort with the most astonishing noble qualities! As the principal consort of the second Buddha, you have fully accomplished the samadhi of nonconceptual awareness. Your miraculous embodiment has sent forth five different manifestations of light, thousand-petalled lotus flowers and lakes filled with amrita. Stainless dakini of five noble qualities, you are a manifestation of self-originating miracles beyond imagination. We now implore all you dakinis gathered in this charnel ground to satisfy this group of wrathful dakinis with the gift of holy Dharma."

Mandarava responded with this vajra song: "Namo Guru Padmakara! In the space of original purity, the azure firmament of the dharmakaya opens to reveal the sambhogakaya of rainbow clouds encompassing all directions. The great rain of the nirmanakaya, which tames in whatever way is deemed necessary, descends upon the unborn earth of the unobstructed garden of disciples. The boundless emanation of the five primordial wisdoms ripens the stainless fruit of the essence of the vehicles. The result, as all-pervasive as space, is the uncompounded state of great exaltation. By the blessings of the Lord, Guru Padmasambhava of Oddiyana, who is unrivaled throughout the three times, I have had the great fortune to obtain this uncontaminated sublime embodiment. Listen now! Although phenomenal existence is based on interdependence, this dakini represents the pure perception of existence, and you wrathful mamos[60] represent impure wrathful expression in the world. Primordially, all of you are without confusion in your essential nature of original purity. Because of your temporary obscurations, however, you have created your present state of self-grasping and the suffering that accompanies it. You must come to recognize that your suffering is derived only from your own confusion.

"Now, wrathful mamos, do not be confused! Your own mind's nature is buddha. Do not disparage because of this confusion, the nature of which is buddha. Wrathful mamos, do not grasp with compulsive attachment at this illusory play of appearances. Wrathful mamos, do not hold to the objects of the conceptual mind as true. This habitual cycle of dualistic grasping and clinging must not be maintained. O wrathful mamos, allow it to collapse. O wrathful mamos, accomplish the nondual state of the five certainties, which is the inherently pure primordial wisdom of self-originating awareness. O wrathful mamos, to be liberated from this inexhaustible ocean of samsara you must employ the antidotes and skillful means. O wrathful mamos, recognize the nature of your own mind to be none other than the original primordial buddha. Knowing this, observe your own nature, O wrathful dakinis! Directly expose your own dharmakaya nature that was previously unseen. O wrathful mamos, accomplish the absolute state of the four kayas!"

After she had thus spoken, all the mamos were liberated. Then her emanations dissolved back into her heart, and the mamos became her faithful attendants. They compiled the hundred and eight secret oral transmission tantras, condensing them into the secret symbolic script of treasure texts. At that time the cannibal mamos offered a raksha rhinoceros hide receptacle. All the yaksha demons offered receptacles marked with the syllable *ksha*, and the rulers offered a receptacle made of stone. Scrolls of the treasure text were placed securely within each receptacle, and the openings were carefully sealed. These containers were entrusted to the mamos, who took them and concealed them within the vase-shaped cone of a stupa.

Then the dakini sat in the shade of a tala tree in the charnel ground known as Simhavana. Seventy-two evil rulers came to test her level of realization and display their magical powers. Then, from the palms of Mandarava's hands, white, yellow, red, and green nectar emerged. Flowing in the ten directions, the nectar invoked ten dakinis, all of whom dissolved into Mandarava's body. Then, from her body, ten wrathful beings emanated—with countless magical manifestations and hand implements—binding the evil rulers to the oath. Additional light rays were sent forth, displaying innumerable miracles that so overcame the evil rulers, they were compelled to surrender their life essence.

At that time, all the glorious protectors received her pointing-out instructions, and the protector Kalaraksha offered a jeweled receptacle. All the instructions were placed within that vessel, which was then sealed in the expanse of space where it dissolved. After that, each of these formerly evil rulers became guardians of the secret mantra doctrine. Then Mandarava met with the precious guru of Oddiyana, reporting what had transpired. Exceedingly pleased, he told her: "Now you must quickly go to the land of Kotavira and bind the great demonic obstructor Vajrabinaka and his followers with an oath. The time has come for you to display your fully-endowed noble qualities!"

She departed immediately for Kotavira, where she seated herself under a kamarupa tree. Then she manifested the vajradhatu mandala, the outer perimeter of which was a mandala of each of the nine vehicles of the doctrine. The inner mandala was a display of the four and six tantric classes; and the secret mandala, a manifestation of the palace of the sphere of great bliss. After she had practiced for seventeen months, the entire mandala of deities actually appeared in complete, vivid detail.

At that time, the mighty demonic obstructor Vajrabinaka, together with his retinue of eight thousand obstructors, began waging a war of black magic against the wisdom mandala of deities. Suddenly, sand, stones, and earth descended like a hailstorm. Unearthly sounds of persistent wailing and screaming filled the air. A fierce dust storm emerged out of nowhere, causing the ground to shake and disturbing the cycle of day and night. Meteorites, hailstones, lightning bolts, and dragon thunder abounded. At night, fires raged, incinerating the mountains. In the day, sinister clouds obscured the sun. Brutal cries of "Kill, kill!" and "Strike, strike!" resounded. Various chimeras began appearing, some seeming to be attractive young men and women, others decrepit goons with fierce expressions. Some of the heads did not fit the bodies, and they all uttered indecipherable, garbled rhetoric. Then the demons approached, riding tigers, leopards, grizzly bears, and apes. Fire and smoke emerged from their mouths and nostrils. So vast was their number that the earth shook beneath them.

Now the dakini Mandarava displayed the full strength of her miraculous powers to attract the demonic obstructors and to prophesy their future. She transformed into a great queen of perfection with a hundred heads and a thousands arms. Fire blazed from her every pore, and her hands wielded various weapons. Her hair pointed upward toward the gods, and she was dressed in charnel ground attire. When she stomped her one hundred legs, the entire world beneath her shook. She set the mandala of primordial wisdom fire ablaze.

Suddenly, she sang this fearless song: "Hum! Hum! Bhyoh! Bhyoh! I am the blazing dakini of the three realms of existence. With my blazing vajra sword I shall slice you wicked malefactors to pieces. My power in this world is boundless and vast as the heavens. My every gesture propels the ocean's waves. My power holds sway over all that is peaceful in the world and beyond; whatever remains I shall press between the palms of my hands. Now, you eagle-like demons and malefactors, prepare for the moment of your annihilation! Rulu! Rulu! Hum! Bhyoh!

Bhyoh! Bhyoh! Bhyoh!" Then she placed her toes on the peaks of all the large and small surrounding mountains, crushing them into dust.

Overwhelmed with fear, the obstructors fell unconscious. When they awoke, they meekly offered her the essence of their lives: "Kye ma! Primordial wisdom dakini, please listen! From time immemorial, by the force of our deluded karma based on lack of awareness, we have brought nothing but harm to sentient beings. We have even opposed you, consort of all the buddhas. Your form, arisen from meditative stabilization, is the supreme manifestation of wrathful compassion. Now, through fear, we offer you our very lives."

Then, in accordance with their words, they offered the essence of their lives, swearing, "Tri tri o na ma ra ka du na," the oath of offering the body; "Nri tri ya ma bi na ya ka dun dza," the oath of offering the essence of their speech as the heart mantra; and "Tri mu ta ya gu yi he tun nik," the oath offering the essence of their minds. In this way, they were sworn to protecting the doctrine thereafter. They also vowed to never intentionally harm the mind of any sentient being. Then they all began meditating upon the mind of altruism—bodhichitta.

At that time she displayed her peaceful manifestation as Mandarava. As a great wave of blessings of the sacred Dharma, she taught more than seven hundred pointing-out instructions to tame their minds. These were condensed into the symbolic script, given into the care of the wrathful female, keeper of the doctrine, and sealed within a rhinoceros hide casket.

Mandarava then met with the guru to tell him everything that had transpired. He gave her one hundred additional pointing-out instructions to be buried within the great Mount Kailash. By speed-walking, Mandarava arrived in Tibet at holy Mount Kailash in seven days. Upon her arrival, the local elementals, nagas, and spirits displayed countless magical deceptions. Then she manifested as the dakini Uma Devi and engaged in union with the keeper of the mountain, Mahadeva.[61] Bestowing the secret empowerment upon him, she bound him to the oath. Giving him one hundred and eight treasures, she departed for the land of Nepal. For seven days, she remained in the mountain cave called Asura, and she encountered eight Nepalese people. Among them was a young Nepalese woman wearing many jeweled ornaments. She showed great devotion to the dakini, saying she had never met her before: "O Dakini, where have you come from? What are the names of your parents? What is the name of the master with whom you have been studying? What is your family's class and lineage? Why have you come here at this time? I request you to please me by answering my queries."

"This is one who has accumulated great merit in the past," Mandarava thought to herself. "She is similar to a woman of the lotus family, a sister of the gods." Omnisciently realizing that the woman's life was close to ending and that in the future she would be reborn as a dakini who accomplishes the benefit of beings, Mandarava sang this song of Brahma, which spontaneously arose from her throat:

"Kye! O noble woman from the land of Nepal! My family class is the royal family of Zahor. My father's name is King Viharadhara, and my mother is Wangmo Ögema. My name is Princess Mandarava. My spiritual teacher is Guru Padmasambhava of Oddiyana. I am pursuing the path of the nine vehicles of the Buddhadharma. My place of residence is uncertain, as I wander from one charnel ground to another. I have no desire for a husband, who increases and encourages the delusions. My son is the son of the primordial wisdom of great bliss. I have no illusory servants or followers. My Dharma protectors are the dakinis and mamos of this world. I have come to this place to conceal the precious secret instructions that the varja master has given on the essence of the secret mantra. I bring them here as an offering. In three years' time, you woman, will die. You will be reborn as the queen of the king of Nepal, and your name will be Shakyadevi. You will meet the great Guru Padmasambhava and become a suitable vessel to receive the teachings on the secret mantra. You will then conceal many profound treasure texts to benefit of the red-faced people of the land of Tibet." Then Mandarava went with the eight Nepalese people to the village and explained her story.

All the people of the kingdom gathered together to see if the dakini was authentic. An older ascetic man addressed her: "Girl, you are someone who has been relying upon a spiritual master. I wonder, just what profound transmissions you have received? Have you taken the time to accomplish any of them? What sign do you possess that may indicate that you hold such transmissions? Perhaps you have really come here in search of a husband?" Asking such probing questions, he stared at her with a fierce expression.

The dakini replied: "Kye! Listen here! I am a pure awareness holder. My class and lineage are even greater than the master's. I have not come here to compete with someone like you. In order to reverse your wrong views, I shall reveal something about myself."

Mandarava rose up into space. Her body blazed with light as brilliant as the rays of the sun. From her mouth the sound of the Dharma spontaneously arose. "Hum! Hrih! Guru Padmasambhava, the supremely kind Lord, born from the lake and free from the stain of attachment, is the representative of the buddhas of the three times. Please look upon this girl Mandarava at the present moment! In order to cleanse the distorted views of worldliness, please hold me with your compassion. My supreme mind is the originally pure primordial awareness nature of Samantabhadri. Throughout the three times I am free from the fear of birth and death. Having obtained the state of the great bliss embodiment of rapture, unstained by attachment, I do not remain in samsara. I know how to work unhindered for the benefit of sentient beings by opening the door to the Dharma that tames without attachment. Those who are still caught in the trappings of samsara and who aspire toward liberation become my followers, for I am a keeper of the perfectly pure secret mantra that brings permanent bliss."

Having thus spoken, she snapped her fingers, and the old ascetic fainted. All the people of Nepal, feeling great devotion, bowed down to her. They respectfully requested her to teach them the Dharma, so she sang this song about severing attachment to samsara: "Kye! Listen, men and women of Nepal! The suffering of this worldly existence is inexhaustible. Whatever happiness is seen is like the honey that the honeybee extracts. Attachment to samsara is like poison. Partaking of it, even unknowingly, is self-destructive. The habitual propensities of karma are like a long-term prison sentence—if one heedlessly falls into such a situation, the chances for liberation are lost. If clung to, temporary pleasures are deceptive and the moment they are gone, suffering ensues. Entanglement with samsaric companions is like meeting an executioner, because one is ultimately led to rebirth in the lower realms. Wealth and possessions are like objects of a hungry ghost's obsession.

Persevering in the hustle and bustle of this world allows no freedom and is like slowly beating oneself to death. Remaining attached to this existence will cause you sorrow as you remain a slave to your own inadequacies. Seize the supreme path now. Rely upon the Three Jewels as your objects of refuge. Your commitment to the holy Dharma will bring you happiness in this and all future lifetimes. I, Mandarava, practice in this way. If you are fortunate disciples, you will persevere accordingly." They all rejoiced at these words.

Then Mandarava traveled by speed-walking to the terrifying Tsang Tsang charnel ground. There, in a cave in the Bhabramari forest, she remained for a week. All the elementals who resided in this charnel ground displayed many disturbing emanations in order to unsettle her. Demonstrating her level of development, the dakini manifested as Simhamukha, the Lion-headed Dakini. She bound all the malevolent spirits and elementals with an oath to protect the Dharma.

Then she went to the country of Bhendha, arriving in the region of Padmavana. This was in fact a city of bloodthirsty butchers called Kumri. They were killing thousands of creatures in order to eat them. In order to show these butchers the path, the dakini went to the crossroads and sat down, making herself appear as a vagrant. Many butchers gathered around her. They talked about how beautiful this beggar girl was and wondered if they could sleep with her. Mandarava said: "I have no desire for an ordinary lover of this world—particularly any of you butchers who dwell here. In this world there is nothing to be cherished more than life itself, yet in this demonic place there is needless killing and death! Any wife of you malevolent flesh-eaters would have to be an elemental from the sinister charnel grounds!"

The cannibals were extremely offended by her answer. They shouted, "Kill her!" Some tried to beat her, attempting to end her life. They threatened to cut off her arms and legs if she did not allow them to rape her. As they grabbed her, Mandarava suddenly manifested as a wrathful dakini. So vast was her presence that her head reached far up into space. Six dakinis emanated from her body, shouting cries of victory and proclaiming that they would liberate all the butchers. Then all the people in the country gathered around. They began paying obeisance to the dakini and promised to do whatever she asked of them.

She told them to cease taking the lives of others, after which they all abandoned their nonvirtuous ways and entered the path of Dharma. The dakini turned the Dharma wheel for three months, and they all achieved liberation by the path of the Buddha's doctrine.

Then Mandarava went to the country called Kalinga. There she met with the vajra master and received the pointing-out instructions on the Key to the Quintessential Secret. He said, "Mandarava, now you must go to the eastern country of Zahor, where there are beings who still need to be tamed. You must satisfy their needs by giving them the gift of Dharma."

Mandarava next went to Bengal, and, as she was approaching the kingdom, passed through a city called Sirana, where she met an elderly couple. The husband was a craftsman, and they had a son named Sarvakara and a daughter named Prabhasattva. For a long time, these two stared at the dakini. Then they touched their heads to her feet in devotion. They asked her to show them the path, since they had not had the good fortune to have previously met her.

Mandarava said: "Listen to what I have to say about you, son who is named Sarvakara. Formerly, in the kingdom of Damaru, I was the queen known as Pemakye. At that time, your father was Yaksha Anandapala, and you became the king Shinta Budho. You were compelled to kill many cannibals, so you took many lowly rebirths, including the present one. The time has come for you to transfer from this state. You, the girl named Prabhasattva, were the queen of Damaru known as Kala. This is why you both feel such fervent regard toward me. Now I will reveal to you the teachings on secret mantra."

After receiving the secret mantra empowerments and teaching, they were liberated. Within three months, they attained the rainbow body. "Now," said Mandarava, "I shall go to see my father and mother once again." Arriving in Zahor, all the outer and inner ministers and their assemblies were practicing meditation in retreat and did not hear of the news of Mandarava's arrival. After some time, she met the craftsman's daughter who was so pleased to see her that she grabbed her legs and cried out the news of her arrival. One by one, all the people of the kingdom began arriving, until the entire kingdom had gathered. All were filled with joy as the king and queen joined the assembly.

Mandarava prostrated to her parents, and they prostrated back to her. Then the dakini displayed her enlightened miraculous activity for their welfare. Opening up her chest, she revealed to them the entire mandala within her heart, a pantheon of long-life deities, lucidly clear. Everyone was astonished and overwhelmed with devotion. For one year, she turned the Dharma wheel unceasingly. During that time, her father and mother, the king and queen, attained the rainbow body, the minister Tsugpa dissolved into the heart of the king, and the entire kingdom of Zahor achieved liberation.

Samaya

This completes the thirty-fourth chapter of
The Lives and Liberation
of the Princess of Zahor, Mandarava,
called *A Precious Garland,*

Explaining how Mandarava showed eight
great miracles in eight countries in order to
tame the beings, thus placing both humans
and spirits on the path of Dharma.

35.
Turning the Wheel of Dharma in Oddiyana

After some time, Mandarava arrived before the great stupa known as Shubhakara Shekhara. The great vajra guru was in residence there, and she took comfort in his presence. He displayed the mandala of immortal life and bestowed empowerment upon the eight great masters.

Following this, the guru and consort traveled together to the land of Oddiyana, where Mandarava manifested herself with the face of a cat. When the inhabitants of Oddiyana heard the news that the vajra master had returned, many were filled with faith and devotion, while others began plotting against the guru. Without telling the king or queen, the evil minister Prakara had the guru and consort sent off to be burned to death.

At that time, Princess Prabhadhara felt jealousy toward Mandarava. She told her parents that the guru, who was always alone in the past, had found a beggar girl and brought her with him into the kingdom, and that the ministers had ordered them to be burned to death. The king and queen, feeling the need to investigate this matter, went to take a look and found that the fire had not burned the guru and consort at all.

Then the guru and consort displayed the miracle of turning the fire into a lake. The king and queen, Princess Prabhadhara, as well as the entire kingdom expressed their great faith and offered many prostrations. The father, King Indrabhuti, bowed down in devotion and offered these words of praise: "Hrih! Dharmakaya guru, uncontrived and free from elaborations; Dharma Lord Guru, sambhogakaya of great bliss; nirmanakaya guru, born from the lotus; I bow down and render praise to the three kayas of the guru vajra holder." Then the king offered the guru and consort nine prostrations and, leading them himself with an incense offering, invited them to be seated upon thrones and requested the Dharma teachings. The guru replied:

"Kye! Jewel King Indrabhuti! To repay the kindness you have shown in the past, I offer the gift of Dharma at this time. To clear the suffering in the mind of Princess Prabhadhara, the dakini Mandarava will teach the Dharma. I must go to the eight charnel grounds to perform accomplishments and to tame many kingdoms with the sacred Dharma. This dakini and I have accomplished immortality together in the long-life Maratika cave: she is a pure awareness holder of immortality. Then we went together to the land of Kotala and gradually, over a period of two thousand years, tamed the minds of countless beings— doing so only for the benefit of others. Now, here in this land of Oddiyana, there are many whose minds are untamed. The Dharma of secret mantra will bring them to liberation."

After speaking these words, he extensively revealed the profound secret mantra to the king, queen, and all their subjects. Then he took Prabhadhara as his consort and bestowed upon her the supreme secret empowerment of union. Mandarava gathered all the females, and, throughout day and night, taught them the six tantric classes. Establishing spiritual discipline, they all were gradually liberated. King Indrabhuti and five hundred in his retinue obtained the rainbow body without remains and were fully enlightened. Eventually the entire kingdom attained the rainbow body, and the land of Oddiyana was emptied from its depths.

Samaya

This completes the thirty-fifth chapter of
The Lives and Liberation
of the Princess of Zahor, Mandarava,
called *A Precious Garland,*

Explaining how she turned the wheel
of Dharma in the land of Oddiyana and
brought every single inhabitant there to
the state of enlightenment.

36.
Turning the Wheel of Dharma in Shambhala

After this, the dakini went to the land of Anandakara, where she met with the great vajra master and respectfully supplicated: "Hrih! O stainless nirmanakaya buddha, born from the lotus! Indivisibly one with the enlightened sphere of the Dharmakaya Buddha, the natural expression of a sambhogakaya, to your feet, O Vajra Master of great kindness, I bow down! My ancestry is that of the supreme Zahor caste. Due to excellent circumstances from previous lives, I am free from the fears of samsara. As one with fortunate karma, I have met with the sacred Dharma. By the force of previous prayers, I hold the Guru at the crown of my head. Due to my excellent good fortune, I have met with you, Lord of Oddiyana. As a suitable vessel, I have received nine profound doctrines of the secret mantra. By the strength of my perseverance, I have obtained the two spiritual attainments. Now I have the power of a stainless nirmanakaya. The time has come for you to go to tame the lands of Tibet and Nepal. The time has come for me to dissolve into the stainless space of absolute reality. For the purpose of furthering the activity of secret mantra, I shall then send forth, once again, many countless manifestations. It must be the time to dissolve into a body of light."

The guru replied: "Kye! Listen, primordial dakini Mandarava! In the Realm of Great Bliss you are the supreme consort Pandaravasini. In the realm of Potala you are the supreme Natyendri. In Chamaradvipa you are known as Dungmen Karmo. In India you are known as the goddess

Shrimala. In Zahor you are the Princess Mandarava. Bodhisattvas like you are exceedingly rare. You are needed yet one more time to accomplish the benefit of others. It is necessary to tame the minds of beings in the realm of Shambhala. You of great strength, please go there now and perform your enlightened activity. For fifteen years you will turn the wheel of Dharma there."

Thus, the consort journeyed to Shambhala. In that land of twenty-five continents, the eastern realm was known as Bhatana, and the king's name was Bhutinara. He and his assemblies of hundreds of subjects came to see her. When the dakini was trying, with difficulty, to cross the Dhiru River, she suddenly she took flight like a bird and went across it. The king and his subjects approached her: "Kye! Maiden who is like the daughter of the gods, your miraculous abilities are unobstructed, since you flew like a bird. You are strikingly beautiful to behold and possess all the major and minor marks of perfection. Please tell us the caste of your parents and from where you have come. Please tell us everything without holding back."

The dakini gave them this response: "Kye! Listen well, O king and your assembly. I am from the supreme land of Bengal, and my caste is that of the lotus dakinis. My ancestry is that of Zahor, and my name is Princess Mandarava. I am the consort of the great guru of Oddiyana. I have come here in order to tame sentient beings. Do you think, O king and subjects, that you have enough faith? If you are suitable vessels, I would like to teach you the Dharma."

The king and his assembly developed faith from hearing her words. Prostrating with great devotion, they humbly made this request: "Kye! O great dakini, please listen to what we have to say. We are attached to the realm of existence. Our lives are expended in pursuit of the confused karma of samsara. Few of us will be able to encounter the Dharma after we pass from this life. Only you, revered mother, will know if we are suitable vessels. Please satisfy us with the nectar of the holy Dharma." Mandarava went into their palace. She established the law of virtue for the entire kingdom. A palace of nine stories was built, and she began turning the wheel of secret mantra. The king, his ministers, and the attendants were all liberated.

Then she traveled to the southeastern continent, to the city known as Mandhana, where she remained near the gate. There she noticed many beings being punished and harmed, and she knew that the time had come to liberate them. The dakini picked up a human corpse, and as she flew off into space it regained its color, began to breathe, and came back to life. All who witnessed this were amazed. One person told another, and eventually the entire kingdom heard of this miracle. They were all then easily placed on the path of Dharma.

Then Mandarava went to the southern continent. There she saw many soldiers engaged in battle. She chanted the syllables *hum* and *phat*, which caused all the dead soldiers to transform into rainbow bodies, and all the weapons to turn into flowers. The soldiers' minds were filled with devotion, and the conflict naturally came to an end. For three years she turned the wheel of the Dharma.

Next the dakini went southwest to the great city known as Gotipa. All the people in the kingdom had contracted leprosy, and everyone was suffering tremendously. The consort anointed them with her urine, and they were instantly cured. Everyone in the kingdom was overcome with faith and all the illness and disease were instantly pacified. Thereafter she became known as "the dakini who liberates disease." Having brought them satisfaction through the gift of the Dharma, she departed for the western continent.

Upon reaching the city called Katana, Mandarava found that everyone there disparaged her. They were saying that a youthful girl such as this should be accompanied by a husband. Then the dakini sent forth many manifestations of her body and engaged in union with everyone there. Bestowing the secret empowerment, she liberated them all in the rainbow body. She placed the prince and all male inhabitants of the kingdom on the path of liberation through the sole method of union. In addition, she placed all the females on the Dharma path.

After this, the dakini went to the northwestern continent. As she approached the city of Khemali,when everyone could see her, she flew up into space and sang this song: "E ma! I am an enlightened embodiment manifest in this world. Like the sun, I come from the supreme class, and my mother is like the moon. This girl can travel in space with no fear of falling! I am an emanation of the buddhas in the form of a princess. My consort is the joyful embodiment of great bliss. I am the girl who performs the dance of igniting the mystic heat. I have no fear of attachment to delusions. I, Mandarava, am the consort of the deities of the three times. The nature of the primordial sphere of the dharmakaya appears as my many miraculous manifestations. I do not fear to turn the Dharma wheel for the faithful disciples here in the northern kingdom of Shambhala. For the powerful king and his famous ministers, I shall turn the Dharma wheel of the equality of understanding and liberation. I do not fear the mind of distorted perception." Having thus spoken, they were all filled with devotion, and she then turned the Dharma wheel.

Then she proceeded to the northern continent. The king saw her approaching. He gathered his ministers and said: "Kye! O ministers, quickly go outside the palace and you will see a young woman approaching. She seems to have the potential to become a queen of this kingdom. You must examine her characteristics and bring her here to me!" Five ministers went to see the dakini. They said: "Girl, where have you come from and why are you here? Would you like to become queen to our king?"

She replied: "I am not a girl who wishes to remain in samsara. Excellent though the king may be, he accumulates negativity in this world of existence. Although the ministers may be excellent, they are like the messengers of hell. Although there are many members in the retinue, they are like an assembly of maras. Although one's endowments may be abundant, they resemble the objects of the hungry ghost's craving, which can never be sated. I have no time to be a queen while traveling on the path of Dharma."

The ministers reported to the king, who was quite angered by her response: "She has humiliated you ministers as well as my subjects. Let us burn this mindless vagrant at the stake!" The ministers captured Mandarava and bound her tightly with the rope of a hemp plant. Then they threw her on a pyre of sandalwood and sesame oil. Suddenly a divine cleansing rain descended, along with the gods and demons of the eight classes. In the center of the fire there appeared a large swirling lake of nectar. In the center of the lake was the stem of a large lotus flower, and seated upon the lotus was Mandarava, blazing with light. Her ropes and chains had become her jeweled adornments. The smoke had become clouds filled with rainbows, and the scent of sweet incense permeated everywhere. The instruments of the gods, vibrating from the clouds, could be clearly heard by everyone in the kingdom of Shambhala. The ministers and their retinues quickly approached. What they beheld was so astonishing that they quickly ran to tell the king that the gods and nagas were making offerings to the dakini. All the ministers were filled with great shame and remorse.

Then the king of the nagas, Nanda, offered the following praise: "Hrih! In Sukhavati you are known as Pandaravasini. You emanated into this world as the daughter of a king. You are the consort of the great guru of Oddiyana. To the form of this female bodhisattva I render praise!" The king and ministers then confessed their negative deeds. Thirteen kingdoms in Shambhala were astounded by news of the dakini's miraculous powers. They all developed strong faith toward her and requested teachings from her.

The king sent Mandarava an invitation to the palace. Once she arrived, he offered this supplication: "Amazing primordial wisdom dakini bodhisattva, sole mother of the buddhas! Obscured by our ignorance and desire, we have committed such a serious negative mistake. Attempting to harm your precious body, we even tried unsuccessfully to burn you alive. You revealed the miraculous activity of a primordial wisdom dakini, remaining upon the lotus in the middle of the lake, praised by the gods, nagas, and men of this world. We remorsefully confess our mistakes and beg your forbearance. Please bestow upon us the precious, profound Dharma!"

At this request, the consort forgave them and gathered together the entire kingdom. She turned the wheel of Dharma for everyone, and for five years they were diligent in practice. Seven hundred thousand inhabitants of Shambhala attained the rainbow body without remains. Then the consort went to the land of Singhala to join the guru, who was residing there.

Samaya

This completes the thirty-sixth chapter of
*The Lives and Liberation
of the Princess of Zahor, Mandarava,*
called *A Precious Garland,*

Explaining how she turned the wheel of
Dharma in the twenty-one great and small
regions of Shambhala, liberating one
million three hundred thousand fortunate
disciples into rainbow bodies.

37.
Becoming the Wisdom Dakini

Then Mandarava respectfully bowed to the great vajra master and made the following request: "Kye! Enlightened embodiment of the buddhas of the three times, unequaled in kindness! O Lord, self-arisen from a lotus, unstained by the womb, your enlightened activities are boundless like space. O Guru Padmasambhava, hold me with your loving compassion! May we never be separated in this and all future lifetimes!

"Now the time has come for me to dissolve into the stainless dharmakaya. Protector, enlightened in the actual nature of the three embodiments, show me the way and support me from behind. Since I am free from the suffering of the cycle of birth and death, I need not follow the exhausting accumulations of karmic propensities. For the benefit of beings, I have displayed the miracle of intentional manifestations. Through the power of my aspirations, I have the miraculous ability to tame beings in whatever way is deemed necessary. Free from illness as the cause of ordinary death, I remain liberated in luminous clear light. Without having to endure the bardo, I travel directly to the pure realms. Still, until the activities of the buddhas become empty, may my efforts to benefit sentient beings remain unceasing."

Then the precious guru replied: "Kye! Venerable mother, wisdom dakini, Mandarava! You, supreme dakini, are the precious eye that views this world. You have naturally perfected the five pure realms[62] of the buddhas; your supreme dharmakaya mind is free from birth and death. O dakini, your essential nature is like space. Free from the limitations of coming and going, sending and receiving, your nature, inexpressible, is the natural sambhogakaya speech that possesses the sixty melodious branches. With a form that effortlessly dissolves into the expanse of great bliss, you, dakini, are free from the need to remain, to die and take rebirth. Like a cloud that dissolves in space, the cycle of birth and death is alien to you. Your sublime form performs the magical dance, the nature of which is like the reflection of the moon in water. Free from the characteristics of going, remaining, or passing, you emanate throughout the three times to tame the minds of beings in whatever way is most needed. O woman made manifest, free from compounded conditions, you intentionally choose your place of rebirth! As the supreme consort of Buddha Amitabha, goddess, your dance brings satisfaction to the sentient beings' senses. Goddess with the miraculous ability to manifest countless noble qualities, although your present embodiment dissolves into the sphere of truth, you will continue to reveal multitudes of individually appearing manifestations in accordance with the needs of the beings to be tamed. No one is capable of determining the measure or limit of your ability. Throughout all aeons of time, venerable mother, may I never be separate from you!" Having spoken, the guru departed on the tenth day of the dragon month for the peak of the highest mountain in the land of Bheche in India.

Mandarava bestowed spiritual transmissions upon the countless remaining disciples who had gathered. Then she addressed them with the following advice: "Kye! O pure friends whose illusory nature is mundane, it is impossible for anyone to remain permanently in this ordinary world. Whatever doubts you may have, please call on me now because my time to remain here for the benefit of beings has reached its completion."

Accordingly, her many disciples made individual queries and received complete instructions until they were fully satisfied. Then a young girl from Zahor came forward and respectfully made this request: "E ma! Daughter of the gods, guide of sentient beings! By passing on to the sphere of truth rather than remaining among us as the protector of beings, what could your enlightened awareness be considering? Is it really possible that you could just leave us here without a protector? Wisdom dakini, precious as our hearts, how can you not remain here to teach the sacred Dharma to your disciples? How can you now consider passing to the place beyond sorrow? Is it possible for your loving-kindness and compassion to abandon those with weak minds, those full of negative karma? Venerable mother, Dakini Mandarava, if you do not stay here now to show the path to sentient beings, what will you accomplish by going instead to a place of great bliss? Is it really possible for you to leave us here in this dark place without eyes to see? For myself and all living beings, you are the only mother, the only guru! How can you not stay here among us in these difficult times? How can you consider dissolving into the sphere of truth? How can you leave us like a mother leaving her only child? O dakini consort, lamp for the Buddha's teachings, how can you consider passing to the paradises of great bliss without remaining here to uphold the teachings on explanation and accomplishment through your enlightened activity? Who will lead beings upon the path away from this place of darkness? Alas, alas! O mother, please remain here with us!"

The girl's words caused everyone present to begin lamenting aloud. This compelled the dakini to speak: "Listen to me, assembly of faithful disciples! No one in this world is permanent. Though a rainbow appears clear and stationary in the sky, it vanishes in an instant. Even though a girl like me appears youthful and full of life now, I am powerless to remain when the time has come for me to go elsewhere in order to help beings. Though the flowers of summer bloom with a brilliant luster, this beautiful sight will quickly vanish as soon as the season changes. Though this girl has health and energy beyond measure, she cannot control her departure when it comes to helping others. Though a king may be a sovereign in this world, such a powerful status is merely temporary: nothing is exempt from the condition of impermanence. Though Mandarava, the Princess of Zahor, was reborn in a high class, she must still travel for a time to another realm for the benefit of beings. Even a perfect buddha's vajra body of major and minor features, which appears for the purpose of taming beings, must also pass beyond the bonds of sorrow. Though the princess has performed many deeds for the welfare of others, she cannot now remain, for she must journey on for the benefit of others. O disciples, listen to these words and consider the meaning of these essential instructions!"

After she spoke, Mandarava's body became a mass of swirling light, and the entire sky filled with shimmering rainbows. The earth shook six times, and from within the massing clouds the sound of musical instruments could be clearly heard. Multitudes of colorful flowers fell like a rain storm. The gods and spirits without exception bowed down in reverence. Many people asked questions and received answers in the language of their own lands.

The dakini's form then seemed to fly like an arrow into space, and once again her speech could be clearly heard: "Listen, my devoted disciples gathered here! Maintain my last testament carefully within your hearts. Without ever wasting this precious human birth, polish it with Dharma and cherish it as the true source through which all wishes are fulfilled! Do not be lazy or indifferent or hold to things as permanent! Without wasting time, train your mind and accomplish the Dharma! Always consider what to accept and reject, and do not confuse virtue and nonvirtue. Be diligent in Dharma and you will find everlasting bliss!

"This realm of samsara is like a dungeon. Always consider what is best for setting yourself free and attaining liberation. The Three Precious Jewels of refuge are undeceiving. Hold fast to this infallible refuge and accomplish the great purpose. Any impure downfalls and negativity you have accrued from time immemorial must be confessed, purified, and never repeated until all negative karma is exhausted. The basis of all noble qualities is the precious accumulation of merit. Bearing this in mind, you will swiftly perfect all the attributes of buddhahood!

"You must keep the great kindness of the precious vajra master in mind until you attain limitless common and supreme spiritual attainments. Uphold the essential nature of the clear light doctrine of trekchö, cutting through, and realize the magical nature of mental projections until the stages on the path are perfected. Meditate unceasingly on emptiness and compassion and become fully endowed with the ability to accomplish the great purpose of benefitting others. If the mind never mistakes the absolute view, then it is easy to reach the state of enlightenment without hardship.

"O disciples, hold these pointing-out instructions as the wish-fulfilling jewel of your mother's heart. Have no doubt that the two purposes can thereby be spontaneously accomplished. This Princess of Zahor, Mandarava, has discovered the uncontaminated body, free from birth and death—not even the subtlest suffering of death need ever be experienced! In the expanse of the primordially pure space of original purity, the mind of Mandarava dwells in its original resting place. In the foundation of the originally pure space of the unborn dharmakaya, the Princess dissolves within the unobstructed nature of non-conceptuality. In union with the primordial protector Samantabhadra, Mandarava abides in the expanse of joyful great bliss. "My appearances are like space, utterly without coming, going, birth, death, eternalism, and nihilism. Likewise, until this realm of samsara is emptied, my miraculous emanations will surpass imagination.

"The minds of all beings are naturally radiant and empty. They remain in the nature of emptiness, inseparable from Mandarava. As the pure expression of the five primordial wisdoms, the nature of mind is never separate from Mandarava in the state of nondual bliss. In the mind of a faithful witness, appearances remain as the unobstructed nature of Mandarava. The wisdom of Mandarava is ever inseparable from the skillful display of the changeless three kayas. As you abide in the equipoise of your own true nature, I, the consort Mandarava, will appear to you in symbolic visions. Pray to me and you shall encounter your own true face!"

After Mandarava spoke, two utpal flowers, white and red, emerged and traveled as light rays from her heart to the lands of Tibet and Nepal. Gradually her body became invisible and then appeared as a delicate sphere of light filling the entire sky. Having departed to Akanishta Paradise of Padmavyuha, she arose in the enlightened embodiment of the supreme secret consort of primordial wisdom. At that moment, nine hundred of her devoted pure awareness followers simultaneously dissolved into rainbow bodies leaving nothing behind.

Samaya

This completes the thirty-seventh chapter of
The Lives and Liberation
of the Princess of Zahor, Mandarava,
called *A Precious Garland,*

Explaining how she perfected the benefit
of beings, how they achieved liberation in
rainbow bodies, leaving nothing behind,
and how she passed to Sukhavati Paradise,
where she arose as the secret primordial
wisdom dakini.

38.
Supplication to Mandarava's Emanations

The dakini Yeshe Tsogyal expressed her deep gratitude to the guru by respectfully offering prostrations and the mandala offering. Supplicating the Lord Guru of Oddiyana, she said: "Kye! Guru Padmasambhava, crown prince in the land of Oddiyana! In Silwatsel, the Cool Grove, and the eight great charnel grounds, you revealed yourself as the eight manifestations.[63] Now you remain in the land of Tibet, turning the wheel of Dharma. In your great kindness, you have given innumerable instructions on the vast wealth of the secret mantra doctrine. I, the supreme head of dakinis, bow down to you, Lord Oddiyana! We express our gratitude to you for giving us the complete teaching on the *Lives and Liberation of the Principal Dakini Mandarava*! Please—for the benefit of those of us who are gathered here, as well as for future generations—I implore you to bestow upon us a concise version of her enlightened deeds that is simple to read and inspires faith. Please speak a few profound words for our welfare, so that we might cleanse the two obscurations and receive blessings and spiritual attainments. I implore you now to speak to us again out of your great kindness and compassion!"

The guru was extremely pleased by her request and he said: "Listen, and I will tell you." He instructed: "Whoever recites this supplication prayer should do so at the break of dawn in a kneeling position, with palms pressed together, in a state of heartfelt devotion." Then the precious guru sang:

E ma ho!

In the previous aeon of Bhaskara,
As the daughter of King Indradeva known as Pandaravasini,
She trained on the path to abandon samsara and actualize
  buddhahood.
To the feet of Mandarava, I supplicate!

Later in the aeon known as Ratnavistirna,
She was born into the holy caste as the princess Natyendri.
Suryagarbha and his entire kingdom was placed
  on the path of Dharma.
To the feet of Mandarava, I supplicate!

In the Bright Aeon of Buddha Kanakamuni's revelation of
  the doctrine,
With the blessings of the buddhas of the three times,
She naturally emanated the five embodiments as manifestations in
the five continents to tame the minds of beings.
To the feet of Mandarava, I supplicate!

Born as the princess of the god Brahma and consort,
She was known as Özer Nangyen.
All the people of the kingdom of Kanika, in India, were placed
  on the path of Dharma.
To the feet of Mandarava, I supplicate!

By the blessings of the aryas, in the land of Damaru,
She was born from a lotus and summoned Hayagriva as her aid.
Through peaceful and wrathful means the kingdom was turned to
  the path of virtue.
To the feet of Mandarava, I pray!

In the abode of the god Indra, in the land of Kangkari,
She was the mother of the Buddha Dampa Togkar, and she
  tamed the hordes of demigods.

She was famed for her subjugation of the entire country, which
was transformed to the path of the Buddha.
To the feet of Mandarava, I supplicate!

In the subterranean region at the peak of the jewel mountain,
She manifested as a nagini to cure all rampant diseases
among nagas.
Known as Dharmindra, she placed all the nagas on the path to
enlightenment!
To the feet of Mandarava, I supplicate!

As an emanation of the princess of the demigods,
She tamed the hordes of jealous demigods.
As the one known as Samantabhadri, she brought the hosts of
demonic demigods to maturity and liberation.
To the feet of Mandarava, I supplicate!

In the presence of Buddha Kashyapa,
She generated the bodhichitta and emanated as the daughter of
King Sukhapala named Shri Sagara.
She was responsible for the perfect enlightenment of one
hundred thousand nuns.
To the feet of Mandarava, I supplicate!

During the time of Shakyamuni Buddha,
She manifested herself twenty-five times; her further emanations
are utterly inconceivable,
Such a one opening the door to the path of the secret mantra
vehicle.
To the feet of Mandarava, I pray!

Then, in the western paradise of Sukhavati,
Here a million manifestations reveal the secret mantra,
Her dakini emanation appears with each of them!
To the feet of Mandarava, I supplicate!

Light from the five places of the supreme consort Pandaravasini
Radiated into all the paradises to become the manifestations of the
    five dakinis of the sphere of truth.
Blessing and empowering the syllable *hrih,* this light emanated
    into the land of Zahor.
To the feet of Mandarava, I supplicate!

Through her miraculous powers, her father and mother, the king
    and queen, had astonishing indications in their dreams.
In the male wood-horse year, on the tenth day of the month,
She was born and immediately recited the sounds of the vowels
    and consonants!
To the feet of Mandarava, I supplicate!

At the very moment of birth, she prostrated to her parents to
    repay their kindness,
And sang a pleasing song for all who had gathered.
The gods came to bathe her, and her fame encompassed
    this world.
To the feet of Mandarava, I supplicate!

Seeing the suffering of birth, old age, sickness, and death, she felt
    deep repulsion,
Her mind turned from samsara, and became well-trained
In the five sciences of the holy Dharma.
To the feet of Mandarava, I supplicate!

In the land of Gautala, in accordance with the prophecies of
Master Drime and Vajravarahi, she debated the heretic Kyabsel.
She defeated and subjugated all heretics at that time.
To the feet of Mandarava, I supplicate!

In the land of Zahor, she brought three hundred women to
    the path
and transformed the suffering of the king and queen at the death
    of Prince Palde.

She discovered the flesh of the holy sage, which became the chief
  object of the people's devotion.
To the feet of Mandarava I supplicate!

She reconciled Bheta and Zahor, ending their war.
In accordance with the prophecy of Pandaravasini, she brought
  her entourage to the Dharma.
She generated fervent prayers to remain in samsara for the welfare
  of others.
To the feet of Mandarava, I supplicate!

Meeting with the king, she discussed the requests for her hand in
  marriage from the royal suitors of every direction.
Without attachment to samsara, she received a prophecy from
  Vajrasattva.[64]
Skillfully escaping, she took the vows of ordination before the
  Abbot preceptor.
To the feet of Mandarava, I supplicate!

Thoroughly investigating the scriptures, she studied the Tripitaka,
And in the pleasure grove she taught the Dharma to her five
  hundred attendants.
She received prophecy directly from the emanation of
  Guru Padmasambhava.
To the feet of Mandarava I supplicate!

Arriving in the flower garden, she actually met face to face with
  the guru.
When she invited him to her palace to teach the Dharma,
  a wandering cowherd took notice.
Rumors ensued, and the king took action to punish them.
To the feet of Mandarava, I supplicate!

Despite king and queen's attempt to burn the Guru Padmasambhava alive, he revealed his miraculous powers.
The king and ministers were filled with deep remorse.

The guru stayed with the king and queen, at which time the king
  formally offered Mandarava as the consort for the guru of
  Oddiyana.
To the feet of Mandarava, I supplicate!

All the males in the land of Oddiyana became disciples of
  the guru;
And Mandarava revealed the Dharma to all the females, who
  achieved liberation.
She reached perfect maturity through receiving the master's
  pointing-out instructions.
To the feet of Mandarava, I supplicate!

Receiving the profound Dharma of indication,
She went to the Maratika cave together with the guru
And truly accomplished the deathless state of becoming an
  immortal pure awareness holder.
To the feet of Mandarava, I supplicate!

In the land of Kotala, she tamed the beings through
  miraculous means
And achieved great victory over the magic of the heretics.
In the charnel ground of Yongdü, she placed the hordes of
  obstructors under oath.
To the feet of Mandarva, I supplicate!

In accordance with the prophecy of Padmasambhava,
She went to the land of Chamara, where she placed all the male
  and female cannibals upon the Dharma path.
They accomplished the rainbow body, and the entire country
  was emptied!
To the feet of Mandarava, I supplicate!

In Ngampatsal and the eight great countries,
And in Kailadrog and the eight minor power places,
She revealed eight major and minor miraculous, enlightened
  physical deeds.

To the feet of Mandarava, I supplicate!

Then the Guru Padmasambhava and consort went together
To the land of Oddiyana to banish all perverted views through
skillful means.
They turned the wheel of Dharma, and everyone was liberated in
the rainbow-light body.
To the feet of Mandarava, I supplicate!

In accordance with the prophecy of the guru,
She went to Shambhala and, with her great skillful means, tamed
beings in the twenty-five paradises.
One million, three hundred thousand fortunate disciples were
liberated in the rainbow body.
To the feet of Mandarava, I supplicate!

Then she traveled to the peak of the highest mountain in
Bheche, India,
Where all remaining transmissions, without exception,
were given.
She manifested herself as two utpal flowers of white and red—one
in Tibet and one in Nepal.
To the feet of Mandarava, I supplicate!

Dissolving in the expanse of space like a rainbow,
without remains,
She departed to the Akanishta Paradise of Padmavyuha.
She transformed into the embodiment of the supreme consort, the
secret primordial wisdom dakini.
To the feet of Mandarava, I supplicate!

Together with nine hundred pure awareness holder disciples,
After dissolving into a rainbow body, she manifested herself once
again for the benefit of others.
Mandarava emanated unceasingly, manifesting herself as a dakini to
tame the minds of beings in every essential way.

To the feet of Mandarava, I supplicate!

In the Realm of Great Bliss, she is known as the secret wisdom
    consort Pandaravasini;
In the realm of Khechari, as Natyendri;
And in Zahor, as Dungmen Karmo.
To the feet of Mandarava, I supplicate!

"May I and all others throughout all future lifetimes never be separate from her, who is the supreme one among dakinis! May we be free
from all temporary and absolute states of fear, may we realize perfect
buddhahood! Just like the example of her many lives, by accomplishing
the Dharma may we all become enlightened! May all hindering obstacles without exception be pacified. May the benefit of others be swiftly
accomplished and perfected! Grant me the blessings to place all beings
in the state of the Victorious Mother, emptying the realms of samsara.
For those who never waver from these words and who persevere single-pointedly, may the negative obscurations accumulated over
countless past lifetimes be cleansed without remains! By perfecting all
noble qualities on the stages and paths and encountering the dakini, the
common and supreme siddhis will be swiftly obtained; the negative
accumulations that cause illness and demonic-force obstructions will be
reversed without exception; there will be the enjoyments of longevity,
excellent health, and a wealth of endowments and prosperity. Whatever
is wished for will be spontaneously present!

"Have no doubt that the mother Mandarava will guide one to the
future place of rebirth in the Realm of Great Bliss. Accordingly, for all
beings, including the fortunate disciples of Tibet, whoever writes or
reads this account of Mandarava's lives and liberation and makes prostrations, offerings, and supplications with faith and devotion will
experience the result of the spontaneous accomplishment of all wishes.
Whoever simply reads this account with pure faith will be free from the
threat of contagious disease, war, misfortune, and drought; black magic,
curses, and detrimental threats will be pacified. The threat of untimely
death and obstacles to one's life will be reversed if one reads this
account a hundred times. If one reads this text, the illnesses that four-

legged beasts endure, as well as those of impoverished beggars, will be pacified, and good fortune and prosperity will abound. If one desires offspring, one's family line will increase by reading this text. Whoever owns this text about her lives and liberation will accomplish all desires without obstacle. Wherever a copy of this account is found—within any monastery, country, city, or family home—the spirits, demonic forces, and elementals will be kept back at a distance, unable to approach any closer than a mile. If this account is recited a hundred times in order to obtain a better future rebirth, there will be liberation from the fear of the lower realms, and the consciousness will travel to the realm of Khechari.

"The actual benefits of this account are so remarkable that they simply cannot be expressed. If it is worn on the body, the effects of obscuration will not occur. There will be no fear of weapons, and poison will loose its potency. Contagious diseases, open, festering sores, and leprosy will all be pacified. Illness, demonic-force possession, obstructing forces, and all such harm will be stripped of strength. If this account is read prior to embarking upon a journey, all mishaps and harm, such as ambush, robbery, and treacherous passageways, will be pacified. If one maintains this text as an object of veneration, making regular prostrations, circumambulations, and offerings, it is certain that rebirth will occur in the Realm of Great Bliss. Therefore, sentient beings of the future generations, persevere accordingly!"

Samaya

This completes the thirty-eighth chapter of
The Lives and Liberation
of the Princess of Zahor, Mandarava,
called *A Precious Garland:*

The concise supplication to
Mandarava's successive incarnations.

Epilogue

Once again, the Lady Tsogyal requested: "Kye ma! Guru Padmasambhava of Oddiyana! Should this precious account of the dakini's lives and liberation become a part of the oral transmission (*kama*) or the rediscovered treasure (*terma*) lineage for future propagation? When is it meant to accomplish the benefit of sentient beings? In your great kindness, please give us an indication for the future."

To this request, the guru responded: "Listen well, Jomo Yeshe Tsogyalma! This account of the dakini's lives and liberation that has never before been revealed will be written down in three copies, which are to be buried and concealed as treasures. In the three places known as the Tsangrong Mebar Drag, Tsarong Drag, and Gowowang Mountain are meditation caves of mine. Conceal the three copies within rhinoceros hide caskets in these three power caves. Authorize the treasure keepers Dü, Tsen, and Lu to guard the treasures.

"The account to be concealed in the cave in Gowowang Mountain will be revealed in the future when the life expectancy of humans is below thirty and above twenty years. At that time, this account will accomplish the benefit of sentient beings. The concise version to be concealed in the cave in Tsangrong will be propagated when the life expectancy is forty years and will be given to one named Karma or Dorje. However, the auspicious circumstances of its discovery will be reversed, and the letters on the golden parchment will eventually vanish.

"The account to be buried in the cave at Tsarong will be widely propagated when the life expectancy is twenty years in the area called Dokham by one named Ratna. Three further accounts will be buried: the extensive account in Tsangrong, the intermediate at Gowowang Mountain; and the concise account at the Tsarong cave.

"The intermediate version will be revealed by the treasure discoverer Samten Lingpa, who will be born in the iron sheep year. As a man of great forbearance, he will be impartial and uphold great, pure perception. His wisdom qualities will be sublime, and he will never keep company with obscured, negative beings. A man utterly free from obscuration, he will be a master of the eye of primordial wisdom. His heart will be marked with the syllable *hum*, his cheek with a syllable *bhrum*, and his shoulder with a swastika.[65] His thigh will have the patterns of bone ornamentation, and his navel will be marked with the syllable *tam*. As a master of all sublime qualities, he will be a subjugator of the maras. In his final rebirth, through the method of concealment he will be a great utilizer of the profound treasure lineage. Through the blessing of my speech he will lead beings; with whomever he makes a connection, may they be placed in the irreversible state.

"After receiving this treasure, he will conceal it for twenty years until meeting with Rigden Dewa, Sonam, Dronma, and the one known as Dharma. Befriending them, he will clearly reveal this account, and they will become Dharma keepers of this treasure. There are five principal texts connected with this account, as well as six branches. Gradually they will all be propagated to bring benefit to countless sentient beings. Now this life account of Mandarava, a terma of Nanam Dorje Düjom, with eight doors, is hidden close to Zegyal mountain in the secret cave of the dakinis. The interdependent keepers of this Dharma treasure are Tso or Chö. If any one of them meet with this, there is no doubt that it will be revealed. Then the small print will clearly indicate the prophesied treasure keepers. This treasure will give bliss and happiness to the people of Tibet. After thirteen additional treasures are discovered, the profound key will be given over by the guardians. Therefore, future generations should abandon any doubt!"

Samaya

Then the dakini Yeshe Tsogyal, acting as the scribe, wrote this on the back of the white birch tree three times in the secret script of symbolic indication. In the cave called Tsangrong Mebar, she concealed the Padma Pungpe Tantra together with reference pointing-out instructions. On Gowowang Mountain, she concealed the five cycles of the Tugdam, as well as the Yangchang Chenmo. In the black Tsarong cave, she concealed the Purba Mitri Tantra with supplementary commentaries; thus entrusting all into the hands of future treasure owners and guardians. Many prayers of auspiciousness were offered!

Samaya gya gya gya ku gya sung gya tug gya da tim
Sealed by the words of honor, enlightened body seal,
enlightened speech seal, and enlightened mind seal.

The tantric adept who appeared at the end of this aeon, the Heruka Orgyen Jigme Migyur Samten Lingpa Trinle Drodul Lerab Dewa Tsal, revealed this treasure from the Gowowang Mountain Lotus Meditation Cave during his fourteenth year, male wood-monkey year. The mind commitment of Yeshe Tsogyal, in five divisions together with this *Lives and Liberation* account, was revealed and then concealed by the treasure revealer until he reached thirty-seven years of age. As prophesied, upon meeting the incarnation of Langlab Gyalwa Jangchub, Dorshul Tsewang Tendzin Pema Trinle the terton received seven strong natural indications to reveal the terma. Then Dorshul Tsewang Tendzin Pema Trinle gave the terton the material with which to record this revelation, and the writing was begun in the hermitage of Gochen Gyalwa, called Düdul Ngag, close to the mountain Dzegyal Mamo. This work continued in the accomplishment place of the guru of Oddiyana, called Maratika, and was completed in the place called Gangshung Yangkyilgar. The entire account was written down on golden parchment of white birch bark the size of two by three finger-widths. May all the accumulated and resulting virtue increase the doctrine of Lord Buddha and may the lotus feet of the great upholders of the doctrine remain firm in this world for one hundred aeons! May all sentient beings experience fully-endowed bliss and happiness!

Sarva Mangalam Geoh!

May There Always Be
Good Fortune and Virtue!

Table of Equivalents

Adzitayi Menche	a dzi ta yi sman bcad
Ajivaija	a dzi bai dza
Akanishtha	'og min
Akanishtha Padmavyuha	'og min padmo
Akshobhya	mi bskyod pa
Akshobhyavajra	mi bskyod rdo rje
Akshobhyavira	mi bskyod dpa' bo
Amitabha	'od dpag med / snang mtha' yas
Amitayus	tshe dpag med
Amoghapasha	don yod zhags pa
Amoghasiddhi	don yod grub pa
Amrita Garden	am ri ta tshal
Anananta	mtha' yas rgyal mo
Anandakara	bde byed
Anandapala	bde skyong
Anandashri	dga' ba'i dpal
Anga	ang ga
Arnapa	arna pa
Arura	a ru ra
Arya Kotra	ār ya ko ḍa
Arya Vikridita	'phags rnam par rol
Asura Cave	a su ra brag phug
Atashi	a ta shi
Avalokiteshvara	spyan ras gzigs / lo ke shwa ra
Bāla Urdhi	bā la u rdhi
Bage Khadog	ba sgad kha dog
Beche	sbed byed
Bengal	bhang ga la
Bhabramari	bhabra ma ri
Bhaiti	bhai tī
Bhaskarasa Hasrakara	snang byed 'od stong

Bhaskarashri	snang byed dpal
Bhatana	bha ta na
Bhatatho	bha ta tho
Bhaumahing	bhau ma hing
Bheche	bhed byed
Bhendha	bhendha
Bheta	bhe ta
Bheta Soge	bhe ta so gad
Bhigche	bhig byed
Bhitotha	bhi to ṭha
Bhutinara	bhu ti nā ra
Brahma	tshangs pa
Buddhalocana	sangs rgyas spyan ma
Buddhi Tsomo	buddhi'i gtso mo
Chakravartin	'khor lo'i bsgyur ba
Chakravartin	'khor lo'i sgyur ba'i rgyal po
Chakravartin	'khor lo'i sgyur rgyal
Chamara	rnga yab
Chamaradvipa	rnga yab gling
Chandala	gdol pa
Charje	'char byed
Chatama	ca ta ma
China	rgya yi yul / rgya nag
Chöden	chos ldan
Chogroza	lcog ro bza'
Chokzangma	mchog bzang ma
Chöma Wangmoche	spyod ma dbang mo che
Copper-colored Mountain Realm of Lotus Light (Chamara Padmabhasa)	rnga yab padma 'od
Dahina	da hī na
Dakadhipati	mkha' gro'i bdag po
Damaru	ḍā ma ru
Damintra	dha mintra
Dampa Togkar	dam pa tog dkar
Dawe Kyeu Drime	zla ba'i khye'u dri med
Dawa Özer	zla ba'i 'od zer
Deche Tseg	bde byed brtsegs
Dekyong Kungawo	bde skyong kun dga' bo
Dema	bde ma
Dema Chogilha	bde ma mchog gi lha
Deshek Yongdu Kagye	bde gshegs yongs 'dus bka' brgyad
Devendra	lha dbang

Devendrashri	lha dbang dpal
Dewata	de wa ta
Dewe Tsalchen	bde ba'i tshal chen
Dhaha	dha ha
Dhahimune	dha hi mu ne
Dhanakosha	da na ko sha / dha na ko sha
Dharmakara	chos kyi 'byung gnas
Dharmakaya	chos sku
Dharmakosala	dharma ko sa lā
Dharmaraja	chos kyi rgyal po
Dharmavata	dhar mā a ba ta
Dharmindra	dhar min dra
Dhateshvari	dbyings phyug ma
Dhatrakosha	dha tra ko sha
Dhiru	dhi ru
Dipamkara	mar me mdzad
Dokham	mdo khams
Dombhi	ḍombhi
Dorje	rdo rje
Dorje Pagmo	rdo rje phag mo
Dorshul Tsewang Tenzin Pema Trinle	rdor shul tshe dbang bstan 'dzin pad ma 'phrin las
Drangsong Lelak	drang srong le lag
Drime Yeshe	dri med ye shes
Dronma	sgron ma
Dronma Yeshema	sgron ma ye shes ma
Dronme	sgron me
Drowa Dulwa	'gro ba 'dul ba
Drushar	gru shar
Dü	bdud
Düdul Ngag	bdud 'dul sngags
Düduldrag	bdud 'dul brag
Düje Garab	bdud rje dga' rab
Düjom	bdud 'joms
Dungmen Karmo	dung sman dkar mo
Dungmen Tsedzin	dung sman tshe 'dzin
Five Texts on Abandonment	spang ba lnga
Four Cycles of Mother and Son	ma bu bskor bzhi
Gache	dga' byed
Gagana	ga ga na
Gama	dga' ma
Ganda	gaṇ ḍa

Ganges	gang ga
Gangshung Yangkyilgar	gangs gzhung g.yang 'khyil sgar
Gangzang Umanti	gangs bzang u mām ti
Garab Nagpo	dga' rab nag po
Garden of Blazing Fire	'bar tshal
Garden of Nectar	a mri ta'i tshal
Garuda	khyung
Gaumi	gau mi
Gautala	gau ta la
Gautama	gau ta ma
Gemapal	dge ma dpal
Gesar	ge sar
Getso Lhamo	dge mtsho lha mo
Getsoma	dge mtsho ma
Glorious Red Palace	bzang mkhar dmar
Gocha Zangpo	go cha bzang po
Gochen Gyalwa	sgo chen rgyal ba
Gotipa	go ti pa
Gowowang Mountain	go bo dbang ri
Guna Indra	gu ṇa indra
Gyalpö Khab	rgyal po'i khab
Gyeche Tsugpupel	dgyes byed gtsug phud dpal
Gyenlekma	rgyan legs ma
Gyepepel	rgyas pa'i dpal
Hadzin	ha 'dzin
Haling	ha ling
Hasabid	ha sa bid
Hasha Dhari	ha sha dha ri
Hashi	ha shi
Hatakin	ha ta kin
Hayagriva	dbang chen khro bo / rta mgrin
Hayagriva Mechar	rta mgrin me 'char
Hematsal	he ma tshal
Heroine Victorious Over the Maras	dpa' mo g.yul las rgyal ma
Heruka Orgyen Jigme Migyur Samten Lingpa Trinle Drodul Lerab Dewa Tsal	dpal khrag 'thung nag po o rgyan 'jigs med mi 'gyur bsam gtan gling pa 'phrin las 'gro 'dul las rab bde ba rtsal
India	rgya gar
Indra	brgya byin
Indrabhuti	in dra bhu ti / in dra bo dhī
Indradam	in dra dam

Indradeva	dbang phyug lha
Indranila	in dra snyil
Jambudvipa	'dzam bu gling
Jihar	ji har
Kailadrog	kai la sgrogs
Kala	ka la
Kala Yaksha	kā la yak sha
Kalachakra	dus kyi 'khor lo
Kalaraksha	ka la raksha
Kalaraksha Marajita	ka la raksha bdud 'dul
Kalasiddhi	kā la siddhi
Kalinga	ka ling ka
Kalingapa	ka ling ka pa
Kalpa Zangmo	bskal pa bzang mo
Kamalashri	ka ma la shrī
Kamaru	ka ma ru
Kamarupa	ka ma ru pa / kā ma ru pa
Kanakamuni	gser thub
Kangkari	kang ka ri
Kanika	ka ṇi ka
Kari	ka ri
Karkatamoha	kar ka ṭa mo ha
Karma	kar ma
Karma Bhadriha	kar ma bha dri ha
Karmadhani	kar ma dhā ni
Karshita	kar shi ta
Kartrari	kar dra ris
Kashmir	kha che
Kashmirakarabha	kha che rnga thug
Katana	ka ta na
Katitsa	ka ti tsa
Katrokopa	ka tro ko pa
Kelpazang	bskal pa bzang
Kharchen Tsogyal	mkhar chen mtsho rgyal
Khasarpana	mkha' skyong
Khasarpani	kha sār pā ṇi
Khechari	mkha' spyod
Khemalia	khe ma lī
Kirti Bhadra	grags pa bzang mo
Koli	ko li
Koshala	ko sha la
Koshi	ko shi

Kotachungwa	ko ta chung ba
Kotala	ko ta la
Kotamati	ko ta ma ti
Kotashri	ko ta shri
Kotavira	ko ta bi ra
Kshemadevi	dge ba'i lha mo
Kuluta	ku la ta
Kumri	kum ri
Kumud Shepetsal	ku mud bzhad pa'i tshal
Kunche	kun byed
Kunga Zangmo	kun dga' bzang mo
Kuntuchang Wangpo	kun tu 'chang dbang po
Kunzig Önang	kun gzigs 'od snang
Kushthasukha	ko tha bde
Kyabche Barwa	khyab byed 'bar ba
Kyabsel	khyab gsal
Kyabsel Nagpo	khyab gsal nag po
Kyema	skyes ma
Lady Tsogyal	jo mo mtsho rgyal
Land of Snow	gangs can
Langlab Gyalwa Jangchub	lang lab rgyal ba byang chub
Lanka	lang ka
Lhamo Yukye	lha mo g.yu skyid
Lhawang Khorpa	lha dbang 'khor pa
Lhayiwang	lha yi dbang
Lion-headed Dakini	seng gdong drag mo
Lotus Light	padma 'od
Lotus-born	padma skyes / padma byung 'gnas
Lu	klu
Mahabala	ma hā ba la
Mahakala	mgon po
Maitri Shrideva	byams pa dpal gyi lha
Maitrikanta	mai tri mdzes pa
Malashri	mā la shri
Malaya	ma la ya
Mamaki	ma mā ki
Mamo	ma mo
Mandarava	man dha ra
Mandhana	man dha na
Mangadha	man ga dha
Manifest Joy (Abhirati)	mngon par dga' ba
Manika	ma ṇi ka

Manjushri	'jam dpal dbyangs
Mara	bdud
Maratika	mā ra ti ka
Marichi	'od zer ldan ma
Maru Singhala	ma ru singga la
Maruta	ma ru ta
Matiratna	ma ti ratna
Mengag Tongdzö	man ngag stong mdzod
Menita	me ni ta
Menmo Rinchenzang	sman mo rin chen bzang
Metog Trengze	me tog phreng mdzes
Mingpo Dawa	ming po zla ba
Mitrarashmi	mi tra rasmi
Mokyau Ching	mo kya'u ching
Molarasa	mū la ra sa
Mount Kailash	te se gangs
Mount Meru	ri rab
Mudrabuhani	mu dra bu ha ni
Mulagyen	mu la brgyan
Murum	mu rum
Naga Nagi	nā ga nā gi
Nagalaru	nā ga la ru
Nagaraja Go Ngön	klu rgyal mgo sngon
Nahuti	na hu ti
Namaru	na ma ru
Nametotra	na ma'i to ṭha
Nampar Nangwa	rnam par snang ba
Nanam	sna nam
Nanda	dga' bo
Narayana Baladhara	sred med stobs 'chang
Natyendri	gar gyi dbang mo
Nepali	bal skad / bal po
Ngampa	rngam pa
Ngampa Tsalchen	rngam pa tshal chen
Ngampachen	rngam pa chen
Ngampatsal	rngam pa tshal
Ngatug	rnga thugs
Nidzu	ni dzu
Nilakantha	mgrin sngon
Nimsani Tsal	nim sa ni tshal
Norkyonglha	nor skyong lha
Nyangzatso	nyang bza' mtsho

Nyime Paldenma	nyi ma'i dpal ldan ma
Nyingthig	snying thig
Oddiyana	o rgyan
Önang Pagme	'od snang dpag med
Ösema	'od sred ma
Özer Barwewang	'od zer 'bar ba'i dbang
Özer Nangyen	'od zer snang brgyan
Padma Drodul	padma 'gro 'dul
Padma Gyalwa	padma rgyal ba
Padma Nateshvara	padma gar gyi dbang
Padma Pelgyitso	padma dpal gyi mtsho
Padma Pungpe Tantra	padma spungs pa'i rgyud
Padma Tsegpa	padma brtsegs pa
Padma Vikridita	padma rnam rol
Padma Yangnying Rolpa Chenpo	padma yang snying rol pa chen po
Padma Yiongkyi	padma yid 'ong skyid
Padmabja	padma skyes
Padmarachana	padma bkod
Padmarashi	padma spungs pa
Padmasambhava	padma 'byung gnas
Padmoshnisha	padma gtsug tor
Palapatre Gyen	pā la pa tras brgyan
Palasha	pā la sha
Palasiddhi	pha la siddhi
Palde	dpal sde
Palmo Ökyigyen	dpal mo 'od kyis brgyan
Palmo Seldron	dpal mo gsal sgron
Palmo Shonnu	dpal mo gzhon nu
Paltseg	dpal brtsegs
Pandaravasini	gos dkar mo
Parardha	pā ra rdha ra
Pawode	dpa' bo'i sde
Pema Tsegpa	padma brtsegs pa
Pemachen	padma can
Pemakö	padma bkod
Pemaköpa	padma bkod pa
Peme Gompar Shegpa	padma'i gom par gshegs pa
Pemetsal	padma'i tshal
Persia	stag gzigs
Pharol Gölwajom	pha rol rgol ba 'joms
Phurba Mitri	phur ba mi tri
Potala	po ta la

Prabhadhara	'od 'chang ma
Prakara	pra ka ra
Pratima	pra ti ma
Precious Jeweled Garden	rin chen yongs 'dus tshal
Pushpalamkara	me tog brgyan ma
Raga Maha	rā ga ma ha
Rakshasa	srin po'i skad
Ratna	ratna
Ratna Shribhadra	rin chen dpal legs
Ratnadhara	ratna 'dzin pa
Ratnajaya	rin chen rgyal
Ratnalamkara	ratnas brgyan
Ratnapala	ratna pā la
Ratnarchi	rin chen 'od zer
Ratnasambhava	rin chen 'byung gnas
Ratnashri	rin chen dpal
Ratnashri	ratna shrī
Ratnavistirna	rin chen brdal ba
Ratnavyuha	rin chen bkod
Rayaya	khar bu
Rigche Dawa Lha	rig byed zla ba lha
Rigche Tsangnema	rig byed tshangs gnas ma
Rigden Dewa	rig ldan de wa
Rigsum Kegui Dagmo	rigs gsum skye rgu'i bdag mo
Rimahala	ri ma ha la
Rinchen Nangche Dronme Ö	rin chen snang byed sgron me 'od
Rinchen Ö	rin chen 'od
Rinchen Pung	rin chen spungs
Rinchendron	rin chen sgron
Roti Kirima	ro ti ki ri ma
Rugma	rug ma
Sāmapatra	sā ma pa tra
Salapatra	sā la pa tra
Samadhiraja	ting 'dzin rgyal po
Samantabhadra	kun tu bzang po
Samantabhadri	kun tu bzang mo
Samato	sā mā to
Samayatara	dam tsig sgrol ma
Samten Lingpa	bsam gtan gling pa
Samye Peloling	bsam yas pā lo gling
Sarasvati	dbyangs can ma
Sartasumtibha	sar ta sum ti bha

Semshogma	sems shogs ma
Senge Dradrog	seng ge sgra sgrogs
Sengetsal	seng ge tshal
Shakya	shākya
Shakyadevi	shākya de bī
Shakyadevi of Nepal	bal mo shākya debī
Shakyamuni	shākya thub pa
Shambhala	sham bha la
Shangka Kotali	shang ka ko ta li
Shangtsen Mayi	zhang btsan rma yi
Shenpa	shan pa
Shinta	shin ta
Shinta Budho	shin ta budho
Shintama	shin ta ma
Shintang	shin tang
Shintipa	shin ti pa
Shiroratna	gtsug na rin chen
Shri Sagara	dpal mtsho / dpal gyi mtsho mo shri sā ga ra
Shribhadra	dpal legs
Shrigani	shri ga ni
Shrimala	dpal 'phreng ma
Shrimati	shri ldan ma
Shubha	shu bha
Shubhakara Shekhara	bde byed brtsegs pa
Shubhamanidhara	dge ba'i nor 'dzin
Shuddhodana	zas gtsang ba
Silwatsel	bsil ba tshal
Singh Sutitra	singh su tī ṭha
Singha	singha
Singhala	singga la
Singmo Gangadevi	sring mo gang gā'i lha mo
Sinpo	srin po
Sirana	si ra na
Sitana	si ta na
Sonam	bsod nams
Songtsen Gonpo	srong btsan sgam po
Srishti	sṛṣṭi ma
Sugata	bde bar gshegs pa
Sukama	su ka ma
Sukhahi	su kha hi
Sukhapala	bde skyong

Sukhavana	bde ba'i tshal
Sukhavati	bde ba can
Suryagarbha	nyi ma'i snying po
tala	tā la
Taluma	ta lu ma
Tanadug	lta na sdug
Tangkar	tang dkar
Tashi Kyidren	bkra shis khye 'dren
Taye Dzesema	mtha' yas mdzes se ma
Tazanya	pra dza nya
Tergo	gter sgo
Thalihangti	thā li hang ti
Thamadu	tha mā rdu
Thubzin	thub 'dzin
Thubzin Wangpo	thub 'dzin dbang po
Togar	tho gar
Tongchen	stong chen
Tratrashri	tra tra shri
Trigna Tighata	trig na trig ha ta
Trignadzin	trig na 'dzin
Tripitaka	sde snod gsum
Trushangdan	'phru zhang ldan
Tsang Tsang	tsang tsang
Tsangchinma	tshangs byin ma
Tsangrong Dorje Drag	gtsang rong rdo rje brag
Tsangrong Mebar Drag	gtsang rong me 'bar brag
Tsantoha	tsha ṇa ḍa ha
Tsarong	tsha rong
Tsen	btsan
Tsoti Bhigche	btso ti bhig byed
Tsugpudzin	gtsug phud 'dzin
Tugdam	thugs dam
Tushita	dga' ldan
Tushtikaradevi	dgyes mdzad lha mo
Udughi	u du ghi
Uma Devi	u ma de wi
Ushnishavijaya	gtsug tor rnam par rgyal ma
Vairocana	rnam par snang mdzad
Vaishravana	rnam thos bu
Vajrabinaka	rdo rje bi na ka
Vajradhara	rdo rje 'chang
Vajragarbha	rdo rje'i snying po

Vajrakula	rdo rje pho brang
Vajrapankti	rdo rje brtsegs pa
Vajrasana	rdo rje gdan
Vajrasattva	rdo rje sems dpa'
Vajravarahi	rdo rje phag mo
Varunasena	chu lha'i sde
Vasundhara Bhadrashri	nor 'dzin dge ba'i dpal
Vidyadhara	rig 'dzin
Viharadhara	gtsug lag 'dzin
Vimala	dri med
Vishnu	sred med bu
Vitanahuta	bi ta na hu ta
Wangchen Pemakyi	dbang chen padma skyid
Wangdrag Rolpa	dbang drag rol pa
Wangmo Ögema	dbang mo 'od dge ma
Yagantha	ya gan tha
Yaksha Ānandapala	yaksha bde skyong
Yampa Dihuta	g.yam pa di hu ta
Yangchang Chenmo	yang byang chen mo
Yangchen	dbyangs can
Yangchen Üpa	yangs can dbus pa
Yangpachen	yangs pa can
Yangsang Demig	yang gsang lde mig
Yeshe Zangmo	ye shes bzang mo
Yidü Tersung	yi dud gter srung
Yongdutsal	yongs 'du'i tshal
Yonten Köpa	yon tan bkod pa
Zabmo Tashige	zab mo bkra shis dge
Zahor	za hor
Zahor Sitana	za hor si ta na
Zakha Haling	za kha ha ling
Zangkye	bzang bskyed
Zangmo	bzang mo
Zegyal	gze rgyal
Zhang Zhung	zhang zhung
Zhonupal	gzhon nu dpal

Notes

Introduction

1 The Tibetan text is entitled *Za hor rgyal po'i sras mo lha lcam man dha ra ba'i rnam par thar pa rin chen phreng ba* and is published in Bsam-gtan-gliṅ-pa Phrin-las-'gro-'dul-las-rab-bde-ba-rtsal, *The life of Lady Mandarava, the Indian consort of Padmasambhava* (New Delhi: Ngawang Sopa, 1973).

2 The seventeenth century lifestory of Yeshe Tsogyal has been translated into English twice: Nam-mkha'i snying-po, *Mother of Knowledge: The Enlightenment of Ye-shes mTsho-rgyal*, trans. Tarthang Tulku (Berkeley: Dharma Publishing, 1983); Keith Dowman, *Sky Dancer: The Secret Life and Songs of the Lady Yeshe Tsogyel* (London: Routledge & Kegan Paul, 1984). I am currently working on several earlier versions of her life.

3 For an overview of the Padmasambhava lifestory tradition, see Anne-Marie Blondeau. "Analysis of the Biographies of Padmasambhava according to Tibetan Tradition: Classification of Sources" in *Tibetan Studies in Honour of Hugh Richardson*, edited by Michael Aris and Aung San Suu Kyi (Warminster, England: Aris & Phillips, 1980), pp. 45–52. See also F.A. Bischoff and Charles Hartman, "Padmasambhava's Invention of the Phur-bu Pelliot Tibétain 44," in *Études tibétaines dédiées à la mémoire de Marcelle Lalou* (Paris: Adrien Maissonneuve, 1971), pp. 11–28. An English rendering of Orgyan Lingpa's life of Padmasambhava is Kenneth Douglas and Gwendolyn Bays, *The Life and Liberation of Padmasambhava* (translated from the French translation of the Tibetan) (Berkeley: Dharma Publishing, 1978), 2 vols. An English summary of excerpts from the version by Sangye Lingpa is to be found in W.Y. Evans-Wentz, ed., *The Tibetan Book of the Great Liberation* (London: Oxford University Press, 1954), pp. 105–192.

4 E.g., Douglas and Bays, vol. 1, p. 236 ff; Evans-Wentz, p. 142 ff.

5 Diana Paul, *Women in Buddhism* (Berkeley: Asian Humanities Press, 1979); Alan Sponberg, "Attitudes toward Women and the Feminine in Early Buddhism," in Jose Cabezón, ed., *Buddhism, Sexuality, and Gender* (Albany:

State University of New York Press, 1992), pp. 3–36.

6 As recounted by Tāranātha: Martin Willson, *In Praise of Tara: Songs to the Saviouress* (London: Wisdom Publications, 1986), pp. 33–4.

7 The work is also associated with another of Padmasambhava's disciple, Nanam Dorje Dudjom (p. 240; see also p. 78)

8 See n. 4 above.

9 Cf. Herbert Guenther, trans., *The Jewel Ornament of Liberation by Sgam.po.pa* (Berkeley: Shambhala, 1971), pp. 64–5.

10 Dowman, pp. 118–9.

11 *Poems of Early Buddhist Nuns*, translated by C. A. F. Rhys Davids and K. R. Norman (Oxford: The Pali Text Society, 1989).

The Lives and Liberation of Princess Mandarava

1 Past, present, and future.

2 *rig 'dzin*, Skt. *vidyadhara*. In the Nyingma tantric system, there are four kinds of pure awareness holders: the pure awareness holder of maturation (*rnam smin rig 'dzin*), the awareness holder of power over life-span (*tshe dbang rig 'dzin*), the pure awareness holder of the great seal (*phyag chen rig 'dzin*), and the pure awareness holder of spontaneous presence (*lhun grub rig 'dzin*).

3 The five buddha families are a tantric Buddhist typology of enlightenment in which the pure enlightened nature of the five psychosomatic constituents of sentient beings—the five aggregates or skandhas of form, feeling, perception, conceptualization, and consciousness—are seen as five male buddhas; these are in union with their female counterparts, who embody five primordial wisdoms, which are the pure enlightened nature of the five poisonous emotions (anger, pride, desire, jealousy, and ignorance). The "buddha" family is symbolized by Vairocana in union with his consort Dhateshvari, who embodies the primordial wisdom of the absolute expanse; the "vajra" family is symbolized by Akshobya in union with Buddhalochana, who embodies the mirror-like primordial wisdom; the "jewel" (*ratna*) family is symbolized by Ratnasambhava in union with Mamaki, who embodies the primordial wisdom of equality; the "lotus" (*padma*) family symbolized by Amitabha in union with Pandaravasini, who embodies the discriminating wisdom that knows the diversity of all phenomena; and the "action" (*karma*) family is

symbolized by Amoghasiddhi in union with Samayatara, who embodies the wisdom capable of accomplishing all activities. (The five buddhas also have their respective paradises; cf. note 62.) Princess Mandarava is considered a manifestation of Pandaravasini, the female counterpart of Amitabha.

4 The three realms of existence are the desire, form, and formless realms.

5 These three enlightened embodiments are the three kayas. The enlightened embodiment of ultimate reality is the dharmakaya, the enlightened embodiment of rapture is the sambhogakaya, and the enlightened embodiment of intentional manifestation is the nirmanakaya.

6 These are the four enlightened activities enacted by bodhisattvas and buddhas.

7 A trident staff held by tantric meditational deities, decorated with symbols of enlightened body, speech, and mind.

8 Sapphire.

9 These five networks of channels are located in the five principal energy centers within the psychic body. They are the chakra of great bliss or network of channels in the crown; the chakra of complete enjoyment in the throat; the chakra of dharma in the heart; the chakra of manifestation in the navel; the chakra of sustaining bliss in the genitals.

10 The rishi posture is a reference to the posture that a sage or holy mendicant assumes while sitting in meditation for extended periods of time. The soles of the feet are down, the feet are crossed at the ankles with knees held close to the chest. The elbows are placed on the knees and the arms are crossed at the chest while the tips of the fingers touch opposite shoulders.

11 The ten stages and five paths are the grounds and paths of the Mahayana Vehicle. The five paths are: the path of Accumulation; Preparation; Seeing; Meditation; and No Further Learning. The ten stages are: Very Joyful; Stainless; Luminous; Radiant; Difficult Training; Manifest; Gone Afar; Immovable; Good Intelligence; Cloud of the Dharma.

12 A chakravartin is a universal monarch who possess the merit to rule the universe. He appears only during the time when the human life span stretches between infinite to eighty thousand years.

13 The five embodiments are the three kayas including the fourth kaya, the svabhavikakaya (essential nature as it is), and the fifth, the abhisambodhikaya

(Tib. *mngon byang sku*, fully awakened enlightened embodiment).

14 The second of the thousand buddhas to appear in our world system in the present aeon.

15 The rainbow body is an accomplishment unique to the practice of crossing over with spontaneous presence (*lhun grub thod rgal*). By accomplishing this practice, which is the main method of the Dzogchen path, the result is the rainbow body, which means dissolving the corporeal body into light energy particles at the time of death. There are two types of rainbow body, both of which are referred to in this revelation. "Rainbow body with remains" refers to leaving behind only the hair and nails at the time of death. "Rainbow body of the great transference" refers to leaving behind nothing and simply vanishing in space.

16 The Ati Vehicle is the path of the Great Perfection (*rdzogs chen*).

17 *Kamarupa* is a region in the western part of modern-day Assam, which is known to this day for its fierce—and sometimes cannibalistic—tribal inhabitants.

18 The dharma protector Tsen (*btsan*) is also referred to as Tsi'u marpo, who is the head of the *yaksha* (wealth deity) realm and the king of the *dgra-lha* (war god) realm. This protector has the capacity to befriend and assist practioners through conferring wealth, prosperity, and the like or, if offended, through inflicting harm.

19 The nine vehicles taught in accordance with the Nyingma School of Vajrayana Buddhism are: the Shravaka or Hearer Vehicle; the Pratyeka or Solitary Realizer Vehicle; the Mahayana or Great Vehicle; Kriya or Action Tantra; Upa or Conduct Tantra; Yoga or Practice Tantra; Mahayoga or Great Yoga Tantra; Anuyoga or Transmission Yoga Tantra; Atiyoga or Great Perfection Yoga Tantra.

20 *rNga yab gling*, synonymous with *zangs mdog dpal ri*, the Copper-colored Mountain where Guru Padmasambhava resides.

21 The demigods are the titans who occupy the lower gods realms. They are also referred to as the warring gods because they are at constant war with one another.

22 Ultimate truth, which is emptiness and primordial wisdom, and relative truth, which is cause and effect.

²³ The father of Prince Siddhartha, who would become Shakyamuni Buddha.

²⁴ The maras are the demonic forces that oppose the direction of virtue.

²⁵ The six paramitas are generosity, discipline, patience, effort, meditation, and wisdom.

²⁶ Nagas are subterranean beings who guard and protect the underworlds.

²⁷ The "rose-apple" continent of Indian cosmology, identified with this world.

²⁸ The Tripitaka, or "three baskets," classifies the Buddha's teachings into three divisions. The Vinaya Pitaka, or Basket on Discipline, mainly emphasizes the training of ethics. The Sutra Pitaka, or Basket on Discourses, mainly emphasizes concentration. The Abhidharma Pitaka, or Basket on Knowledge, mainly emphasizes wisdom.

²⁹ *bde gshegs lha*, lit. "sugata deities."

³⁰ Perhaps refers to Kamarupa; cf. n. 17.

³¹ The eight pure qualities of water are: coolness, sweetness, clearness, freedom from impurities, lightness, softness, soothing to the stomach, clearing and freeing the throat.

³² These are three important wisdom protectors of Vajrayana Buddhism. Mahakala (Gonpo), the Great Black, has as many as seventy-five forms and is classified as a wisdom Dharma protector, as well as a meditational deity. Ging is a protective deity of the environment who assumes the form of a skeleton, and Tsen was mentioned earlier in note eighteen.

³³ Faith, moral discipline, generosity, learning, conscience, shame, and wisdom.

³⁴ The five primordial wisdoms are the five wisdoms of a buddha. They are: *adarshajñana* (*me long lta bu'i ye shes*), mirror-like primordial wisdom; *samatajñana* (*mnyam nyid ye shes*), the primordial wisdom of equality; *pratyavekshanajñana* (*so sor rtog pa'i ye shes*), discerning primordial wisdom; *dharmadhatujñana* (*chos dbyings ye shes*), primordial wisdom of the sphere of phenomena; *krityanusthanajñana* (*bya ba nan tan du grub pa'i ye shes*), primordial wisdom of consummate activity.

³⁵ The five colors are white, yellow, red, green, and blue.

³⁶ The five empowerments are the empowerment of enlightened body, speech, mind, noble qualities, and activities.

³⁷ The eight fields of consciousness are the consciousness of the eye, ear,

nose, tongue, body, mental events, passion-based mental events, and the basis of all.

38 The four dogmas are the four extreme views of believing in existence, non-existence, both, and neither.

39 The four immeasureables are love, compassion, joy, and equanimity.

40 The four joys are experienced as the result of meditative stabilization. They are joy, supreme joy, specific joy, and co-emergent joy.

41 The term passion is a reference to the five passions or poisons, which are ignorance, pride, desire, anger, and jealousy.

42 The ten airs are the five root vital energies: all-pervasive, life sustaining, upward motion, downward motion, and heat assimilating; and the five branch airs, which correspond to the elements of earth, fire, water, air, and space.

43 The vajra chain of awareness is a vision that is experienced during the practice of crossing over with spontaneous presence (*lhun grub thod rgal*). This is the principal method used on the path of Dzogchen, through which the rainbow light body is realized.

44 The four self-manifesting visions are the stages of realization that occur during the profound practice of crossing over. They are the vision of the direct perception of the nature of phenomena, the increasing vision, the full measure of pure awareness, and the completion of all phenomena in the nature of phenomena.

45 "Nature of the ground" is a reference to the fundamental nature of reality, the source from which all phenomena arise.

46 The eight classes of spirits are the Gongpo (*'gong po*), Th'utrang (*the'u brang*), Ngayam (*nga yam*), Sadag (*sa bdag*), Yul Lha (*yul lha*), Man (*sman*), Tsan (*btsan*), and Lu (*klu*).

47 The three white substances are curd, milk, and butter, and the three sweets are sugar, honey, and molasses.

48 Meditation deity (*yi dam*; Skt. *deva*), the principle deity that one generates in the practice of tantra.

49 The bardo is the transitional period that the consciousness experiences in between lifetimes.

50 The Lord of Death refers to Yama, the messenger of death in the Buddhist pantheon.

51 *dkar rtsis nag rtsis*. These deal with the mathematical and interpretive aspects of astrology, respectively.

52 Tormas are ritual offering cakes, typically cone-shaped.

53 The three doors are the body, speech, and mind.

54 The ten non-virtues are killing, stealing, adultery, lying, slander, harsh speech, gossip, craving, ill-will, and wrong view.

55 The three poisons are ignorance, desire, and anger.

56 The thirty-seven branches of enlightenment are thirty-seven noble qualities that are developed on the path to liberation. They include the four close contemplations, the four perfect abandonments, the four miraculous legs of transformation, the five purified mental faculties, the five forces, the seven limbs of enlightenment, and the eight-fold noble path.

57 Both this and the preceeding chapter are numbered twenty-six in the Tibetan text. For clarity, we have numbered this chapter twenty-seven. Subsequent chapters are consequently one number higher than the chapter numbers in the Tibetan text.

58 Great adepts.

59 Speed-walking is one of the eight mundane spiritual accomplishments.

60 A type of carnivorous female spirit.

61 Tib. *lha chen*, or Shiva.

62 The five paradises of the buddhas are the realms of the five buddha families. They are the Realm of Dense Array in the central direction, the Realm of Manifest Joy in the east, the Realm Endowed with Glory in the south, the Realm of Great Bliss in the west, and the Realm of Perfectly Complete Activity in the north.

63 The Eight Manifestations of Guru Padmasambhava are: Guru Tsokye Dorje (The Lake-Born Vajra Guru), Guru Orgyan Dorje Chang (The Vajra Holder Guru of Uddiyana), Guru Lodan Chogse (Guru Endowed with Supreme Intelligence), Guru Padma Gyalpo (Guru Lotus King), Guru Shakya Senge (Guru Lion of the Shakyas), Guru Nyima Özer (Guru Light Rays of the Sun), Guru Senge Dradrog (Guru Lion's Roar), Guru Dorje

Trolö (Guru Vajra Wrath).

64 Buddha Vajrasattva is the head of all Buddha Families and classes of Meditation Deities. He is the synthesized essence of all one hundred deities of the pantheon of forty-two peaceful and fifty-eight wrathful deities. As the crown jewel of the sambhogakaya buddhas, Vajrasattva is responsible for the dissemination of the doctrine in the world systems and is the principle deity of purification.

65 Tib. *g.yung drung*. The swastika (from Sanskrit *su* 'good' + *asti* 'it is') is an ancient symbol known from prehistoric times. In the Indian context it symbolizes the sun, prosperity, and good luck. In the Buddhist context the swastika may also represent the double-crossed vajra, which in turn symbolizes the seat of the Buddha's enlightenment, called the "vajra-seat" (*vajrāsana*). Since for Tibetans the swastika bears none of the negative connotations that it does for twentieth-century Westerners and, thus, will continue to be an important symbol in their religious iconography, we have elected to use the most literal and descriptive term to translate *g.yung drung*.

About the Contributors

LAMA CHONAM is an ordained Khenpo in the Nyingma school of Vajrayana Buddhism. He was born in Golok as the son of a nomadic family and joined the monastery in his early teens. His root teacher was the late Khenpo Munsel, one of the revered senior teachers of the Great Perfection Tradition. He left Tibet in 1991 and was invited to come to the U.S. in 1992. He serves as an authority and interpreter of the epic of Gesar of Ling, which he is translating with colleagues at the Tibetan Institute of Literary Studies. He is an advisor to the Nalanda Translation Committee and works closely with Sangye Khandro in the translation of many important texts.

SANGYE KHANDRO has been a student and practitioner of Buddhism since 1972. She has dedicated her life to the study and practice of Vajrayana Buddhism for the last twenty-six years and has served as a world-reknowned translator for many great senior Tibetan teachers over the last eighteen years. In 1979 she met H.H. Dudjom Rinpoche, who became her root teacher. Prior to that she also met the Venerable Gyatrul Rinpoche and became his spiritual companion. Under the guidance of H.H. Dudjom Rinpoche and his family, Gyatrul Rinpoche and Sangye Khandro helped establish the Yeshe Nyingpo Dharma centers in America and build Tashi Choling retreat center in southern Oregon. Her recent translations include *Perfect Conduct*, a translation of one of the most important Vajrayana texts on the subject of the three vows and commentaries found in the new treasures of Dudjom Rinpoche. In addition, she is one of three scholars engaged in the lengthy translation of the classical epic of King Gesar of Ling.

JANET GYATSO is Associate Professor of Religion at Amherst College. She has studied with many Tibetan teachers and has received her doctorate in Buddhist studies from the University of California at Berkeley. Her recent research interests have focused on Tibetan visionary practices, lifestories, diaries, and female religious masters. Her most recent book is *Apparitions of the Self: The Secret Autobiographies of a Tibetan Visionary* (Princeton, 1998).

About Wisdom Publications

WISDOM PUBLICATIONS, a not-for-profit publisher, is dedicated to making available authentic Buddhist works for the benefit of all. We publish translations of the sutras and tantras, commentaries and teachings of past and contemporary Buddhist masters, and original works by the world's leading Buddhist scholars. We publish our titles with the appreciation of Buddhism as a living philosophy and with the special commitment to preserve and transmit important works from all the major Buddhist traditions.

If you would like more information or a copy of our mail-order catalog, please contact us at:

Wisdom Publications
199 Elm Street
Somerville, Massachusetts 02144 USA

Telephone: (617) 776-7416   Fax: (617) 776-7841
E-mail: info@wisdompubs.org   Web Site: http://www.wisdompubs.org

THE WISDOM TRUST

As a not-for-profit publisher, Wisdom Publications is dedicated to the publication of fine Dharma books for the benefit of all sentient beings and dependent upon the kindness and generosity of sponsors in order to do so. If you would like to make a donation to Wisdom Publications, please do so through our Somerville office. If you would like to sponsor the publication of a book, please write or email us for more information.

Thank you.

Wisdom Publications is a non-profit, charitable 501(c)(3) organization and a part of the Foundation for the Preservation of the Mahayana Tradition (FPMT).